SMART GLOBALIZATION

The Canadian Business and Economic History Experience

Today's globalization debates pit neoliberals, who favour even deeper integration into the global economy, against neo-mercantilists, who call for a relatively selective approach to globalization and the return to more interventionist industrial policies. Both sides claim to have the facts on their side.

Inspired by the work of economists Ha-Joon Chang and Dani Rodrik, editors Andrew Smith and Dimitry Anastakis bring together essays from both historians and economists in this collection to test claims that wealth comes from either protectionism or free trade.

With empirical research that spans more than a century of Canadian history, *Smart Globalization* demonstrates that Canada's success stemmed neither from complete openness to globalization nor from policies of isolation and self-sufficiency.

ANDREW SMITH is a lecturer in international business at the University of Liverpool Management School.

DIMITRY ANASTAKIS is an associate professor in the Department of History at Trent University.

EDITED BY ANDREW SMITH
AND DIMITRY ANASTAKIS

Smart Globalization

The Canadian Business and Economic History Experience

UNIVERSITY OF TORONTO PRESS
Toronto Buffalo London

© University of Toronto Press 2014
Toronto Buffalo London
www.utppublishing.com
Printed in Canada

ISBN 978-1-4426-4804-3 (cloth)
ISBN 978-1-4426-1612-7 (paper)

Printed on acid-free, 100% post-consumer recycled paper
with vegetable-based inks

Library and Archives Canada Cataloguing in Publication

Smart globalization : the Canadian business and economic history
experience / edited by Andrew Smith and Dimitry Anastakis.

Includes bibliographical references and index.
ISBN 978-1-4426-4804-3 (bound). – ISBN 978-1-4426-1612-7 (pbk.)

1. Canada – Commerce – History.   2. Business enterprises – Canada –
History.   3. Industries – Canada – History.   4. Canada – Economic conditions.
5. Globalization – Canada – History.   I. Smith, Andrew, 1976–, editor of
compilation   II. Anastakis, Dimitry, 1970–, editor of compilation

HF3224.S63 2014   330.971'05   C2013-908072-4

University of Toronto Press acknowledges the financial assistance to its
publishing program of the Canada Council for the Arts and the
Ontario Arts Council.

 Canada Council   Conseil des Arts
for the Arts   du Canada

University of Toronto Press acknowledges the financial
support of the Government of Canada through the Canada Book Fund
for its publishing activities.

Contents

Contents

Figures, Maps, and Tables

Figures

Maps

Tables

Foreword

In early 2010, a group of business and economic historians gathered in Kitchener-Waterloo to present papers and to discuss "Smart Globalization: The Canadian Business and Economic History Experience."

Globalization has been a part of Canada's business and economic history since the first interaction between European traders and Indigenous peoples. This book focuses on the late nineteenth and early twentieth centuries and the post–Second World War period – both important periods in the history of the globalization of business. The book is a starting point, not an end point, and it is hoped that in the future there will be more conferences on Canadian business and economic history, as well as more publications.

The Rotman School of Management at the University of Toronto had an interest in business history and nearly a decade ago established the L.R. Wilson/R.J. Currie Chair in Canadian Business History, Canada's first such chair at a graduate school of business.

The chair was to fund courses and research that explored the evolution of business in Canada and examine the legal, economic, and political events that shaped the course of its history. The business school also launched a research program in Canadian business history and provided research resources including data collection, data processing, and access to published information.

Since then the school has designed, developed, and delivered a basic course in Canadian business history, prepared and published a casebook for the study of Canadian business history, and participated actively in the business history community both domestically and internationally, including participating in the Kitchener-Waterloo Conference.

Because of the importance of the subject matter of the Kitchener-Waterloo Conference, Rotman's Canadian Business History Program was pleased to provide financial support for the publication of the proceedings.

Joe Martin, Director of Canadian Business History,
Rotman School of Management, University of Toronto

Acknowledgments

We would like to thank and acknowledge a number of individuals and institutions who helped to make this collection possible. Our thanks go to the three external reviewers of the collection, Len Husband and everyone at the University of Toronto Press. We also thank Joe Martin of the Rotman School of Business, who provided support for the publication of this book through the Canadian Business History Program. Of course, we thank the contributors, as well.

The genesis of this project was a conference on globalization and Canadian business and economic history held at the Centre for International Governance Innovation in Waterloo in January 2010. Our thanks to the conference contributors, including Eugene Beaulieu, Jevan Cherniwchan, William D. Coleman, Robin Gendron, and Michael Huberman, and to the student volunteers, Mike Commito, Rita Weise, Clare Glassco, and Mary-Ellen Godfrey. Laurentian and Trent Universities (the latter through the Symons Trust Fund) provided funding for this conference. We would also like to thank John English.

SMART GLOBALIZATION

The Canadian Business and Economic History Experience

Introduction
Smart Globalization: The Canadian Business and Economic History Experience

ANDREW SMITH AND DIMITRY ANASTAKIS

What is globalization and how do we understand it in a Canadian context? Globalization has become one of the most commonly used and contentious terms in recent popular, political, and academic discourse. From civil society groups, to economists, to international diplomats to laid-off factory workers, the word *globalization* has a diversity of meanings. For Canadians, globalization has simultaneously represented economic opportunity and economic uncertainty; it has taken the form of mercantilism, continentalism, and other forces; it has become synonymous with global communications interconnectivity and deindustrialization; it has been condemned for fostering cultural homogeneity, while creating a global village of cultural consumption; it has sparked protest, and at the same time, been heralded as Canadian as touchstones such as multiculturalism and internationalism.

The definition of the word *globalization* is contested. In this book, the word denotes the integration of previously autarkic areas into the global economy through the removal of natural and human-made barriers to the movement of goods, capital, and people. Historically, globalization has been driven by two interconnected forces. On the one hand, over time technological change has reduced the costs of moving goods, information, and people, cutting transport and communication costs and thereby facilitating the growth of long-distance economic linkages. Simultaneously, governments have taken decisions that have made political boundaries less significant to firms, consumers, and other economic actors. The result is that the world economy has moved towards the borderless state of affairs that many liberal economists regard as ideal.

Of course, we are still a long way from a borderless world economy. For instance, there are still many trade barriers between Canada and the United States, notwithstanding the much-ballyhooed Canada-US and North American Free

Trade Agreements, in 1989 and 1993, respectively. These barriers bias much of the trade of Canada's provinces towards each other and away from American states, albeit to a lesser extent than in the 1980s.[1] Moreover, transportation costs still have a massive impact on global trade. Indeed, an increase in oil prices prompted the economist Jeff Rubin to speculate in 2009 that decades of globalization might be reversed.[2] Although it remains to be seen whether this prediction will be fulfilled, Rubin was entirely right that globalization is not an irreversible process. History suggests that a spike in oil costs is not the only thing that could reverse globalization: major wars have rolled back globalization in the past. The half century before 1914 is widely regarded as the first "golden age" of globalization. By some measures, the world was more globalized in 1913 than it is today, although this interconnected global economic system was shattered by the First World War. The interwar period saw the creation of many barriers to international trade and is widely regarded as an era of "deglobalization." Globalization did not resume until the late 1940s. The second great wave of modern globalization, beginning in the late 1940s, accelerated around 1980. The world is far from "flat" (i.e., totally globalized), as the journalist Thomas Friedman once claimed, and the reports of the death of distance have been greatly exaggerated. The borders of nation-states still matter a great deal in the business world. Nonetheless, the world is undoubtedly far more interconnected today than it was several centuries ago, though the nature and diversity of this interconnectedness remains amorphous.[3]

This book will use the Canadian historical experience to speak to present-day debates about globalization. Unquestionably, globalization is a fact of daily life: few would argue that it would be wise for a country to attempt to reject globalization in its entirety, nor would it be credible to suggest that countries should erase their borders entirely. The real debate is about how we manage globalization. Instead of complete economic liberalization (i.e., the elimination of all tariffs and other trade barriers) or protectionism, there are those who advocate development through the selective embrace of globalization and the intelligent use of industrial policy. The latter is the argument of Ha-Joon Chang, a heterodox economist who argues the industrial democracies developed by using a selective mixture of protectionist and nonprotectionist policies, rather than through a wholesale embrace of globalization.[4] The management theorist Pankaj Ghemawat has also recommended a selective approach to globalization. He suggests that nations seeking to prosper in the global economy need to adopt a middle course between complete laissez-faire openness to foreigners and old-fashioned protectionist autarky. In his recent book, *World 3.0*, he suggests that globalization is beneficial when it involves the removal of tariffs and other barriers to the movement of physical goods. However, he argues that the financial globalization that followed the removal of international capital controls in the 1970s and 1980s has produced more problems than benefits.[5]

The theorist of globalization whose ideas have had the greatest direct influence on this book is the Harvard economist Dani Rodrik, who speaks of smart globalization and positions himself in between antiglobalization zealots and the neoliberal ideologues who believe in the wholesale elimination of barriers to international trade and investment. Rodrik shows that in the three decades after the Second World War, the world economy experienced globalization: barriers to international commerce were removed, and overall human welfare was improved. However, he argues that countries in this period did not move in the direction of eliminating all barriers to the movement of people, capital, and goods. Instead, national governments practiced selective globalization, choosing to eliminate some barriers to international trade, especially tariffs, while retaining others, such as restrictions on international capital flows and foreign ownership. Rodrik argues that the rapid growth in living standards Western countries witnessed in this period proves that selective globalization is the best approach.

In the three decades after 1945, nation-states operated within the Bretton Woods system, which gave policymakers a wide degree of latitude when it came to how they were going to integrate into the global economy. Rodrik's view is that after the 1970s the capacity of nation-states to manage their degree of integration into the global economy was undermined. The period after the Bretton Woods system saw the advent of rigorously enforced rules-based trade regimes and the so-called Washington Consensus of the 1990s. The Washington Consensus privileged free-market fundamentalism over selectivity in economic policymaking. Rodrik argues that the "hyperglobalization" of the past few decades has been destructive, unlike the more limited globalization of the immediate post-war period. Rodrik does not advocate a return to autarky or an end to all forms of globalization. Instead, he supports selective or smart globalization. Such an approach would allow policymakers to manage globalization more effectively, to overcome the challenges to democracy and national decision-making that unregulated globalization represents, and to avoid the economic excesses and periodic crisis that have marked post-1980 hyperglobalization.[6]

Rodrik points to a number of historical examples to support his theory that selective globalization is the best way for a country to develop. Many of his examples come from East Asia, a region that has seen dramatic improvements in the past half century through the implementation of a judicious mixture of pro-globalization and protectionist/interventionist policies. Rodrik shows that the trailblazer for development in the region, Japan, practiced selective globalization. From the 1950s to the 1980s, the Japanese state cultivated infant industries in export-led sectors such as automotive and electronics. It also protected home markets, funded research and development, and actively supported export-oriented growth, often in contravention of international trade rules at the time. As another example, from the 1970s to the 1990s, the Chinese government replicated Japanese efforts to build its own export industries and added other techniques, such as an encouragement of joint ventures and technology transfers. Only after establishing many key industries on a secure footing did the Chinese acquiesce and join the World Trade Organization in 2001. Rodrik's point is that while China reintegrated into the global economy after 1978, it embraced neither globalization nor neoliberalism in its entirety. Instead, it developed a mixed economy that participated very selectively in globalization.[7]

Although Rodrik does not explicitly address the Canadian historical experience, it certainly fits solidly within his notion of smart globalization. Canada is one of the world's most successful countries in terms of average living standards. The chapters in this collection will show that Canada's success stems from neither complete openness to globalization nor policies of autarky or self-sufficiency. Since the time of Sir John A. Macdonald, Canada has developed through a policy mix that corresponds to Rodrik's concept of "smart globalization." Macdonald's National Policy involved a mixture of protectionist tariffs, encouragement of foreign investment, and infrastructure projects designed to facilitate exports. The National Policy in Canada corresponds closely to what the global economic historian Robert C. Allen calls the "standard model" of nineteenth-century national economic development. According to Allen, the standard model was first adopted by the United States, where it was outlined in 1792 by Alexander Hamilton, one of the founding fathers of the new republic. Hamilton's goal was to allow the United States to catch up with the world's first industrial nation, Great Britain. In the late nineteenth century, the standard model was adopted by countries ranging from Australia to Germany to Russia. The constituent policies of the standard model were elimination of internal trade barriers, a protective tariff to encourage manufacturing, creating a uniform national currency, subsidies for transportation infrastructure, and mass education. According to Allen, the successful catch-up economies of the nineteenth century all adopted the standard model rather than trusting the unregulated free market to deliver growth.[8] In the twentieth century, the precise policy mix in Canada changed, but the country continued to practice selective globalization. Although Canadians championed the post-war Bretton Woods order – becoming leading figures at the General Agreement on Tariffs and Trade (GATT), the United Nations, and other globalizing institutions – they maintained a distinctively selective approach to their trade practices and kept a steady hand on the level of globalization in which the country took part. Since 1945, Canadians have been particularly shrewd practitioners of selective globalization. In the 1960s, they opened their flagship auto industry to a continentally managed trade regime with the United States only after securing a good dose of protectionist measures that ensured a viable Canadian assembly industry and an indigenous auto parts sector. In the 1980s, when protectionism threatened their most important markets, Canadians selectively embarked on the aforementioned regional trade initiatives with the United States and Mexico.[9]

Other examples of Canadian "smart globalization" in this period abound. Even in an era of decreasing barriers to trade, Canadians selectively sold their wheat to Cold War adversaries and created wheat-marketing boards. They also fought to maintain marketing boards on various other agricultural products such as eggs, poultry, and dairy. They assiduously protected their banking and financial services sectors from international competition and sought exemptions in their trade treaties to protect cultural and other sensitive industries. On monetary policy, Canadians also exhibited a willingness to employ selective globalization. During the break-up of the Bretton Woods system in the early 1970s, as the United States and other countries attempted to impose some sort of order on currency flows, Canada steadfastly maintained its floating currency policy, much to the chagrin of American policymakers.[10]

Using Rodrik's approach as a framework for this collection allows us to do a number of things that help to better conceptualize Canadian business and economic history. First, the book provides an opportunity to test Rodrik's hypothesis against the Canadian experience by using concrete examples of how Canadian policymakers embraced selective globalization as a technique to advance Canadian interests. Second, this collection allows us also to push the notion of Canadian smart globalization back into the pre–Bretton Woods era, into the Gilded Age era of globalization, therefore expanding on Rodrik's approach and further deepening the analysis. Third, the collection also allows us to focus on the question of smart globalization not only at the level of national policy but also at the level of the individual and utilize business history to examine the role of corporations in this these Canadian efforts to selectively embrace globalization in the period from the late nineteenth to the twenty-first century. Finally, the book utilizes case studies to situate and contextualize the Canadian environment within the Chang-Rodrik selective/smart thesis. Case studies are a long-standing approach in business and economic history, having been used for decades as a method by which to more effectively disseminate research findings and provide a pedagogical tool for scholars and students alike. Some of the most famous tomes in the business history canon and more recent works that have focused on Canadian business history have used the case method.[11] In this collection, the case method allows readers to test the evidence of selective globalization at work in Canada on a host of examples, while at the same time providing a snapshot of particular firms, industries, or economic issues. Further, when taken as a whole, the cases give the reader a compelling sense of the changes over time that Canadians experienced as they grappled with globalization. Thus, the book takes a particular methodological approach to help us understand how Canada's economic history fits into the wider story of the history of globalization.

The book also offers an interdisciplinary approach, as historians and economists collaborated in this collection. In the second half of the twentieth century, business history and economic history became estranged from one another. There was a breakdown in communications between business historians, who used mainly qualitative research methods, and econometric historians, who developed increasingly sophisticated tools of quantitative analysis. Business historians have traditionally used the firm as their main focus of analysis, whereas economic historians have often focused either on macroeconomic data or on particular sectors of the economy and on building models that test economic relationships. Scholars in both subdisciplines have called for an end to the disciplinary segregation between business and economic history.[12] The editors of this collection believe that blending business historical and economic historical approaches will increase the work's utility to people in a wide range of disciplines. As an article by three business school academics recently and persuasively argued, qualitative and quantitative approaches should be amalgamated when studying economic systems.[13] This book provides a bridge between disciplinary groups in an effort to illustrate that although they might have differing approaches, the problems they seek solutions for are often similar. In this instance, both business historians' and economic historians' work is being used to test the Canadian experience against the selective globalization thesis. Though the approaches and subjects are diverse, chronologically our collection is focused on two recent phases of globalization, the pre–First World War period and the post-war era from 1945 to the present.

In our introduction, we begin by offering a brief overview of globalization that will contextualize the essays in this collection and show that Canada has been both a product of and agent in globalization. Second, we examine some of the key themes in globalization historiography, and in Canadian business and economic historiography, and connect these literatures as a way of linking Canada more forcefully into any understanding of the currents and drivers of globalization and to the broader selective globalization approach offered by Rodrik. The last section of this introduction will provide a brief overview of the chapters in this collection, fitting them within broader aspects of globalization, among one another, and within the selective globalization approach. Our focus is on globalization as an underlying and organizing theme in Canadian business and economic history, and how best to understand this theme.

I

Globalization is often viewed as an exclusively "modern" phenomenon.[14] To some readers, it may seem odd to write of globalization when referring to any era before the advent of the GATT or the jumbo jet. The reality is that globalization has had a long history. The archaeological evidence of long-distance trade has led some scholars to speak of "archaic globalization," a period that began several thousand years before the Common Era and lasted until the start of the early modern period of globalization, conventionally dated to the 1492 voyage of Christopher Columbus. The Roman Empire made a greater volume of trade possible as long as it existed, but its collapse ushered in a period in which trade stagnated. Similarly, the short-lived Mongol Empire, which united much of Eurasia under a common government and set of laws, allowed trade between western and eastern Eurasia to flourish, albeit for a brief period.[15] Moreover, sea voyages were a relatively minor feature of archaic globalization, long distances being covered mainly by overland caravans.[16] The Western Hemisphere was thus almost entirely cut off from the trading systems of the Old World, notwithstanding a few pre-Columbian voyages. Nonetheless, there is much archaeological evidence of long-distance trade taking place in precontact North America.[17] Unfortunately, for historians seeking to reconstruct the activities of individual First Nations entrepreneurs, there are challenges, given that First Nations societies were orally based and did not generate the contracts, ledgers, and other documents available to historians interested in business in Europe and Asia during the same period.

Early modern globalization, from the sixteenth to the nineteenth centuries, had several outstanding features. At the outset, intercontinental commerce was dominated by a small group of nations in Western Europe whose economic connections to other continents was frequently accompanied by the extension of colonial rule to those territories. This was most obvious in the case of the British, French, Spanish, and Portuguese colonial empires in the New World whose lead in military technologies in this period allowed them to dominate other cultures.[18] Moreover, global commerce was influenced by the rivalries of the colonial powers and the desire of governments to closely regulate commerce and reflected an early variety of selective globalization. International trade was intensively regulated through tariffs, statutory monopolies, and other regulations known collectively as "mercantilism," a set of policies most commonly associated with Jean-Baptiste Colbert (1619–83), the French minister of finance from 1661 to 1683. Colbert's philosophy was that governments had to spend money to get money: a policy of laissez-faire would not be enough to develop France. Under Colbert's leadership, public funds were lavished on subsidized factories, domestic infrastructure, and overseas colonies, including New France – even to the point of subsidizing breweries.[19] Finally, much international trade was mediated by large, state-chartered corporations that enjoyed legal privileges in their home market. These firms, which included the Hudson's Bay Company (and marked an important early Canadian contribution to the development of globalization), have been compared to today's multinationals.[20] To a certain extent, this analogy is a misleading one, for the chartered trading monopolies were both rulers of territories as well as commercial enterprises.

In the nineteenth century, the global economy changed dramatically. "Steam-era globalization" reminds us of the important role the British Empire played in promoting an open international economic order during Queen Victoria's reign from 1837 to 1901 and how intimately tied to technology such imperial power was. During the heyday of its relative power, Britain was able to use its political clout and influential example to open the markets of many countries to external commerce.[21] The substantial differences in the intellectual climate of the nineteenth century also helped to make steam-era globalization very different from early modern globalization.[22] In the nineteenth century, a quasi-religious faith in the benefits of free trade and economic laissez-faire diffused from Britain to other countries. In the 1820s and 1830s, the ideas of Adam Smith and other classical political economists began to influence public policy in a variety of Western countries, especially English-speaking ones.[23]

In the 1840s, this move towards free trade accelerated, as the British dismantled their own mercantilist colonial edifice. The end of this earlier form of selective globalization had a direct impact on Canada because the end of colonial preference and the embrace of free trade was a major blow for producers of wheat and timber in British North America.[24] Indeed, resentment at the loss of protection caused a large section of the English-speaking business community in Montreal to sign a petition that called for Canada to become an American state.[25] Thereafter, the idea that Canada could ensure prosperity through some sort of merger, perhaps a customs union with or even outright annexation by the United States, was a perennial idea in Canadian politics. For instance, in the late 1880s, a section of the Liberal Party became fixated on the idea of unrestricted reciprocity with the United States, and the idea of continentalism – itself a form of selective globalization – has remained a constant in Canadian business and political discourse since that time.

Technological change was, as the name suggests, a major factor in steam-age globalization. The date of the first successful ocean crossing using steam power is contested, but by the late 1830s, paddle wheelers were offering a regular transatlantic service.[26] In the late 1850s, Sir Hugh Allan of Montreal introduced a fleet of iron-hulled screw propellers to connect Canada to Britain.[27] Steamboats had earlier appeared on North America's inland waterways. The first steamship in British North America, John Molson's *Accommodation*, was launched on the Saint Lawrence in 1809.[28] The great advantage of steamers was in moving people and mail, fields in which time was of the essence. For the movement of goods, steamships were adopted first for short voyages, but progressive improvements in technology made steamships increasingly competitive on longer routes.[29]

The late nineteenth century was a great age of globalization. Commodities, capital, information, and labour flowed much more easily across national boundaries. Rail, telegraph, and telephones facilitated communication across continents. Europeans came to rely on products from the farms of Canada, the ranches of Argentina, and the massive slaughterhouses of Chicago. European capital flowed into infrastructure, mining, and other projects throughout the world, and international brands and technologies, such as Singer sewing machines and Massey tractors, became familiar in households and on farms on many continents.[30]

In the early twentieth century, however, the geopolitical underpinnings of this global economy came under threat. The world's high degree of globalization circa 1900 was, in part, a function of the Pax Britannica: the world was dominated a by a single superpower, a global hegemon capable of policing the world's oceans, discouraging piracy, maintaining a fairly stable international financial system tied to the gold standard, and otherwise providing the global public good of security. But by the late nineteenth century, British hegemony began to be challenged by other states. Moreover, the eclipse of British authority after 1890 was paralleled by a growing tide of protectionism. The First World War, which saw the sudden appearance of exchange controls, submarine warfare, and the cessation of trade between belligerents, ended this golden age of globalization. During and after this conflict, the breakdown of British power coincided with the onset of a period of *deglobalization*, when nation-states that had previously been tightly integrated into the global economy reverted towards autarky.[31]

Despite the growth of global connections, the late nineteenth century also saw that political developments within states had already begun to undermine globalization. Counter-intuitively, the most important of these internal developments was democratization. Democracy, as Rodrik has argued, can sometimes be incompatible with globalization. Steam-era globalization began in the early nineteenth century, when Britain had consolidated its hold over a vast empire. In the 1840s and 1850s, Britain granted considerable internal autonomy to its colonies of white settlement in North America and Australia: although Britain continued to control the foreign relations of these regions, control over economic policies was devolved to legislatures elected by local property holders. The new constitutional order meant that if local voters were determined to expropriate an asset controlled by a British investor, the imperial government would be powerless to stop this from taking place. In practice, colonial parliaments usually displayed a respectful attitude to the interests of British investors, largely because private property was regarded as sacrosanct. However, the late nineteenth century witnessed the rise of movements that were, broadly speaking, social democratic, in many countries. Moreover, many business groups were increasingly keen to use the powers of the state to further their own ends. For instance, as we shall see in Chapter 1, in Ontario businesses that were consumers of electricity and frustrated by high prices began to demand that the province's electrical industry be taken into public ownership. This campaign was fiercely resisted by locals and Britons who had invested in this industry.

At the same time, the spread of democracy itself also worked to undermine globalization. The global economic order had been constructed at a time when only a small proportion of adult males had the right to vote in most Western countries.[32] In the late nineteenth and early twentieth centuries, there was a global trend towards democracy. In Canada, the 1921 federal election was the first election without property or other economic qualifications for voters (or gender qualifications). Democratization slowed globalization in several ways. Globalization created winners and losers within national economies. Working-class people faced challenges in insulating themselves from the effects of globalization because they had few financial resources. Workers whose jobs were threatened by foreign competition were therefore likely to vote in favour of protectionist policies, notwithstanding the cogent arguments made by academic economists about free trade being the best way to maximize overall growth in a national economy.

At the same time, the tension between democracy and globalization also helped the latter. In the pre-1945 period, the booming population growth in a farming Canadian West fuelled an emerging free-trade movement. In the post-1945 period, as Rodrik has shown, countries used their welfare states to broaden support for globalization, the implicit social contract being that if individuals lost jobs because of foreign competition, they would receive a form of compensation out of government revenues. Not surprisingly, the twenty-first-century industrialized countries with the strongest redistributive social programs, such as Scandinavian ones, are the states in which popular opinion is least hostile to globalization.[33] In the period of deglobalization that characterized the first half of the twentieth century, however, such social programs were in their infancy, which meant that those groups that were most likely to lose out from globalization were especially fierce in their opposition to the sorts of policies needed to maintain an integrated global economy.

As a result, working-class people used their new electoral power to challenge globalization by voting in favour of parties that supported protectionist tariffs. Working-class voters also demanded restrictions on immigration because the arrival of more workers in the country threatened to undercut the bargaining power in the labour market. In the middle of the nineteenth century, the liberal states around the North Atlantic imposed very few restrictions on immigration, except for quarantine rules for those with infectious diseases. This laissez-faire approach encouraged workers to move: millions of workers flowed across international boundaries without visas, passports, or indeed any official documentation. This policy contributed to the rapid population growth of North America and other resource-rich settler societies, such as Canada, Australia, and Argentina.[34]

Starting in the late nineteenth century, legislatures in the settler societies of the New World began to impose progressively more severe restrictions on immigration, largely because of pressure from organized labour.[35] Asians were the first target of these policies. In 1885, Canada imposed a special tax on Chinese immigrants, and the United States and Australia introduced similar laws in this period.[36] Over time, the restrictions on immigration grew progressively more severe and were broadened to other classes of economic migrants, including those from Western Europe: in the 1930s, which saw the peak of protectionism in all of its forms, the settler societies shut their doors to almost all immigration. The United States responded to high unemployment by deporting large numbers of Canadians and Mexicans. Canada, it should be noted, deported migrants from the Dominion of Newfoundland, which was even more troubled economically than Canada.[37]

The first era of globalization ended abruptly in August 1914, as the global economy was profoundly disrupted by the First World War.[38] Deglobalization was a major theme of the interwar period. Many countries responded to the 1929 economic downturn by raising tariffs, a process triggered by the infamous Smoot-Hawley Tariff enacted by the US Congress in 1930. Although this law and the retaliatory tariffs it sparked did not single-handedly cause the Great Depression, they did choke world trade and helped to turn a recession into a much more severe economic crisis.[39] Since 1945, globalization has resumed, thanks in part to the institutions that the United States put in place at the end of the war and that emerged from the famous Bretton Woods conference. These institutions represented, in Rodrik's view, a form of "shallow globalization" but allowed nation-states to maintain national policies and some protectionism measures. The most important of these institutions was the GATT, a United Nations agency for promotion of free trade between member states. GATT was, in part, the brainchild of Cordell Hull, the ardent free trader who was President Franklin Roosevelt's secretary of state from 1933 to 1944. Hull was convinced that free trade would have political as well as economic benefits. Indeed, he believed that economic nationalism was the primary cause of war and had been lobbying American presidents for something similar to the GATT since 1916.[40] Hull's belief that international trade would promote peace as well as prosperity informed post-1945 US policy. The GATT involved a multilateral trading system for trade in both goods and services through a series of negotiations, called "rounds."[41] Though the GATT represented a great step forward in eradicating protectionism, it was non-binding and had no remedial powers, and its membership grew slowly.

The post-1945 period also saw the rise of regional trading blocs, of which the North American Free Trade Agreement and the European Union are just two.[42] These trading blocs emerged in part because American policymakers perceived that the blocs would help the world as a whole move towards their ideal of free trade. The United States strongly supported the creation of the European Economic Community by pressuring Western European countries to join.[43] Academic proponents of globalization are divided as to whether regional free-trade zones are stumbling blocks or stepping stones towards their goal of total free trade: some people fear that the continent-wide free-trade zones may eventually turn into protectionist entities surrounded by high tariff walls. Others regard the creation of continent-wide free-trade zones as congruent with the eventual elimination of all international barriers to trade and investment.[44] It is too soon to say which theory is correct. The Canadian historical experience, however, suggests that the continental trading blocs have primarily been a force for trade liberalization, not protectionism. Since the signing of its free-trade agreement with the United States in 1988, Canada's integration into the American economy has intensified. However, Canada has retained and exercised its freedom to negotiate similar preferential trade agreements with other countries. It remains to be seen as to whether the net effect of the regional trading blocs will be to advance or to impede globalization.

There seems to be a consensus that globalization has accelerated since the late 1970s, when the deregulation of global financial markets began to re-shape the international economy. The period has also seen rising inequality in many developed countries, most notably the United States. In the Gilded Age of the late nineteenth century, the United States was a society of extremes of wealth and poverty. Income inequality there remained high until the New Deal–Second World War era when the United States rapidly became a country with low income inequality, or what the economist Paul Krugman has called the "middle-class society" of his youth.[45] This situation persisted until roughly 1980, when the distribution of income in the United States became more un-equal once again. In the United States, the Gini coefficient, a common measure of inequality, has increased from 0.32 in the middle of the 1970s to 0.46 today. Intergenerational social mobility is also now lower in the United States than in other Western countries, a reversal of the historical pattern. Canadian society has also become more unequal. Canada's Gini coefficient increased from 0.29 in the middle of the 1980s to 0.32 in 2008.[46] A recent study found that techno-logical change and globalization in the form of "offshoring" were the "major factors contributing to the growth in wage inequality in Canada." The authors also noted that Canada's relatively robust system for the redistribution of wealth prevented a marked increase in inequalities of earned income from translating into inequality of disposable income.[47]

Economists have offered a wide range of explanations for the recent growth in inequality. Some scholars attribute most of the increase to changes in taxa-tion and social policy that began with the breakdown of the New Deal con-sensus in the United States.[48] Some argue that it is a function of technological change or the increasing returns for those who have invested in high educa-tion.[49] Many North Americans, however, blame globalization and immigration from low-wage countries for rising inequality. The underlying theory here is simple: cost-conscious businesses are shifting work to factories in the Third World or are hiring Third World migrants to do jobs inside the First World. Moreover, there is some evidence to support this belief, as even Krugman, who is a staunch advocate of globalization, has conceded.[50] Critics of hyperglobal-ization have also noted that its emergence has coincided with the "financializa-tion" of many economies.[51] The period since 1980 has witnessed a change in the centre of gravity within the private sector and the growth of the financial ser-vice industry at the expense of other sectors of the economy. In terms of their relative importance in the economy, firms that engage in nothing more than electronic financial transactions have displaced companies that make tangible products. The ability of nation-states to regulate this sector is limited: unlike a factory or a mine that is tied to one location, a bank can relocate to another financial centre if regulation becomes too onerous. In the eyes of some critics, such as the economist James Tobin, much of this frantic financial activity, although profitable for the firms involved, produces few, if any, benefits to society.[52] Since 2008, some industry insiders have conceded that much of the global financial sector is in fact socially useless. They have also noted that the period between 1945 and 1975, when governments deliberately restricted the growth of the global financial sector, saw a faster rate of economic growth than the subsequent thirty years.[53] There is also widespread concern that globalization is destroying an entire social group, the former "blue-collar middle class," and has contributed to the tremendous growth in interest in globalization among both academics and the general public. Our collection will not provide simple answers or grandiose statements to the effect that globalization is either good or bad. What it will do is to help place contemporary policy debates about globalization into a Canadian historical context.

II

Although Dani Rodrik's recent work has focused on "selective globalization" as a way to explain why post-1945 globalization was a success, and *how* it can guide the future of globalization, much of the recent international historical literature on globalization has addressed the scholarly debate over *what* is the primary driver of globalization. Vaclav Smil's explanation for why globalization takes place is narrowly focused on technology. In fact, he focuses on just two technologies, diesel engines and gas turbines.[54] Some critics might regard Smil as coming dangerously close to technological determinism.[55] This is not to say that that he is entirely wrong. Clearly, technological innovation has been a major factor in the various phases of globalization. The globalization of the early modern period, which saw wooden sailing vessels leaving Europe for the spice islands of the East and the fur-trapping grounds of North America, was made possible by the advent of the magnetic compass and more seaworthy ships. Steam-age globalization was made possible by the development of ocean-going steamships and the railways that brought commodities (e.g., prairie wheat) to ports. The technologies implicated in post-1945 globalization, such as containerization and fibre-optic cable, will be familiar to most readers. Technology has progressed steadily over the past few centuries, but the fact that the world has experienced successive cycles of globalization and deglobalization shows that globalization is, in essence, the product of political decisions. Technological change is a necessary but not sufficient cause of globalization because governments can decide whether or not to allow technologies to be used to facilitate trade.

Consider the late nineteenth century, when improved technology made it much cheaper to ship agricultural commodities across oceans. The falling costs of shipping a bushel of wheat across prairies and oceans meant that the Illinois, New York, and Liverpool prices of wheat converged, which was very good news for European consumers but bad news for European farmers, who were unable to compete with New World producers. Some European countries, most notably Britain, adhered to a policy of free trade that essentially involved sacrificing their domestic farmers in the interests of cheap food for urban consumers.[56] Germany, in contrast, responded to the same influx of cheap food imports by imposing tariffs designed to protect its farmers. These tariffs, which have been called "artificial oceans," effectively counteracted the effect of the secular decline in the costs of shipping food across the ocean.[57] Most historians of Europe would argue that explaining why Germany adopted this policy involves looking at the German electoral system, the nation's intellectual climate, and the shifting attitudes of key political personalities, most notably German chancellor Otto von Bismarck.

The career of Sir John A. Macdonald has some definite parallels with that of Bismarck. Macdonald and Bismarck played pivotal roles in the unification of their respective nations in the 1860s and early 1870s. Moreover, both men adopted protectionist policies (in part because of lobbying by business interests), in an era often referred to as a golden age of globalization, and both men had unquestionable political and economic successes. The protectionist "National Policy" legislated by the Macdonald government in 1879 and perpetuated by his successors is rightly regarded as a major turning point in Canadian business history. The existing secondary literature shows that the tariff had a profound influence on Canadian economic life, incentivizing the growth of infant industries and, ironically, contributing to the phenomenon of the branch plant economy.[58] The National Policy can be regarded as an "artificial ocean," one that prevented American companies from using the relatively new transportation technologies of the period (e.g., railways) to flood the Canadian market with their goods. In this case, politics trumped technology as Macdonald embraced a form of selective globalization.

John Maynard Keynes once said that "ideas shape history." He elaborated that "practical men, who believe themselves to be quite exempt from any intellectual influences, are usually the slaves of some defunct economist."[59] Doug Irwin has applied this insight to the study of globalization's history. In sharp contrast to Smil, who sees technology as the prime mover, Irwin's research has focused on the evolution of the changing climate of economic opinion as the key variable that explains the successive waves of globalization and deglobalization. He attributes, in part, the late nineteenth-century "golden age" of globalization to the fact that growing numbers of people after 1815 were persuaded by the classical economists' arguments in favour of free trade.[60] It would be possible for a historian of globalization to advance an extreme version of this theory of globalization's causation by arguing that intellectual history is the key to understanding globalization. Irwin, however, does not go this far and recognizes that the powerful interest groups that had been created by the technologies of the Industrial Revolution also played a big role in shaping trade policy. Any workable explanation for either globalization as a general phenomenon or a case study of a region's engagement in the global economy needs to incorporate a wide range of factors and to draw on the history of ideas as well as the history of technology.

Canadian scholars have contributed to our understanding of both the techno-material and the cultural/intellectual causes of globalization. The cultural and communications critic Marshall McLuhan is the Canadian who probably made the largest contribution to the theory of globalization. His work on technology and its impact in the 1950s and 1960s provided a language to describe globalization: McLuhan coined the term *global village*. Economist Harry Johnson was a long-time advocate of free trade and provided a vibrant intellectual and economic justification for open borders, especially between Canada and the United States.[61]

The University of Toronto political economist Harold Adams Innis had a rare ability to combine the study of material and cultural factors, which is perhaps why he is still read with profit today. In the interwar period, Innis developed the staples paradigm, which laid out a grand political economic narrative that provided a view of business in Canada, business-government relations, and Canada's place in the world economy.[62] The staples paradigm, which is sometimes inaccurately called the "staples thesis," emphasized the dependent relationship between hinterland Canada and its successive imperial "metropoles" (France, Britain, and finally the United States) and was, in its own way, a precursor approach to selective globalization. Innis described how Canada's mercantilist-driven economic development had centred around a succession of natural resource industries, beginning with fish and fur and later expanding to include timber, wheat, minerals, and newsprint.[63] Innis argued that resource extraction did not lead to the development of the "backwards and forwards linkages" (banking, finance, technology, etc.) that created a diverse economy. In other words, Canada remained in the staples trap, condemned to exporting raw materials to the industrial economies. W.A. Mackintosh, on the other hand, was more optimistic and argued that staples had, in fact, led to the development of a diversified modern economy in Canada.[64]

The debate over the staples thesis was rekindled in the 1960s when Marxist academics embraced staples approaches to help explain Canadian "dependency" on the United States. These scholars emphasized Canada's dependence on US multinational corporations, the domination of the Canadian economy by the United States (particularly in natural resource extraction), and the "weakness" of Canadian industry, which was largely dominated by US branch plant operations. The left nationalists, who christened their views the "New Canadian Political Economy," found allies around the globe in the 1970s, particularly in developing nations, which also viewed their own "backwardness" as an indication of their dependence on foreign capital.[65] In the 1990s, the idea that resource-led development is ultimately harmful for a country was popularized by the economist Jeffry Sachs, who spoke of nations being cursed with too many natural resources.[66] Chapter 4 in this collection addresses the so-called resource curse thesis and will be discussed subsequently.

III

The first three chapters of this collection not only tackle questions surrounding globalization, but also revisit the role of natural resource industries in Canadian economic and business history. The state's interventionist role in shaping economic development was at the centre of H.V. Nelles's now-classic *The Politics of Development: Forests, Mines and Hydro-Electric Power in Ontario, 1849–1941.* A seminal work in the field of Canadian history, *The Politics of Development* engaged economic, business, and environmental history and strongly linked both extractive and manufacturing industries into a continental and international context, fixing Ontario's core sectors into an implicitly globalized framework and reflecting much of the Canadian economic and business historiography of the 1970s. Although Nelles did not use the term *selective globalization,* his book is essentially about how the Ontario government used a toolkit that included some protectionist measures to convert the province's abundant natural resources into thriving export-oriented sectors and value-added industries. For instance, Nelles shows that the Ontario government prohibited the export of unprocessed logs to the United States so as to encourage the development of sawmills. Nelles's research, which emphasized the power of the state to do good, is congruent with the Chang theory of how countries prosper in the global economy. The first three chapters in this collection are about Ontario-based industries, whose experiences also support Chang's theory.

For instance, the collection's first piece, Andrew Dilley's examination of the Ontario government's battles with the City of London, uses a transnational approach in exploring some of the dynamics surrounding Ontario's decision to take its hydroelectric industry into public ownership. A major issue in Ontario politics in the early twentieth century was hydroelectric power: Should foreign, mostly British-owned, utilities be able to charge high rates to their industrial customers? Or should the industry be nationalized so that manufacturers could have access to power at cost? After 1905, Ontario's government decided that the needs of the province's value-added and electricity consuming industries would be prioritized over those of the firms that produced electricity. Dilley's chapter (Chapter 1) is essentially about a conflict between a group of foreign investors and elected politicians who wanted to revise the terms on which their jurisdiction participated in the international economy. Within the City of London, there was widespread hostility to the proposed nationalization of Ontario's hydroelectricity industry: nationalization and the retroactive alteration of contracts were anathema with the institutions and values that underpinned the golden age of globalization. Despite the City's opposition, Ontario persisted with the policy of nationalization, which was popular with the electorate. Rooted in recent historiographic debates about Britain's colonial legacies and the place of capital markets in structuring centre-periphery relations, Dilley reminds us that tightly knit transnational networks wove local Ontario concerns into broader imperial dynamics and debates about capital, property, and notions of imperialism and identity.

Moreover, Dilley's research forces us to revise the view that the interests of overseas investors always took precedence in the pre-1914 golden age of globalization and convincingly closes the distance between Toronto, Montreal, Ottawa, and the City of London, giving a fresh view on how the politics of development in Canada reached outward in its impact and importance. Dilley's research is particularly important in light of Dani Rodrik's argument that settler societies such as Argentina, among the most prosperous in the world in 1900, fell behind economically because they failed to use the powers of the state to diversify beyond primary production and to redistribute wealth within their societies. As a country of recent European settlement located in the temperate zone of the world, Argentina was similar to Canada in many ways. Unlike Argentina, politicians in Canada and the other dominions of the British Empire increasingly used tariffs and other forms of state intervention to foster industrial development and value-added industries. Rather than simply letting the free market determine how their economies participated in the global economy, these jurisdictions practiced selective globalization. Ontario's hydroelectric industry is a classic case of development through selective globalization.[67] Dilley suggests that the Ontario case highlights important differences between late nineteenth-century and contemporary financial globalization based on the flexibility of the rules of the investment game. Indeed, the rules within which Canada operated in this period resemble the looser framework at the heart of Rodrik's "Capitalism 3.0" – a laxity that to some extent resolved the tension between democracy and globalization noted by Rodrik. Dilley's chapter also deepens our understanding of the making of policy in Ontario beyond the account provided by Nelles.

Another key aspect of Nelles's work examined the forestry sector. Forestry products were Canada's greatest international export before the Second World War and one of Ontario's key sectors in this period – both as a provincial extractive industry and as an early indicator of the extent of multinational (i.e., American) penetration into the Canadian staples firmament. In Chapter 2, Mark Kuhlberg engages the debate over the effectiveness of Ontario's "manufacturing condition" – outwardly an example of selectivity – by making the case that any prohibition on exports of unprocessed pulpwood was actually something of a mirage. Kuhlberg shows that successive Ontario governments were only slightly more interested in fostering colonization than they were in imposing barriers on the voracious appetites of lumbermen, which is to say, very little. The case illustrates another example of the how the making of policies governing commodities such a pulpwood reflected a kaleidoscope of local, provincial, and international factors at play – from homesteaders and northern lumber interests, to Queen's Park politicians and public servants, to giant American enterprises. The example also illustrates the limits of selectivity; sometimes, the idea of smart globalization was more politics than real policy. For much of the pre–Second World War period, the global took on many different forms, even in a sector as provincial and seemingly parochial as pulpwood.

Hydroelectric power and pulpwood were important, essential, and profitable industries, but they were never considered strategic in a military sense. Nickel, on the other hand, became a very valuable and politically sensitive commodity during that most global of events, a world war. Daryl White's chapter (Chapter 3) on the International Nickel Company, Inco, during the First World War acts as a capstone to Nelles's troika of resource-based industries. Like Dilley's and Kuhlberg's work, White's chapter takes a new approach to this sector of the Canadian economy at a precipitous moment and also reveals a relatively understudied yet telling episode. Inco, a multinational firm headquartered in an avowedly neutral country, but with its main product mined (but not refined) in Canada – which was at war – faced a political, legal, and public relations dilemma: If it did not allow extraterritorial control over its operations and exports (i.e., by Canada and the British) during a time of war, Inco ran the risk of having the sole source of its only product cut off entirely. On the other hand, even if it did allow Canadians to investigate the sale of processed nickel from its New Jersey plant, the company could not control who bought the product, and it could wind up in German hands. Canadians' outrage at the idea that Canadian nickel was being used to kill Canadian troops in France threatened to upset the delicate balance that the company was trying to maintain in this difficult period. The Inco case during the First World War illustrates that corporate entanglements in a globalized world – be it potash corporations, ports, or intellectual property – are as much subject to nationalism as they are legal necessities, then as now, in wartime and in peace. Globalization, for all of its border-destroying creative destruction, often has its limits.

Economists have provided some of the most sustained and provocative explorations of globalization and its impact, both in the present and in the past. International comparisons and sector-specific studies are both useful tools to examine how global industries have been affected by geographical considerations or technological changes, or how they have been shaped by local, regional, and national political circumstances. In their examination of another great staple industry, wheat production, Livio Di Matteo, J.C. Herbert Emery, and Martin P. Shanahan explore an age-old question, one that catapulted its original Canadian inquisitors, Harold Innis and W.A. Mackintosh, into the first rank of political economists. In Chapter 4, Di Matteo, Emery, and Shanahan utilize tools less often used by business and economic historians (though, not sources) to analyse the comparative levels of wealth generated by wheat production between Canada's Lakehead region and South Australia. Their aim is to grapple with the "resource curse," and the authors find that a resource-exporting region is more likely to derive permanent benefits from a resource boom if people in that region control economic policy. South Australia, which was a self-governing colony at the time of its wheat boom, benefited from the ability to control the rules of the game. The Lakehead region of Northern Ontario, which was governed from distant Toronto and Ottawa, derived far fewer benefits from its resource boom precisely because it was not a self-governing jurisdiction.

Similarly, Michael Hinton's microstudy of the Canadian cotton industry challenges another long-standing shibboleth of Canadian economic history, namely, that Canadian manufacturing before the First World War was inefficient because it was tariff protected. The traditional view that Canada's infant industries never grew up reflects the classical liberal view that protectionism is harmful to a country's overall level of development. Hinton's chapter (Chapter 5) presents new quantitative and qualitative evidence that suggests that far from being an unsuccessful infant industry, Canadian cotton mills are actually an example of successful infant industry protection. Hinton's research supports

Chang's thesis that government intervention and a degree of protectionism are necessary for the country to prosper in the global economy. Although they do not directly address Chang's theory, the chapters of Dilley, Kuhlberg and White can also be used to support Chang's position.

Hitherto, the chapters in this collection have examined Canada's place in the first great age of globalization prior to the First World War. But globalization renewed itself vigorously after 1945, and Canadian firms and industries played key roles in this revitalized economic internationalism, even within a Cold War context. One key area of global growth was the auto industry: Canada's sector became very much export oriented until the late 1950s but faced internal challenges and international competition in the 1960s as Europe and Japan recovered from war. In Chapter 6, Greig Mordue examines the long course of Canada's public policy evolution towards the auto industry, explaining and exploring how the tariff measures of Macdonald's nineteenth-century National Policy, imperial entanglements, and Canada's interwar and post-war multilateralism complicated the policies governing Canadian car production well into the twentieth century. By focusing on Vincent Bladen's seminal 1961 royal commission into the auto sector, Mordue shows how domestic concerns were always also defined by external and global trends and developments – from protectionism to imperial preference to imports and, eventually, to a form of continentalism found in the 1965 Canada-US auto pact. This treaty was, in some ways, an exemplar of the selective globalization at work: even at the height of Bretton Woods internationalism, Canadians demanded and achieved ingenious ways to protect their industries from the harsh efficiencies of globalization. Nonetheless, the auto pact was a precursor to the North American rules-based free-trade regimes that proliferated in the 1980s and 1990s and that marked, in many eyes, a particularly American-dominated strain of economic globalization.

Indeed, Canadians have often been a part of the American-dominated globalization that characterized the post-1945 period. As Graham Taylor shows in Chapter 7, the Canadian distiller Seagram's succeeded by marketing its products as tangible, branded consumables that reflected a worldwide thirst for what many saw as the American dream. Seagram's was a bona fide Canadian multinational and a success story, albeit one that became essentially American by its third generation. By exploring the reasons for Seagram's eventual demise as a firm (though many of its brands live on), Taylor posits useful questions about the nature of "modern" globalization, the role of the multinational, and the volatility and changing tastes of the worldwide market for consumer goods. It also begs the question of whether family-run firms – no matter their provenance and past successes – have a natural lifespan.

Taylor's chapter provides a useful comparison and counterpoint with another sector of the Canadian alcoholic beverage industry, one that did not succeed on the same global scale as did Seagram's spirits but has also been dominated by family-run firms. Neither the Canadian beer industry nor its brands ever really made a global impact but instead became a takeover target of multinational brewers, especially in the 1990s and thereafter. Matthew Bellamy (Chapter 8) explores some reasons why by looking at industry-specific, country-specific, and firm-specific determinants of growth and survival. Both Taylor's and Ballamy's chapters examine Canadian failures on a global stage, though those paths to failure are very different: it is from those different paths that Canadians can draw lessons on the broader implications and consequences of globalization for a country that, by and large, remains on the periphery of the world economic order.

The chapters in this volume cover only a small number of the innumerable global entanglements that shaped Canadian business and economic history. We offer them as a starting point for additional research on globalization as a theme in Canadian history. These chapters and this collection have attempted, in a small way, to provide some shape to a theme that remains as profoundly important today as it did since the time of the first trading interactions among indigenous peoples in Canada, the first contacts with European explorers, the emergence of the first branch plants, or the successes – and failures – of the latest Canadian multinational firms.

NOTES

1 James Anderson, "Gravity with Gravitas: A Solution to the Border Puzzle," *American Economic Review* 93, no. 1 (2003): 170.
2 Jeff Rubin, *Why Your World Is About to Get a Whole Lot Smaller: Oil and the End of Globalization*, 1st ed. (New York: Random House, 2009).
3 Our definition of and thinking about globalization has been informed by Pankaj Ghemawat, *World 3.0: Global Prosperity and How to Achieve It* (Cambridge, MA: Harvard Business School Press, 2011).
4 Ha-Joon Chang, *Kicking Away the Ladder: Development Strategy in Historical Perspective*. (London: Anthem, 2002).
5 Ghemawat, *World 3.0*.
6 See, for example, Rodrik's *The Globalization Paradox: Democracy and the Future of the World Economy* (New York: Norton, 2011) where he writes that "[t]he Bretton Woods regime was a shallow multilateralism that permitted policy makers to focus on domestic social and employment needs while enabling global trade to recover and flourish," one that was replaced by a "hyperglobalization" that removed

regulations on international capital markets and saw economic globalization "as an end in itself" (p. xvii).

7 Rodrik, *Globalization Paradox*, 144–56.

8 Robert C. Allen, *Global Economic History: A Very Short Introduction* (Oxford: Oxford University Press, 2011), 79–81.

9 On Canadian trade policies in this period, see Michael Hart, *A Trading Nation: Canadian Trade Policy from Colonialism to Globalization* (Vancouver: University of British Columbia Press, 2003) and Bruce Muirhead, *Dancing Around the Elephant: Creating a Prosperous Canada in an Era of American Dominance, 1957–73* (Toronto: University of Toronto Press, 2007). On the auto industry in this period, see Dimitry Anastakis, *Auto Pact: Creating a Borderless North American Auto Industry, 1960–71* (Toronto: University of Toronto Press, 2005) and Mordue in this collection (Chapter 6).

10 On Canada's role in the Bretton Woods system and currency questions, see Robert Bothwell, *Alliance and Illusion: Canada and the World, 1945–84* (Vancouver: University of British Columbia Press, 2008).

11 See, for instance, classic treatments such as Alfred D. Chandler's *Scale and Scope: The Dynamics of Industrial Capitalism* (Cambridge, MA: Harvard University Press, 1990) and *The Visible Hand: The Managerial Revolution in American Business* (Cambridge, MA: Harvard University Press, 1977) and Graham Taylor and Peter Baskerville's *A Concise History of Business in Canada* (Toronto: Oxford University Press, 1994), all of which have utilized a firm or sectoral case-study approach to some extent in their work. A recent Canadian business history that utilized the case study approach is Joe Martin's *Relentless Change: A Casebook for the Study of Canadian Business History* (Toronto: University of Toronto Press, 2010), whereas one of the most enduring Canadian economic histories, Harold Innis's *The Fur Trade in Canada: An Introduction to Canadian Economic History* (Toronto: University of Toronto Press, 1930) was an extensive case study. The case method has been, of course, the primary pedagogical approach at business schools such as Harvard's and Western for decades.

12 On the issue of bridging business and economic history, see Naomi R. Lamoreaux, Daniel M.G. Raft, and Peter Temin, "New Economic Approaches to the Study of Business History," *Business and Economic History* 26, no. 1 (Fall 1997): 57–79.

13 Julian Birkinshaw, Mary Yoko Brannen, and Rosalie L. Tung, "From a Distance and Generalizable to Up Close and Grounded: Reclaiming a Place for Qualitative Methods in International Business Research," *Journal of International Business Studies* 42, no. 5 (2011): 573–81.

14 Jurgen Osterhammel and Niels P. Petersson, *Globalization: A Short History* (Princeton, NJ: Princeton University Press, 2009), 13.

15 Deepak Lal, *In Praise of Empires: Globalization and Order* (New York: Palgrave Macmillan, 2004), 17.

16 Karl Moore and David Charles Lewis, *The Origins of Globalization*, 1st ed. (London: Routledge, 2009).

17 John Upton Terrell, *Traders of the Western Morning: Aboriginal Commerce in Precolumbian North America*, 1st ed. (Los Angeles: Southwest Museum, 1967).

18 Daniel R. Headrick, *Power over Peoples: Technology, Environments, and Western Imperialism, 1400 to the Present* (Princeton, NJ: Princeton University Press, 2009).

19 A.J. Sargent, *The Economic Policy of Colbert* (New York: B. Franklin, 1968); Glenn Joseph Ames, *Colbert, Mercantilism, and the French Quest for Asian Trade* (DeKalb, IL: Northern Illinois University Press, 1996); Matthew Bellamy, "'Rich by Nature, Poor by Policy'? The Premature Birth and Quick Death of Commercial Brewing in Canada, 1667–1675," *Brewery History* 137 (Fall 2010): 48–70.

20 The Hudson's Bay Company is one of the few Canadian examples that Rodrik discusses in his *Globalization Paradox*. See also Ann M. Carlos and Stephen Nicholas, "'Giants of an Earlier Capitalism': The Chartered Trading Companies as Modern Multinationals," *The Business History Review* 62, no. 3 (1988): 398–419.

21 Jeffry A. Frieden, *Global Capitalism: Its Fall and Rise in the Twentieth Century*, new ed. (New York: W.W. Norton, 2007), 57–61.

22 Douglas A. Irwin, *Against the Tide: An Intellectual History of Free Trade*, new ed. (Princeton, NJ: Princeton University Press, 1997).

23 Anthony Howe, "Restoring Free Trade: The British Experience, 1776–1873" in *The Political Economy of British Historical Experience, 1688–1914*, ed. Donald Winch and Patrick K. O'Brien (Oxford: Oxford University Press, 2002), 193–214.

24 Robert Livingston Schuyler, *The Fall of the Old Colonial System: A Study in British Free Trade, 1770–1870* (Oxford: Oxford University Press, 1945).

25 L.B. Shippee, *Canadian-American Relations, 1849–1874* (New Haven, CT: Yale University Press, 1939), 1–12; Jacques Monet, "French Canada and the Annexation Crisis, 1848–1850," *Canadian Historical Review* 47 (1966): 249–64.

26 David Budlong Tyler, *Steam Conquers the Atlantic*, (New York: D. Appleton-Century Co., 1939), 2, 86–7; Francis E. Hyde, *Cunard and the North Atlantic, 1840–1973: A History of Shipping and Financial Management* (London: Macmillan, 1975), 36.

27 "The Canadian Mail Line of Steamers," *Mitchell's Steam Shipping Journal*, 4 December 1863, 776.

28 Frank Mackey, *Steamboat Connections: Montreal to Upper Canada, 1816–1843* (Montreal: McGill-Queen's University Press, 2000), 3.

29 Joel Mokyr, *The Lever of Riches : Technological Creativity and Economic Progress* (New York: Oxford University Press, 1990), 129.

30 A.G. Kenwood and A.L. Lougheed, *The Growth of the International Economy, 1820–2000: An Introductory Text* (London: Routledge, 1999).

31 Niall Ferguson, "Sinking Globalization," *Foreign Affairs* 84, no. 2 (2005): 64–77.

32 Barry Eichengreen, *Globalizing Capital: A History of the International Monetary System*, 2nd ed. (Princeton, NJ: Princeton University Press, 2008), 33.

33 Rodrik, *The Globalization Paradox: Why Global Markets, States, and Democracy Can't Coexist* (Oxford: Oxford University Press, 2011).

34 See for example, Ninette Kelley and Michael Trebilcock, *The Making of the Mosaic: A History of Canadian Immigration Policy* (Toronto: University of Toronto Press, 1998), 61–111; Timothy J. Hatton and Jeffrey G. Williamson, "A Dual Policy Paradox: Why Have Trade and Immigration Policies Always Differed in Labor-Scarce Economies?" in *The New Comparative Economic History: Essays in Honor of Jeffrey G. Williamson*, ed. Timothy J. Hatton, Kevin H. O'Rourke, and Alan M. Taylor (Cambridge, MA: MIT Press, 2007), 217–40.

35 Kevin H. O'Rourke and Jeffrey G. Williamson, *Globalization and History The Evolution of a Nineteenth-Century Atlantic Economy* (Cambridge, MA: MIT Press, 1999), 185; David Goutor, *Guarding the Gates: The Canadian Labour Movement and Immigration, 1972–1934* (Vancouver: University of British Columbia Press, 2007).

36 Kornel Chang, "Circulating Race and Empire: Transnational Labor Activism and the Politics of Anti-Asian Agitation in the Anglo-American Pacific World, 1880–1910," *Journal of American History* 96, no. 3 (2009): 678–701.

37 The relevant regulation was P.C. 695 (Canada) (1931), as mentioned in Kelley and Trebilcock, *The Making of the Mosaic*, 220.

38 Ferguson, "Sinking Globalization."

39 Douglas A. Irwin, *Peddling Protectionism: Smoot-Hawley and the Great Depression* (Princeton, NJ: Princeton University Press, 2011).

40 Frieden, *Global Capitalism*, 248–55.

41 Hart, *A Trading Nation*, 125–44.

42 Richard Pomfret, "Chapter 3 Regional Trade Agreements," *Research in Global Strategic Management* 12 (2006): 39–54.

43 Geir Lundestad, *"Empire" by Integration: The United States and European Integration, 1945–1997* (Oxford: Oxford University Press, 1997).

44 Brian T. Hanson, "What Happened to Fortress Europe? External Trade Policy Liberalization in the European Union," *International Organization* 52 (1998): 55–85; Anne O. Krueger, "Are Preferential Trading Arrangements Trade-Liberalizing or Protectionist?" *The Journal of Economic Perspectives* 13, no. 4 (Autumn 1999): 105–24.

45 Claudia Goldin and Robert A. Margo, "The Great Compression: The Wage Structure in the United States at Mid-century," *The Quarterly Journal of Economics* 107, no. 1 (1992): 1–34; Paul Krugman, *The Conscience of a Liberal: Reclaiming America from the Right* (London: Allen Lane, 2008), 5.

46 Organisation for Economic Co-operation and Development (OECD), *Growing Unequal? Income Distribution and Poverty in OECD Countries* (Paris: OECD, 2008), country notes on Canada.

47 Nicole Fortin, David A. Green, Thomas Lemieux, Kevin Milligan, and W. Craig Riddell, "Canadian Inequality: Recent Developments and Policy Options," *Canadian Public Policy* 38, no. 2 (2012): 138.

48 Douglas S. Massey, "Globalization and Inequality: Explaining American Exceptionalism," *European Sociological Review* 25, no. 1 (2009): 9–23.

49 Claudia Dale Goldin and Lawrence F. Katz, *The Race between Education and Technology* (Cambridge, MA: Harvard University Press, 2008), 45–6.

50 Paul Krugman, "Trade and Wages, Reconsidered," (Washington, DC: Brookings Institute Paper, 2008).

51 Harry Magdoff and Paul M. Sweezy, *Stagnation and the Financial Explosion* (New York: Monthly Review Press, 1987).

52 James Tobin, "On the Efficiency of the Financial System," *Lloyd's Bank Review* 153 (1984): 14–15.

53 "Reforming Finance: Are We Being Radical Enough?" (speech by Adair Turner, Chairman, Financial Services Authority, Clare College, Cambridge, UK, 18 February 2011), http://www.fsa.gov.uk/pubs/speeches/0218_at_clare_college.pdf

54 Vaclav Smil, *Two Prime Movers of Globalization The History and Impact of Diesel Engines and Gas Turbines* (Cambridge, MA: MIT Press, 2010).

55 Merritt Roe Smith and Leo Marx, *Does Technology Drive History? The Dilemma of Technological Determinism* (Cambridge, MA: MIT Press, 1994).

56 Frank Trentmann, "Political Culture and Political Economy: Interest, Ideology and Free Trade," *Review of International Political Economy* 5, no. 2 (Summer 1998): 217–51.

57 Paul Bairoch, "European Trade Policy, 1815–1914," in *The Industrial Economies: The Development of Economic and Social Policies*, ed. Peter Mathias and Sidney Pollard (Cambridge, MA: Cambridge University Press, 1989), 55.

58 Works that look at the emergence of large Canadian firms include W. Kaye Lamb, *The History of the Canadian Pacific Railway* (Toronto: Macmillan, 1977); Lawrence Mussio, *Sun Ascendant: A History of Sun Life of Canada* (Montreal: McGill-Queen's University Press, 2008); Joy L. Santink, *Timothy Eaton and the Rise of His Department Store* (Toronto: University of Toronto Press, 1990). Works that examines the role of branch plant operations in Canada include Dimitry Anastakis, "From Independence to Integration: The Corporate Evolution of the Ford Motor Company of Canada, 1904–2004," *Business History Review*, 78 (Summer 2004): 213–53; Graham D. Taylor, "From Branch Operation to Integrated Subsidiary: The Reorganization of Imperial Oil under Walter Teagle, 1911–1917," *Business History* 34 (July 1992): 49–68.

59 John Maynard Keynes, *The General Theory of Employment, Interest, and Money* (New York: Harcourt Brace and World, 1964), 383.

60 Irwin, *Against the Tide.*

61 On McLuhan's work, see *The Mechanical Bride: Folklore of Industrial Man* (New York: Vanguard Press, 1951) and *The Gutenberg Galaxy: The Making of Typographic Man* (Toronto: University of Toronto Press, 1961); Harry Johnson's voluminous work included *The Canadian Quandary: Economic Problems and Policies* (Toronto: McGraw-Hill 1963).

62 See his classic *The Fur Trade in Canada: An Introduction to Canadian Economic History* (New Haven, CT: Yale University Press, 1931, various reprints) and his *The Cod Fisheries: The History of an International Economy* (New Haven, CT: Yale University Press, 1940). Another example of the staples thesis, conceptualized as the "Laurentian thesis," is Donald Creighton, *The Commercial Empire of the St. Lawrence* (Toronto: Ryerson Press, 1937, various reprints). There is also R. Craig Brown's *Canada's National Policy, 1883–1900: A Study in Canadian-American Relations* (Princeton, NJ: Princeton University Press, 1964).

63 Other examples of work on particular staples (and/or particular regions) include Vernon C. Fowke, *The National Policy and the Wheat Economy* (Toronto: University of Toronto Press, 1957); Graeme Wynn, *Timber Colony: A Historical Geography of Early Nineteenth Century New Brunswick* (Toronto: University of Toronto Press, 1981).

64 Mackintosh expounded on the staples thesis and laid out his version of it in a report tied to the famous Rowell-Sirois Royal Commission on Dominion-Provincial Relations, entitled *The Economic Background of Dominion-Provincial Relations* (Ottawa: Queen's Printer, 1937).

65 On the ongoing staples debates, including the contributions of the "New Canadian Political Economy" advocates, see, for instance: Melvin H. Watkins, "The Staples Theory Revisited," *Journal of Canadian Studies* 12, no. 5 (Winter 1977): 83–95; W.J. Eccles, "A Belated Review of Harold Adams Innis," *Canadian Historical Review* 60 (1979): 419–41; Mel Watkins, "The New Canadian Political Economy: Classic and Beyond" in *Reclaiming Democracy*, ed. Marguerite Mendell (Montreal: McGill-Queen's University Press, 2005); Neil Bradford and Glen Williams, "What Went Wrong? Explaining Canadian Industrialization" in *The New Canadian Political Economy*, ed. Wallace Clement and Glen Williams (Montreal: McGill-Queen's University Press, 1989), 54–76. Marxists critics also conceptualized the Canadian state as being a handmaiden to capital. See Leo Panitch, "The Role and Nature of the Canadian State," in *The Canadian State: Political Economy and Political Power* (Toronto: University of Toronto Press, 1977).

66 Jeffrey Sachs and Andrew M. Warner, *Natural Resource Abundance and Economic Growth* (Cambridge, MA: Harvard Institute for International Development, Harvard University, 1995).

67 The differing economic experiences of the British settler colonies and Latin America became important elements in late debates about dependency thesis, a literature on which Rodrik touches. See D.C.M. Platt and G. Di Tella, eds., *Argentina, Australia and Canada: Studies in Comparative Development 1870–1965* (London: Macmillan, 1985); H.M. Schwartz, *In the Dominions of Debt: Historical Perspectives on Dependent Development* (Ithaca, NY: Cornell University Press, 1989).

1

Politics, Power, and the First Age of Globalization: Ontario's Hydroelectric Policy, Canada, and the City of London, 1905–10

ANDREW DILLEY

In the spring of 1910, the premier of Ontario, J.P. Whitney, was celebrating. Canada's attorney general, A.B. Aylesworth, had recently announced the rejection of a petition by the Canadian Privy Council to disallow an act staying court cases challenging contracts recently signed between municipalities and Ontario's publically owned Hydro-Electric Power Commission.[1] Whitney's government had established the commission in 1906, and, under the leadership of Adam Beck, it sought to distribute electrical power generated at Niagara Falls cheaply throughout Southern and Western Ontario.[2] This had brought the government of Ontario into conflict with financial interests in Canada and in the City of London. As Whitney told the Toronto *Mail and Empire*:

> From the beginning, the electrical interests were the bitter opponents of this legislation. All the stock gamblers were against it. An emissary from England was sent over and the so-called financial journals there blossomed out with editorials made up largely of misrepresentation, and frigid, calculated, falsehood. The result, however, has proved disastrous to the idea that these journals have any real power or influence. Every imaginable influence over there – social, political, private and public – was retained where possible, and all who realise the strength of such combined influences in London will at once appreciate what this meant.[3]

This struggle reflected Canada's global connections in the early twentieth century. At its heart lay dependence on the London capital markets (something

I would like to thank Ian Phimister, John Darwin, Sarah Stockwell and Phil Buckner for their generous comments on earlier versions of this chapter, and Andrew Smith and Dimitry Anastakis for drawing my attention to Rodrik's work. The errors and views expressed remain my own.

widely recognized in Canada), while ideas of shared British and imperial iden-
tities were frequently evoked. By re-examining the controversy, this chapter
seeks to highlight the ways in which provincial and national economic development and the economic, political and cultural aspects of Canada's connection
with Britain (surely among its most significant global connections) were interrelated and clashed at the start of the twentieth century.

By exploring these connections, it becomes possible to draw broader con-
clusions about the Canadian experience in the period before 1914, which is
now widely recognized as the "first age of globalization."[4] Historians and social
scientists have pointed out the parallels between the first age of globalization
and the more recent wave of globalization through which we are now living.
The pre-1914 global economy, which Dani Rodrik calls "Capitalism 1.0," oc-
cupies a prominent place in his account of globalization's past. Rodrik presented this historical narrative in the course of calling for the replacement of
deep globalization by "smart globalization."[5] Rodrik's narrative opens with an
account of the Hudson's Bay Company, but Canada subsequently disappears
from his account.[6] This is problematic because Canada's experiences with
Capitalism 1.0, along with those of Britain's Australasian colonies, arguably
could provide several important data points to support Rodrik's overall thesis
that selective globalization coupled with democracy is the best strategy for
economic development. For example, Rodrik regards the possession of democratic institutions as a key variable that explains why some nations are better
able to negotiate the global economy than others. The experience of Canada
and the other British dominions in the pre-1914 period would tend to cor-
roborate this view, and the self-governing colonies of the British Empire had
open franchises for men and, in Australasia, were advanced in enfranchising
women (although these franchises remained racially circumscribed).[7] Rodrik shows that under Capitalism 1.0, some of the settler societies of the New
World, most notably Argentina, failed to diversify beyond primary production and failed to redistribute wealth.[8] This was less true of the British settlement colonies, which increasingly used tariffs and state intervention – such
as Ontario's hydroelectric policy – to foster industrial development.[9] Canada
had advanced furthest along this road by 1914 when Capitalism 1.0 entered
a period of prolonged crisis.[10] Historians of Canada, and of the connections
between Canada and London, which is the hub of Capitalism 1.0, are therefore
well placed to contribute to this debate and particularly to examine the interplay of democratic institutions and global economic forces so important to
Rodrik's recommendations for the present.

To tease out these implications, this chapter draws on the recent historical
literature that has reiterated the importance of links between Britain and the

settlement empire. Within their reinterpretation of the contours of modern British imperialism, P.J. Cain and A.G. Hopkins argue that the dependence on British capital created a form of "structural power" and required settler societies – including Canada – to conform to the rules of the financial game set in the City of London. Various critics have suggested that this model understates the "agency" exercised by settler societies in their relations with London, although Cain and Hopkins are clear that the ability to write the "rules" was perfectly compatible with considerable colonial agency in particular bargains.[11] Elsewhere I have argued that the dimensions of this structural *power* depend on the nature and content of the "rules of the game," and that these are best understood as the partially formulated assumptions held in the City on aspects of political economy, rather than as a neat and clear package. This encompassed a range of issues, including property rights, defence, budgetary orthodoxy, immigration, and a fear of excessive "socialism." The City only rarely agreed on how to apply these conceptions in practice, something limiting its potential influence.[12] This analysis in the main confirms Rodrik's argument that late nineteenth-century "financial globalization was the product of convergent beliefs within a close-knit club of central bankers who made all the important decisions"[13] but suggests that a broader set of financial actors than (central?) bankers contributed to the production and application of the rules, and that they were the product of evolving discourses based on experience rather than deliberate acts of creative design.[14] As we shall see, this produced latitude in their application in a country like Canada, which gave states latitude in many aspects of economic policy particularly when shifting the focus from general principles to particular policies.

The operation and application of these rules in Canada was also conditioned by Canada's membership in the British Empire and what a number of scholars have recently termed the "British World."[15] Carl Bridge and Kent Fedorowich, and Phillip Buckner and R. Douglas Francis have highlighted the roles played by ideas of Britishness and dense social networks connecting settler societies with Britain.[16] Membership in this British World eased Canada's access to the London capital market and lowered bond yields. As the eminent British statistician George Paish argued: "We have loaned this great sum of £500 millions sterling to Canada at an interest rate of only slightly over 4 per cent; we should have given it to any other country, at any rate, any other foreign country, for 5 per cent. That means that although you owe us 500 millions sterling yet this costs you not more than 400 millions sterling would cost any foreign country; in other words you have the advantage of borrowing an extra 100 millions for nothing."[17] However, Canada did not enjoy the advantages outlined by Paish as the result of an "empire effect" (to use Ferguson and Schularick's term) based on the operation of institutions of control.[18] Under Responsible Government, the British government had virtually no control over Canadian domestic policy-making. Indeed, Canadian prime minister Wilfred Laurier described the British Empire as "a galaxy of free nations."[19] Conversely, Andrew Thompson and Gary Magee have recently argued that the social networks and shared culture of the "British World" created a "cultural economy" that facilitated investment, in an analysis that, at times, encompasses the United States.[20] Both I and Andrew Smith have pointed out that the legal framework provided by the empire, as well as its strategic guarantees, also served to reassure British investors.[21] Certainly, as we shall see, the Ontario hydroelectric affair revealed the importance of transatlantic networks, and ideas of imperial loyalty and Britishness as adjuncts of the operation of the rules. To borrow from Rodrik, these shared belief systems and ideologies reassured investors of Canadians' probity. Yet, as will become apparent, the idea of responsible government and British liberty was evoked to emphasize Ontario and Canada's right to adapt and bend (if not break) the rules.[22] The implications of this often neglected aspect of the "empire effect" in the dominions will be revisited in the conclusion.

With these lines of interpretation in mind, this chapter seeks to show through a re-examination of the hydroelectric affair the degree to which political life in Ontario, and in Canada more broadly, was bound up with, and shaped by, global connections, particularly financial connections with Britain. Moreover, through a close reading of the affair in the light of historians' recent writings on structural power and the British World, the chapter concludes that, when the affair is viewed through the prism of Rodrik's work, our understanding of the first age of financial globalization may require significant revisions. First, it is necessary to sketch the broader economic and political context within which the dispute took place.

Beginning in 1867, with the exception of Newfoundland, the British colonies and territories of North America were united into a single, federal state: the Dominion of Canada. Each former colony retained its own provincial government (Ontario and Quebec, united from 1841 to 1867, had their separate assemblies and administrations restored), while a new federal (or dominion) government was created to deal with issues of common concern. Although the Fathers of Confederation expected that the system would be dominated by the centre, the provinces remained a powerful alternative focus for politics and, with the support of the Judicial Committee of the Privy Council in London, challenged federal dominance.[23] Thus, in 1898, a judgment by Privy Council effectively ended the federal government's right to disallow provincial legislation on the grounds of injustice unless the matter affected the whole dominion.[24] During its first three decades, control of the federal government generally remained in the hands of the Canadian Conservative Party, a dominance not matched in the provinces. In 1896, Wilfred Laurier's Liberals defeated the Conservatives in a federal election on a banner of provincial autonomy in an election dominated by education policy in Manitoba, an issue closely associated with provincial rights.[25]

Confederation was an economic project as well as a political one. Federal politicians, and especially the federal Conservative Party, hoped that the transcontinental state would become an integrated economy. The state sponsorship of the construction of the Canadian Pacific Railway and former Canadian prime minister Sir John A. Macdonald's "National Policy" of tariff protection sought to reorientate the Canadian economy along an east–west axis. The National Policy also embodied a vision in Ontario of the Canadian west as a natural extension of the province and as a market for its manufacturing industries.[26] This vision relied on British capital, especially for the construction of infrastructure (most notably for transcontinental railways). Domestic capital markets were, and remained, too shallow to supply the vast sums required.[27] Between 1871 and 1914, foreign capital flowed to Canada in three long swings, peaking in the early 1870s, the late 1880s, and just prior to the First World War (see Figure 1.1). Each time, more than 50 per cent of capital formation relied on imported capital at the peak of the swing. Most of this capital came from Britain, even after 1900 when American investment expanded. According to Jacob Viner, Britain accounted for 71 per cent and the United States 23 per cent of $514,979,000 invested in Canada between 1901 and 1913.[28] By then the Canadian economy had changed gears. Between 1877 and 1896, Canadian GNP per capita grew at only 1.5 per cent per annum. By contrast, between 1896 and 1913, the figure leapt to 4.5 per cent.[29] Canada became a major recipient of British investment, much placed in Canadian railways because, after 1903, two new transcontinentals were constructed with the support of the Liberal government.[30]

Montreal's and Toronto's leading financial institutions possessed strong ties to the London capital market. From 1891, the Bank of Montreal had organized the dominion government's borrowing there, and Viner estimated that between 1900 and 1914 the bank's activities accounted for about 50 per cent of all British capital exported to Canada.[31] The Canadian Bank of Commerce, the Bank of Montreal's Toronto rival, had an active business in London, as did an allied institution, Dominion Securities – a bond house that acquired an office in the City in 1908.[32] Leading Canadian financiers openly argued that, in the words of Byron Edmund Walker (general manager and, from 1907, president of the

Figure 1.1. Capital inflows, Canada, 1870–1927

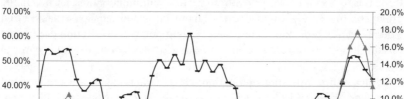

Source: Calculated from M. C. Urquhart, "New Estimates of Gross National Product, Canada, 1870–1927: Some Implications for Canadian Development," table 2.4, 20–5, in *Long-Term Factors in American Economic Growth*, ed. Stanley L. Engerman and Robert E. Gallman (Chicago: Chicago University Press, 1992), 9–95.

Canadian Bank of Commerce), "[w]e are a borrowing country, and we cannot be reminded of that too often."[33] In 1908, E.R. Wood (president of Dominion Securities) estimated that the sale of $500 million bonds in Britain that year showed that "we must meet the British investor not merely with the good faith to which his confidence and enterprise entitle him, but with such abundant good faith as shall keep our financial reputation second to none."[34] Such views were largely accepted by Canadian politicians and a large section of the Canadian press.[35] In 1907, the Conservative leader Robert Laird Borden argued that "the sanctity of public contracts must always be respected" because "Canada requires for the development of its enormous resources a vast amount of money ... It must, therefore, remain for many years a borrowing country. To sanction or enact legislation of a confiscatory character would be the worst possible service that any government or parliament could render."[36] Economic growth, British investment, and "national development" were intimately linked. It was in this context that the hydroelectric dispute took place.

By the early twentieth century, Ontario was the most populous province in Canada and had long sought to become the dominion's industrial heartland. These aspirations partly underpinned support in the province for the development of transcontinental railways linking central Canada with the prairies and the Pacific coast. The development of the Canadian west through improved communications was widely expected to stimulate Canadian manufacturing.[37] Ontario was better positioned to tap this new market than rival centres farther east. However, the province suffered from one fatal weakness: the absence of an adequate supply of energy.[38] By 1900, the new technology of hydroelectric power meant that the answer lay on the province's doorstep at Niagara Falls, which offered an inexhaustible and inexpensive means for the province to cement its place as Canada's industrial heartland.[39] Anyone seeking to obstruct the development of hydroelectric power would have to face down provincial and national aspirations.

By 1902, American companies had obtained two of the three potential sites for generating power at the Canadian side of the falls. In response, a movement emerged in the municipalities of West-Central Ontario opposing the export of power. During a coal shortage that autumn, three deputations (composed of provincial bourgeoisie) visited the province's Liberal premier, George Ross, demanding that the government distribute electricity to ensure its cheapness. Ross resisted this but reassured the deputation that the third lot had been allotted to a Canadian company.[40] The Electrical Development Company of Ontario (EDC hereafter) was promoted in February 1903 by William Mackenzie (former Canadian Pacific Railway contractor), Henry Pellatt (stockbroker), and Fred Nicholls (engineer) with capitalization of $11 million ($6 million in shares and $5 million in bonds). The new company obtained a contract from the Toronto Power Company, another of Mackenzie's enterprises (also established in 1903) to distribute power to two more of his concerns: the Toronto Electric Light and Power Company (TELPC hereafter) and the Toronto Railway Company.[41] Mackenzie placed EDC bonds in the United States and in Britain. In March 1906, the merchant bank Chaplin, Milne, Grenfell floated $2.5 million of 5 per cent First Mortgage Bonds.[42] This created an important connection with one of the bank's partners: Arthur Grenfell, son-in-law of Governor General Earl Grey and one of the leading British players in the market for Canadian securities.[43]

Ross was wrong in thinking that the Canadian-registered EDC's formation would defuse criticism. Adam Beck, a cigar box manufacturer from Berlin, Ontario, quickly emerged as the de facto leader of a populist campaign for cheap public power. As H.V. Nelles has shown, almost from the start the campaign saw the need for power in biblical terms.[44] In 1903, Beck dominated a power commission established by Ross, who Beck increasingly accused of abandoning the consumers of Ontario to stock watering monopolists exemplified by the EDC.[45] This movement attracted the attention of Ontario's Conservatives.[46] Their leader, James Pliny Whitney, spoke in support of the power movement from 1902. In 1905, his party won sixty-nine seats and a majority in the provincial elections. Although the power question did not feature heavily in the campaign, Whitney soon made clear his alliance with Beck's movement, declaring, "The water power of Niagara should be as free as air."[47] Whitney's new government placed Beck at the head of a new Hydro-Electric Power Commission to enquire into every aspect of Ontario's electrical needs.[48] Beck and Whitney devised a scheme to force down prices by establishing a public distribution network to break the EDC's monopoly. Through 1906, towns across the region voted to purchase power from Beck's commission. The EDC's American rival, the Ontario Power Company, agreed to sell power to the commission.[49]

The EDC sought to defend itself from this new competitor, and almost from the start, the connection between capital imports, Canadian credit, and development was invoked in defence of the EDC. On 11 May 1906, the opening of a new power plant allowed prominent men to speak out on the company's behalf. The lieutenant governor of Ontario, Sir William Mortimer-Clark, hoped that "these gentlemen will be permitted to enjoy the legitimate fruits of their enterprise."[50] B.E. Walker, general manager of the Canadian Bank of Commerce, defended promoters who had attracted capital to Ontario.[51] In 1907, with a default threatened on the EDC's bonded debt, the *Canadian Annual Review* (closely connected to the denizens of Montreal and Toronto finance) noted that the EDC's "credit was pledged in financial circles where any failure to make good the expectations raised would, presumably, be hurtful to the province as well as the company."[52]

Ontario's actions could potentially be portrayed as violations of property rights motivated by "socialism": they could be seen to violate several cardinal "rules of the game."[53] Unsurprisingly, evidence of disquiet in London soon began to filter across the Atlantic. In late May 1906, Earl Grey, Canada's governor general, had to reassure a visiting friend that the Ontario cabinet understood the importance of the London market.[54] The EDC's predicament also attracted the attention of Grey's son-in-law, Arthur Grenfell.[55] Grenfell wrote to Grey in March 1907 warning of "very anxious if not critical times in the City" in part attributable to "the want of confidence which has been gradually growing up as a result of State Socialism and interference by Municipal and Government bodies in trade and against Capital." This, Grenfell suggested, might rebound to Canada's favour as long as Canada were not supposed susceptible to the same "socialist" threat to property. As a result, he hoped, "We shant (sic) have many episodes like the Electric Power one" which had "left a nasty taste in our mouths." He continued, "One big Co. refused to look at Mackenzie's [Canadian Northern Ontario Railway] bonds guaranteed by Ontario, because it set a black mark against the richest province in Canada!"[56] Implicitly, Grenfell warned that railway construction might be prevented by the fallout from a public power policy. Whitney travelled to London in July 1907 to allay such concerns. A meeting between with the London bondholders and shareholders of the EDC did not calm fears, and a subsequent letter to the premier from Chaplain, Milne, Grenfell repeated the central charge that by laying down its own lines to supply the power, the government was seen to be unfairly competing with the company.[57]

By then, the EDC's finances were in dire straits. Late in 1906, the Canadian Bank of Commerce lent the company $400,000, and in April 1907, $100,000 followed from Canada Life. In June that year, $900,000 from the Bank of Scotland paid off the Bank of Commerce, renewed in December.[58] Despite these loans, the company faced problems meeting $203,750 in interest due on its bonds in March 1908. Moreover, in 1907, the City of Toronto began a campaign to overturn its contract with TELPC (associated with the EDC) and purchase power for lighting from Beck's commission.[59]

With a default looming and public competition continuing from the Hydro-Electric Power Commission and the City of Toronto, British bondholders again became alarmed. The London-based English Association of American Bondholders (EAAB hereafter) met to discuss the matter.[60] Grey informed B.E. Walker of the "desire" of "certain members ... to pillory Ontario business on the ground that the government of Ontario could not be relied upon to stand to their agreements, or to abstain from plunder."[61] Walker replied that Whitney did not understand "business matters" and was "utterly unable to realize the mischief he has done," continuing that "we are deeply conscious of the mischief that would be done to every Canadian interest if the English Association of American Bond and Shareholders should take the action suggested."[62] At the EAAB meeting, Arthur Grenfell averted direct intervention, which would "prejudice Canadian enterprises," securing agreement that his Canadian Agency partner and brother-in-law, Guy St Aubyn, would visit Whitney to establish the "facts."[63] Despite preparatory talks with Grey, Walker, and J.S. Willison of the *Toronto News*, St Aubyn failed to persuade Whitney (who thought him poorly informed) to expropriate (in modern parlance, nationalize) the EDC and TELPC.[64] Instead, in February 1908, William Mackenzie (one of the original promoters) stepped in and, with a loan from the Bank of Commerce, reconstructed the two companies, securing funds to meet the EDC's bonded debt.[65] Thus, from 1905 to 1908, a confrontation developed between Ontario and the EDC, and from the start, expressions of alarm in the City were central to the campaign.

Ontario's hydroelectric scheme was the most prominent among many instances of popular dissatisfaction with large corporations, especially politically exposed utilities.[66] Leading members of the Toronto and Montreal financial communities became increasingly concerned. Returning from a business trip, the Bank of Montreal's president, Edward Clouston, praised Mexico's treatment of capital and warned that "particularly in Ontario, we can see that the application of socialistic theories might well produce the gravest conditions with respect to the investment of capital."[67] In March 1908, Walker spoke out against the "dangers of democracy" at the Canadian Club in Halifax.[68] He pointed out that "as our West develops, however, we shall need to sell our securities abroad in increasing amounts, and ... we shall obtain money or fail to obtain it in proportion to the maintenance of our high credit." Walker warned: "If any country is *supposed* to be filled with agitators who are opposed to capitalists and to corporations generally, and if the politicians in such a country are *supposed* to be listening to the ground swell from the newspapers and are ready to do what such newspapers recommend, *whether the integrity of contract is violated or not*, it is not likely that such a country will obtain capital as against those countries which maintain the sacredness of contract and which do not exhibit hatred of corporate wealth [my italics]."[69] Thus, Walker argued, overseas (especially British) investors suspecting that a populist policy violated contracts (whether or not this was the case) was sufficient reason to abandon the policy in order not to obstruct economic and national development.[70]

The electorate of Ontario failed to heed such warnings. On 8 June 1908, the fruits of Beck's labours were tested in provincial elections.[71] The opposition of financiers lent the public power policy a populist twist, played on by Whitney who praised Beck: "we love the work he has done and we love the enemies he has made."[72] Whitney's government was returned with seventeen extra seats, taking its total to eighty-six.[73] The *Canadian Annual Review* had no doubt that "[t]he masses of the people were almost a unit in desiring 'white coal' ... in recognising the labours of the honourable Adam Beck along the lines of public control and in approving the policy of the Whitney government in furthering that principle."[74] Whatever its opponents argued, cheap public power was popular.

Meanwhile, Beck and Whitney rapidly expanded the Hydro-Electric Power Commission's remit. In March 1908, Beck signed a deal on behalf of the commission securing power from the Ontario Power Company. Many municipalities secured voters' approval (in referenda) to purchase power from the hydrocommission. In August 1908, the government announced the construction of a new power line from Niagara to Toronto and Southwestern Ontario. The EDC-backed court challenged the validity of the contracts between the various municipalities and the Ontario Power Company. Under great pressure to maintain momentum, the government legislated on 23 March 1909 to end challenges in the courts.[75]

As public competition increased, criticism revived in the City. On 17 November, Grenfell informed Whitney that investors "again became nervous when – as far as they could learn – the security granted by that charter was menaced by the authority that granted it."[76] On 20 November, W.R. Lawson of the *Financial Times* interviewed a now impatient Whitney. The encounter was acrimonious and closed with Lawson telling Whitney that his government "did not know what it was doing" and the premier accusing his interviewer of "impertinence."[77] Lawson soon became Whitney's scourge in the London press, blaming the public power policy for difficulties in getting Canadian issues absorbed in London.[78] When the government suspended the court cases in March 1909, allegations that due legal process had been thwarted and hence property rights were in jeopardy reached a new level. Lawson launched a coruscating attack on the insecurity of contracts revealed by Canadian provinces' ability to thwart due legal process – a central guarantor of property rights.[79] In one article, entitled "Abolishing Magna Charta in Ontario," Lawson gibed that "King John would simply have declared that the courts of Ontario shall be 'forever closed,'" and the fact that "a conservative legislature and Scotch to boot could ever have been cajoled into passing it is a psychological puzzle."[80] These comments played on assumptions that Ontario was British (indeed Scottish), and that Britishness (and Scottishness) along with conservatism *ought* to have provided additional security for property rights and private enterprise.

Whitney received frequent updates from London about the effects on the province's credit. Some suggested that the storm in London was artificially engineered by interested parties. In late March 1909, one traveller recently returned from London told Whitney that London financiers' "indignation" focused on the EDC promoter, not his government.[81] Others were more ambivalent. In May, Williams-Taylor informed Whitney that "the feeling expressed to me by those who have given the matter judicial thought, is that your Government has gone too far," and that further capital for utilities might be hard to obtain "through 'fear' of adverse legislation." The Bank of Montreal's London manager continued, "Whether these fears are without ground is not at the moment material ... the effect is the same."[82] Whitney expressed confidence that the rumblings were the work of a small group of interested parties, confident that "fair minded men" there would not be influenced by unfounded "expert attacks," and, for a time, he accepted Williams-Taylor's advice that any response would simply enable his critics to repeat their attacks.[83] He warned W.J. Hanna, a colleague departing for London, to say only that "the Ontario government does not see fit to engage in a newspaper controversy with interested people from Toronto who are making charges which for recklessness and want of truth are simply monstrous."[84]

Whitney did forward a memorandum to Williams-Taylor to help him reassure his contacts in London.[85] He also applied pressure behind the scenes. He sent a coruscating letter to A.J. Dawson of the *London Standard*, when its financial editor joined the attack, registering his "deep-seated feeling of resentment at the treatment we have received" and describing how "our ideas of the London press and of the, at least, decent treatment to which we are entitled ... have been shattered." He continued: "Material reasons have no place in the feelings which animate us. We are quite independent of the London Money Market, but the treatment we have received has been such that I doubt if the feeling which once existed on our part can be restored. It is indeed a ghastly joke to charge the Ontario Government with being socialistic etc. when it is the bulwark in Canada by means of which such influences will be shattered."[86] A defensive Dawson agreed to withdraw the *Standard* from the ranks of Whitney's critics.[87] In July, while rejecting an offer to publish a response from the *Canadian Mail* (a minor financial paper), Whitney noted that "there are other financial centres besides London," and he accused the London press of betraying the "present movement to draw together sections of the Empire in a truly imperial spirit."[88]

Further reports of London's views reached Whitney through the summer. Hanna had met W.L. Griffith, the deputy high commissioner and a supporter of the public power policy, who argued that a public statement should be made because "some influential London financial men were being persuaded that Ontario is 'traversing the eternal principles of business in its Hydro policy.'"[89] By late July 1909, Hanna informed Whitney that the tide of opinion in London was turning. Grenfell had been standing by the province and denouncing the EDC promoters. Although 55 per cent of the last Dominion of Canada loan remained with the underwriters, no one connected this with the Ontario affair.[90] Perhaps in this context, Whitney decided to break his silence. He had already been in contact with E. Farrer, the *Economist*'s Canadian correspondent.[91] In early August, he forwarded a short statement to the journal that expressed disquiet that the London press had been duped by "interested parties" seeking to sour the credit of the province, re-iterated that property rights in Ontario would be "upheld in all circumstances," and accused the financial press of betraying the empire:

> The people of Ontario, and all of Canada as a body, at this moment earnestly desire to aid in the Imperial work of re-casting and consolidating relations between the great communities and groups which together compose the empire, and to that end are willing and anxious to assume their share of Imperial burdens. The Jeddart justice which a few British newspapers have meted out to us in this matter is not in the nature of encouragement, and may, I fear, cause some three millions of British subjects in Ontario to ask themselves *cui bono*?[92]

The allusion to "consolidating relations" and "imperial burdens" had strong resonances in the context of British debates about tariff reform and the demand for a more consolidated imperial defence aroused by the dreadnought crisis.[93] In public, as well as in private, Whitney deployed imperial loyalty against attempts at financial imperialism.

The statement, published on 28 August, failed to have the desired effect. The *Economist* accompanied it with a stinging editorial. If Whitney accused the London press of being under the influence of financiers, the editorial accused him of being under the influence of those "who see all private utilities as greedy monopolists." Whitney's action on the court cases, it said, showed that Canadian provinces were "independent and supreme to the extent that [they] could ignore Magna Charta and the Ten Commandments." It called for an amendment to the British North America Act to rectify this, "for the sake of ... credit on the English money market."[94] An enraged Whitney had little doubt that Farrer wrote the editorial.[95] Perhaps stung by the accusation that he had violated God's law as well as British tradition, he complained to Dawson that the editorial, in what he had seen as "a very high class financial and commercial journal," contained "more unfairness and deception than any previous attack." The *Economist* had "out Heroded Herod," and it was "[p]ositively sickening ... that the financial journals of London instead of being as we would like to believe quite beyond reproach and honest beyond the possibility of doubt are the opposite. However, it is merely another idol cast down."[96] The biblical imagery again reveals Whitney's anger, and anger aroused by the violation of assumptions about British fair play.

Despite Whitney's anger, the province's financial situation lessened the impact of these criticisms. It had last been to the British market in March 1906 for £1,200,000 and was not to return until July 1914. In 1909, the province's capital markets were proving more than adequate for its needs.[97] As Whitney commented to Williams-Taylor, "We are not concerned in any way with what is going on in financial circles in London. If we were there negotiating a loan, we should feel bound to answer all such questions as would be put to us."[98] It is difficult to explain why Whitney paid so much attention to the City. In part, the previous comments suggest the disquiet of a Conservative and imperialist at accusations that implied a breach of British codes of probity. Perhaps the need of Ontario for inward investment and the widespread acknowledgment that Canada was a "borrowing country" made it hard to ignore criticisms in London. However, if Ontario were temporarily independent of the City, the dominion government was looking to borrow vast amounts in its own right and through bond guarantees to railways.[99] A campaign in London, as Whitney implied, could not be ignored if loans were imminent. It is unsurprising then that the focus of lobbying now shifted from Toronto to Ottawa.

If Whitney's popularity flowed in part from the waters of Niagara, transcontinental railways attracted voters to the Liberal Party. The federal government's deal with the British-owned Grand Trunk to construct the National Transcontinental Railway from Moncton to Prince Rupert was a central issue in the 1904 election. The Liberal Party fought the 1908 election urging the need for the continued railway construction under the slogan "Let Laurier finish his work."[100] Borrowing from Britain enabled these popular projects. Weakening credit raised costs, and if investors ceased to favour Canada, completion of the railways might be jeopardized. This danger had been highlighted at the start of 1909. In January 1909, the Canadian government had struggled to place a £6 million loan as the City became increasingly concerned about falling revenues and expanding government expenditure. The loan was only underwritten after Laurier and Fielding provided assurances that no new loan or guarantee railway bonds would be issued for three years. Even then, 59 per cent of the loan remained with the underwriters.[101] Thus, when in mid-1909 some in the City questioned the security of property in Canada, there were good reasons to expect Laurier's government to take note. Perhaps the politics of national development would trump the politics of provincial development.

Laurier's government was lobbied heavily to disallow the March 1909 act through 1909. As we have seen, by May 1909, the London financial press followed Lawson and called for the dominion to disallow the legislation.[102] The dominion government was kept well informed and, on 2 September, the Canadian High Commission forwarded cuttings of Whitney's exchange in the *Economist* to Laurier.[103] Letters of protest were sent to members of the government. Sir Seymour King (banker and MP), H. Evens Gordon and Co., (an investment company), J.W. Palmer (the Duchess of Marlborough's manager of estates), C.F.K. Mainwaring (an "investor"), and H. Brent Grotian (a trustee investment company director) all asked what security remained for property if a province could obstruct court appeals.[104] A.W.M. Marshall (not the Cambridge economist but a trustee with considerable holdings in the EDC and TELPC) argued that by obstructing the right of appeal to the Judicial Committee of the Privy Council, the March legislation act violated one of the "rights and privileges of every person living in a British colony or dependency."[105] Lord Ridley, president of the Tariff Reform League, warned that the effect "on the mind of the British investor may be most prejudicial, and that it is a matter of imperial concern that this effect should not be produced."[106]

The higher echelons of Canadian finance joined the chorus. Clouston wrote to Lord Stratcona (Canadian High Commissioner and former president of the Bank of Montreal) labelling the government's policy "confiscatory."[107] Walker informed Laurier that contrary to some accounts, "[t]here can be no stronger evidence of alarm at what shows a willingness to go astray with the soundness of contract than that we [find?] in our [?] financial friends. Bankers, bondholders, and financial writers all feel that part of the foundation on which they relied for safety in Canadian investments is being swept away."[108] E.R. Wood, of the Toronto-based National Trust Company (which had close links to the Canadian Bank of Commerce) and a leading expert in Canadian bonds, emphasized the danger for Canadian development.[109] Wood concluded that because British capital was "essential" to develop Canada's wealth, the offending legislation must be disallowed "to save the credit of the dominion in the financial centre of the world."[110] Toronto's leading financiers, including Walker and Wood, had traditionally allied with the Liberals.[111] They had every reason to expect their views to be noted. Rather more cynically, the veteran continentalist and anti-imperialist Goldwin Smith added in the Toronto *Weekly Sun* that "[the] British connection has been of untold value to us if only as a means of introducing us to the English bankers; and should they ever baulk at our paper, we shall find ourselves in a predicament too serious to contemplate just now."[112]

Several petitioners (both to Laurier and Whitney) also raised the point that credit in the United States might be imperilled. At the end of 1907, one Boston financial company, Baker, Ayling and Co., which had placed EDC bonds in New England, wrote to Whitney. They complained that having put "considerable work" into overcoming their clients' "prejudices and objections" to Canadian bonds, these efforts were "injured" by a policy "more socialistic than any action taken against corporations in our country." By way of support, they noted that London bondholders were "upset."[113] The company later made a similar case to Laurier in June 1909, as did the Wall Street–based N.W. Harris and Co. and F.W. Vanderlip (of the National Bank of New York). All emphasized (as Baker, Ayling and Co. put it) that Ontario's legislation would "seriously deter the advancement of Canadian enterprises that should in the future desire to secure capital in the United States, England or even within the boundaries of your dominion."[114] Some Canadians also alluded to the US capital market. A Torontonian petitioned the governor general to disallow the March 1909 legislation because it would "impair the credit of the Dominion of Canada in the money markets of England and the United States" and because it was of "unsound and vicious in character and violates fundamental principles of legislation recognised and accepted throughout the Anglo-Saxon world."[115] Thus, the impacts of credit in the United States featured in the campaign, most often in conjunction with the London market, and they were alluded to in order to confirm that universal (or at least Anglo-Saxon) principles had been breached.[116]

The lobbying left Laurier in an awkward position. He needed to maintain Canada's credit and the favour of powerful financial allies in Toronto. Laurier wrote to Walker that "if, as you say, the Act of Ontario passed last session has the result of affecting seriously the credit of the country, it may be held to be against good order, and as such subject to disallowance," but he continued that a clash with a provincial legislature would be a "calamity."[117] There were indeed considerable risks in obstructing a popular provincial policy. Ontario had 86 out of 221 seats in the Canadian Parliament. In 1908, 36 Liberals were returned there in federal elections, contributing to an overall majority of 45.[118] Federal intervention risked alienating voters in Ontario. Moreover, in 1896, the Liberals had come to power on a platform of provincial rights, which helped secure support in Quebec, where provincial rights were seen as a bulwark against anglophone domination. On 16 October, one correspondent pointed out to the prime minister that Ontario had held two elections, resulting in resounding endorsements for Whitney and Beck.[119] Not only was the Liberals' (somewhat shaky) position in Ontario in jeopardy, but so too was their hold in Quebec (which returned 53 Liberal MPs in 1908).[120] Ontario's government was alive to this. On 14 December 1909, it threw a banquet for Jean Lomer Gouin, Quebec's premier, and was delighted when his speech emphasized the need to preserve provincial rights.[121] One of Whitney's correspondents predicted that the banquet speech would offer Laurier food for thought.[122] The prime minister could not afford to frustrate economic aspirations in Ontario and political and cultural sensibilities in Quebec. When a Liberal barrister from Toronto urged disallowance, Laurier curtly replied, "If you had the task of guiding the party, you might be of the opinion in that to depart from the principles which have always guided us is a serious responsibility."[123]

By then, Laurier was already considering the case for disallowance, first presented on 9 October 1909. Ontario's opponents presented a case emphasizing particularly that the risks to Canada of depreciating credit threatened the well-being of the whole dominion (one of the few valid grounds for federal intervention).[124] In support of this case, the Toronto Power Company published a compilation of British and Canadian press opinion and open letters from financiers on both sides of the Atlantic.[125] The pamphlet lacked one element: any evidence from stock exchange transactions demonstrating that credit was suffering as a result of Ontario's actions. As one opponent of Whitney and Beck later reflected – somewhat ruefully – it was very difficult to establish objectively that credit had slipped or why.[126] Laurier increasingly doubted that Canada's credit was at stake. As he wrote to one New York financier, "[T]he results of the legislation of the province of Ontario could [not] affect all Canadian securities any more than repudiation by a state of the Union could affect the securities of the United States."[127]

On 7 December, Ontario presented a tight case against the dominion's right of disallowance. The province cited thirty-four British cases where access to the courts had been restricted without affecting credit, and it quoted Mackenzie, Walker, and E.B. Osler (a director of the Canadian Pacific Railway) stating that Canadian finance was in buoyant condition.[128] The case concluded by eliding British liberties and constitutional niceties: "For upwards of 200 years the Lords and Commons of Great Britain have legislated without fear of royal veto, although its existence has been undoubted, and therefore, in full accord with the spirit and genius of British institutions the people of the province are entitled to all rights of British subjects elsewhere." Disallowance by the federal government would be the equivalent of a royal veto, and, if exercised "[w]ould mean that there are different grades of British subjects in the empire; that people of the several provinces of the Dominion have not and are not entitled to the full and free enjoyment of those civil rights and liberties which are enjoyed by British subjects in the Mother country, a condition of things which would be intolerable."[129] In March 1910 the case for disallowance was dismissed on the grounds that the right to act was unclear; that the effect of the 1909 legislation on Canadian credit was unclear; and that if credit had suffered, it was attributable to the entire hydroelectric policy rather than the legislation under consideration.[130] The constitutional niceties and practical realities of Canadian politics had triumphed over the risks associated with the need for British capital.

This chapter has focused on an ultimately unsuccessful campaign to obstruct the Ontario government's sponsorship of publicly distributed electric power. It has shown at every turn that the long-standing perception of economic and "national" dependence on the London capital market shaped – structured – this contest, which armed opponents of the policy with an argument based on "national interests." In the City, it was argued that Ontario's actions called security of property into question. Evidence of disquiet in the City was repeatedly used to pressurize the Ontario and federal governments. The campaign was thus fought in London as well as Toronto and Ottawa, reflecting the close links generated by reliance on British capital. In a similar vein, the frequent references to notions of Britishness and to the empire reflected the degree to which Canadians positioned themselves, and were perceived to belong to, two broader global units: the British World, or "Greater Britain," and the British Empire. Yet although economic, political, and cultural connections with the City, and Britain, shaped the form taken by the contest over the hydroelectric policy, and the cases made by both sides, local circumstances played a crucial role in determining the outcome. The popularity of cheap power drove Whitney's policy; the political risks (in Ontario and Quebec) of intervening combined with constitutional realities to prevent Laurier's intervention. In this instance as so many others, the British connection played a crucial role in shaping developments, yet these connections were also tempered by more localized forces. Even so, the power drawn from these global connections suggests that the campaign against Ontario was rather more powerful than H.V. Nelles's classic account allows.

In order to establish its significance, it is worth examining this affair through the prism of the recent historiography outlined at the start. Superficially, the failure of the campaign against Ontario seems to further undermine Cain and Hopkins's arguments about structural power, yet this would be a misreading. In the end, it was not clear that credit was threatened in a significant way, and Cain and Hopkins suggest that structural power manifested itself most powerfully at times of clear economic crisis.[131] A more subtle reading and revision is required, and two points may be made. First, the analysis here suggests that internal political dynamics were a crucial force tempering the impact of the connection with British financiers in Canada (and elsewhere). Second, the very fact that the views of the City became the strongest card to play against Ontario, and that transatlantic networks were mobilized by both sides, reflects the way in which an Anglo-Canadian politics of finance was generated by the *structural* economic dependence on Britain, even if this politics could only generate moments of control. It was mediated by the constantly reiterated recognition of that dependence and its association with nation-building projects. All of this leads on to the British World, which, in a very different way, has highlighted the significance of the British connection in Canadian history. As we have seen, ideas of Britishness, and of a shared imperial identity, were deployed heavily by both sides of the debate – far more so than notions of a common English-speaking identity encompassing the United States. Expectations of behaviour (whether those of the Ontario government or of the London financial press) were conditioned accordingly. The implicit accusation that the other party was behaving in an un-British manner clearly had some currency. Although it would be wrong to place too much weight on Whitney's tempestuous suggestions that the London financial press might prompt people in Ontario to question the British connection, his suggestions do show the extent to which economics (especially the economics of dependence) could introduce discordant notes into Anglo-Canadian relations. Moreover, it shows that ideas of Britishness were both contested and used in contests, and that ideas of British liberty and responsible government were deployed as means to resist pressures from financial markets in the interests of local economic and political goals.

What might this case study tell us about the interaction of states and global financial markets in the first age of financial globalization? At first glance, Ontario and Canada seem successful at "managing their dependence" on British financial markets, whose influence, it has been argued, was ultimately trumped by the gyrations of electoral politics.[132] This accords well with Rodrik's emphasis on the importance of robust democratic institutions to mediate globalization but might seem to suggest less of a necessary contradiction between nation states, hyperglobalization, and democratic politics than his account suggests.[133] However, if the analysis here holds, the Canadian implications of the Canadian case should be read in a very different, and potentially more interesting, manner. The hydroelectric dispute highlighted that a divided City of London (divided not so much on whether property rights were violated, but on whether, given Canada's economic prospects, this division mattered) provided Canadian governments latitude within the rules of the game. This was a result of the ad hoc way in which the rules of governing the first age of globalization were produced. This in turn highlights an important difference between this period and contemporary globalization – that in practice the first age of globalization itself was governed not by a "straitjacket" (as many accounts, including Rodrik's, imply) but by a loosely fitted set of rules. In other words, at certain times and in certain places, Capitalism 1.0 may have been closer to Capitalism 3.0 than has hitherto been acknowledged. Ontario's wiliness to sponsor public competition to private power generation departed from received norms about public ownership, but not to an extent that its credit became compromised. Indeed, the looseness of the rules of political economy under Capitalism 1.0 meant that at times they more closely resembled the "traffic rules" that Rodrik advocates than the tighter twentieth-century frameworks of Bretton Woods or the Washington Consensus. This created a situation that acknowledged a certain freedom for "countries ... to protect their own social arrangements, regulations, and institutions."[134] In the Canadian case, democratic politics in Ontario and Quebec (and the associated ideologies of provincial rights) had the unintended consequence of further limiting the powerful influence of bankers within this loose framework (although it was never intended as such). Within the British dominions, this latitude was buttressed by the ideology of responsible government and British liberty, an interaction of political culture and economic policymaking unparalleled in contemporary globalization or beyond Britain's self-governing empire. Herein lies an "empire effect" diametrically opposed to that outlined by Ferguson and Schularick and underpinned in part by the sociocultural forces discussed by Magee and Thompson: an effect that permitted subtle but potentially significant *deviations* within the rules.

The broadest implication is that, at least in places (not least Canada and also in the other British dominions), the first age of financial globalization emerges as possessing interesting differences from its successor a century later. Rodrik concludes, "We can and should tell a different story about globalisation. Instead of viewing it as a system that requires a single set of institutions or one principal economic superpower, we should accept it as a collection of diverse nations whose interactions are regulated by a thin layer of simple, transparent, and common sense traffic rules."[135] Intriguingly, it is a story that historians examining Canada's experiences of the first age of globalization may already be well placed to tell.

NOTES

1 Aylesworth to Governor-General, 29 March 1910, RG3/2/10-11 (Premier James Whitney Office Records), Public Archives of Ontario (PAO hereafter), Toronto.
2 H.V. Nelles, "Beck, Sir Adam," in Dictionary of Canadian Biography, vol. 15 (University of Toronto/Université Laval, 2003), accessed 22 October, 2013, http://www.biographi.ca/en/bio/beck_adam_15E.html.
3 "Ontario's Two Victories", *Mail and Empire*, 25 April 1910.
4 K.H. O'Rourke and J.G. Williamson, *Globalization and History: The Evolution of a Nineteenth-Century Atlantic Economy* (Cambridge, MA: 1999); A.G. Hopkins, "Introduction: Globalization, an Agenda for Historians," in *Globalization in World History*, ed. A.G. Hopkins (London: Pimlico, 2002), 6–7.
5 D. Rodrik, *The Globalization Paradox: Why Global Markets, States, and Democracy Can't Coexist* (Oxford: Oxford University Press, 2011), 24–66, 233–4.
6 Ibid., 3–8.

7 Ibid., xviii, 189–90, 238–50, 280.

8 Ibid., 138–42.

9 The differing economic experiences of the British settler colonies and Latin America became important elements in late debates about dependency thesis, a literature on which Rodrik touches. See D.C.M. Platt and G. Di Tella, eds., *Argentina, Australia and Canada: Studies in Comparative Development 1870–1965* (London: Macmillan, 1985); H.M. Schwartz, *In the Dominions of Debt: Historical Perspectives on Dependent Development* (Ithaca, NY: Cornell University Press, 1989).

10 K. Norrie, D. Owram and J.C.H. Emery, *A History of the Canadian Economy* (Toronto: Harcourt Brace, 2002), 358–87. In the period 1910–14, manufacturing constituted 13.7 per cent of Australian GNP and 21.1 per cent of Canadian GNP. Calculated from N.G. Butlin, *Australian Domestic Product, Investment, and Foreign Borrowing, 1861–1938/39* (Cambridge: Cambridge University Press, 1962), 9–10; M.C. Urquhart, "New Estimates of Gross National Product, Canada, 1870–1927: Some Implications for Canadian Development," in *Long-term Factors in American Economic Growth*, ed. S.L. Engerman and R.E. Gallman (Chicago: Chicago University Press, 1992), 11–15.

11 For Cain and Hopkins's evolving interpretation, see P.J. Cain and A.G. Hopkins, *British Imperialism, 1688–2000*, 2nd ed. (Harlow: Longman, 2001), 40–2, 71–4, 205–16; P.J. Cain and A.G. Hopkins, "Afterword: The Theory and Practice of British Imperialism," in *Gentlemanly Capitalism and British Imperialism: The New Debate on Empire*, ed. Raymond E. Dumett (London: Longman, 1999), 204–5; A.G. Hopkins, "Gentlemanly Capitalism in New Zealand," *Australian Economic History Review* 43, no. 3 (2003): esp. 292; A.G. Hopkins, "Informal Empire in Argentina: An Alternative View," *Journal of Latin American Studies* 26, no. 2 (1994): 276–82. For the main criticisms, see L.E. Davis, "The Late Nineteenth-Century British Imperialist: Specification, Quantification and Controlled Conjectures," in *Gentlemanly Capitalism and British Imperialism*, ed. Dumett, 82–112; R.V. Kubicek, "Economic Power at the Periphery: Canada, Australia, and South Africa, 1850–1914," in *Gentlemanly Capitalism and British Imperialism*, ed. Dumett, 113–27; A. Redish, "British Financial Imperialism after the First World War," in *Gentlemanly Capitalism and British Imperialism*, ed. Dumett, 127–41; J. McAloon, "Gentlemanly Capitalism and Settler Capitalists: Imperialism, Dependent Development and Colonial Wealth in the South Island of New Zealand," *Australian Economic History Review* 42, no. 2 (2002): 204–24.

12 A.R. Dilley, "'The Rules of the Game': London Finance, Australia and Canada, c.1900–1914," *Economic History Review* 63 (2010): 1003–31; A.R. Dilley, *Finance, Politics, and Imperialism: Australia, Canada, and the City of London, c.1896–1914* (Basingstoke: Palgrave Macmillan, 2012).

13 Rodrik, *The Globalization Paradox*, 37.

14 For a classic analysis, see S.G. Checkland, "The Mind of the City, 1870–1914,"
    Oxford Economic Papers 9, no. 3 (1957): 261–78.

15 The main edited collections are C. Bridge and K. Fedorowich, eds., *The British
    World: Diaspora, Culture, and Identity* (London: F. Cass, 2003); P.A. Buckner and
    R.D. Francis, eds., *Canada and the British World: Culture, Migration, and Identity*
    (Vancouver: University of British Columbia Press, 2006); P.A. Buckner and R.D.
    Francis, eds., *Rediscovering the British World* (Calgary: University of Calgary Press,
    2005).

16 C. Bridge and K. Fedorowich, "The British World," in *The British World*, ed. Bridge
    and Fedorowich, 7; P.A. Buckner and R. Douglas Francis, "Introduction," in *Redis-
    covering the British World*, ed. Buckner and Francis, 16.

17 Quoted in J. Castell Hopkins, ed., *Canadian Annual Review of Public Affairs –
    1913* (Toronto: The Annual Review Publishing Company,1914), 28. See also R.A.
    Lehfeldt, "The Rate of Interest on British and Foreign Investments," *Journal of the
    Royal Statistical Society* 76, no. 2 (1913): 196–207; L.E. Davis and R.A. Huttenback,
    *Mammon and the Pursuit of Empire: The Political Economy of British Imperialism,
    1860–1912* (Cambridge: Cambridge University Press, 1987), 81–97; N. Ferguson
    and M. Schularick, "The Empire Effect: The Determinants of Country Risk in
    the First Age of Globalization, 1880–1913," *Journal of Economic History* 66, no. 2
    (2006): 283–312.

18 Ferguson and Schularick, "Empire Effect." See also N. Ferguson, "The City of
    London and British Imperialism: New Light on an Old Question," in *London and
    Paris as International Financial Centres in the Twentieth Century*, ed. Y. Cassis and
    É. Bussièr (Oxford: Oxford University Press, 2005), 57–78.

19 Quoted in R. Jebb, *Studies in Colonial Nationalism* (London: Arnold, 1905), 1.

20 G.B. Magee and A.S. Thompson, *Empire and Globalisation: Networks of People,
    Goods and Capital in the British World, c.1850–1914* (Cambridge: Cambridge Uni-
    versity Press, 2010), esp. 170–231. For critiques, see S. Ward, "Review of Empire
    and Globalisation: Networks of People, Goods and Capital in the British World,
    c.1850–1914," *Reviews in History* 100 (2010), 1-6; A. R. Dilley, "Empire, Globalisa-
    tion, and the Cultural Economy of the British World," *Journal of Maritime Research*
    14, no. 1 (2012): 37–41.

21 A. Smith, "Patriotism, Self-Interest and the 'Empire Effect': Britishness
    and British Decisions to Invest in Canada, 1867–1914," *The Journal of
    Imperial and Commonwealth History* 41, no. 1 (2013): 59–80; Dilley, *Finance, Poli-
    tics, and Imperialism*, 91–110.

22 For a recent collection on "English liberty," see J.P. Greene, ed., *Exclusionary Em-
    pire: English Liberty Overseas, 1600–1900* (Cambridge: Cambridge University Press,
    2010).

23 G. Martin, "Canada from 1815," in *Oxford History of the British Empire*, vol. 3, *The Nineteenth Century*, ed. A.N. Porter (Oxford: Oxford University Press, 1999), 540–1.

24 J. Mavor, *Niagara in Politics: A Critical Account of the Ontario Hydro-Electric Commission* (New York: E.P. Dutton, 1925), 150–60.

25 E. McInnis and M. Horn, *Canada: A Political & Social History* (Toronto: Holt, Rinehart and Winston of Canada, 1982), 431–3.

26 A.A. Den Otter, *The Philosophy of Railways: The Transcontinental Railway Idea in British North America* (Toronto: University of Toronto Press, 1997).

27 W.L. Marr and D.G. Paterson, *Canada: An Economic History* (Toronto: MacMillan of Canada, 1980), 66–94, 224.

28 J. Viner, *Canada's Balance of International Indebtedness, 1900–1913* (Cambridge, MA: Harvard University Press, 1924), 139.

29 G.P. Marchildon, *Profits and Politics: Beaverbrook and the Gilded Age of Canadian Finance* (Toronto: University of Toronto Press, 1996), 9, table 1.2.

30 I. Stone, *The Global Export of Capital from Great Britain, 1865–1914: A Statistical Survey* (Basingstoke: Macmillan, 1999), 52–62, table 2; D.C.M. Platt, "Canada and Argentina: The First Preference of the British Investor, 1904–1914," *Journal of Imperial and Commonwealth History* 8 (1985): 77–88.

31 M. Denison, *Canada's First Bank: A History of the Bank of Montreal*, 2 vols. (Montreal: McClelland & Stewart 1966), ii, 61; Viner, *Canada's Balance*, 118.

32 G.P. Marchildon, "'Hands across the Water': Canadian Industrial Financiers in the City of London, 1905–20," *Business History* 34, no. 3 (1992): 69–95.

33 "Canadian Bank of Commerce AGM," *Economist*, 26 January 1907, 153.

34 Quoted in J. Castell Hopkins, ed., *Canadian Annual Review of Public Affairs – 1907* (Toronto: The Annual Review Publishing Company, 1908), 604.

35 For a typical press commentary along these lines, see F.W. Field, *Capital Investments in Canada*, 3rd ed. (Montreal: Monetary Times of Canada, 1914), 223–9.

36 Quoted in D.O. Carrigan, *Canadian Party Platforms, 1867–1968* (Urbana: University of Illinois Press, 1968), 57.

37 See Wilfred Laurier's comments while speaking in favour of the National Transcontinental, *Official Report of the Debates of the House of Commons of Canada* (Ottawa: S.E. Dawson, 1903), 7659.

38 G.D. Taylor and P.A. Baskerville, *A Concise History of Business in Canada* (Oxford: Oxford University Press, 1994), 293.

39 H.V. Nelles, *The Politics of Development: Forests, Mines, and Hydro-Electric Power in Ontario, 1849–1941* (Toronto: Macmillan of Canada, 1974), 216.

40 Ibid., 237–8.

41 R.B. Fleming, *The Railway King of Canada: Sir William Mackenzie, 1849–1923* (Vancouver: University of British Columbia Press, 1991), 113.

42 T. Skinner, ed., *The Stock Exchange Yearbook* (London: T Skinner and Co, 1915),591.
43 In 1905, Grenfell had founded the Canadian Agency to float Canadian bonds. Grenfell also had links with J.S. Morgan (J.P. Morgan's London branch) and (through his business partner and brother-in-law Guy St Aubyn) with the underwriting firm Robert Nivison and Co., which dominated the market in colonial government stocks (and from 1908 underwrote the dominion of Canada's loans). See Dilley, *Finance, Politics, and Imperialism*, 60–1.
44 Nelles, *Politics of Development*, 277.
45 Ibid., 256.
46 Randall White, *Ontario, 1610–1985: A Political and Economic History* (Toronto: Dundurn Press, 1985), 179–80.
47 J. Castell Hopkins, ed., *Canadian Annual Review of Public Affairs – 1904* (Toronto: The Annual Review Publishing Company,1905), 289. For the campaign, see *Canadian Annual Review* (1905), 196–218. See also C.W. Humphries, "Whitney, Sir James Pliny," in Dictionary of Canadian Biography, vol. 14 (Toronto: University of Toronto/Université Laval, 2003)–, accessed 22 October 2013, http://www.biographi.ca/en/bio/whitney_james_pliny_14E.html.
48 Nelles, *Politics of Development*, 258–9.
49 Ibid., 259–79.
50 Mavor, *Niagara in Politics*, 65.
51 Ibid., 66.
52 J. Castell Hopkins, ed., *Canadian Annual Review of Public Affairs – 1906* (Toronto: The Annual Review Publishing Company, 1907), 515.
53 Dilley, "Rules of the Game," 1020–6.
54 Nelles, *Politics of Development*, 268.
55 Grenfell frequently advised Grey on investment matters. See Ranald C. Michie, "The Social Web of Investment in the Nineteenth Century," *Revue Internationale d'Histoire de la Banque* 18 (1979): 165–8.
56 Grenfell to Grey, 29 March 1907, enclosed with Mortimer-Clark to Whitney, 2 April 1907, Whitney Papers, MU 3122, PAO, Toronto. For further discussion, see Fleming, *Railway King*, 121–3.
57 Williams-Taylor to Whitney, 1 August 1907; Chaplain, Milne, Grenfell, and Co. to Whitney, 10 August 1907, Whitney Papers, MU 3123, PAO, Toronto.
58 Nelles, *Politics of Development*, 282.
59 On Toronto's actions, see Mavor, *Niagara in Politics*, 33.
60 On the EAAB, see *Stock Exchange Yearbook* (1915), 1842.
61 Grey to Walker, 27 January 1908, Walker Papers, 1/A/7/31, Thomas Fisher Rare Books Library (TFRBL), Toronto.
62 Walker to Grey, 29 January 1908, Walker Papers, 1/B/20/41, TFRBL, Toronto.

63 Canadian Agency to Whitney, 11 January 1908, Whitney Papers, MU 3124, PAO, Toronto.

64 St Aubyn to Whitney, 30 January 1908; Whitney to St Aubyn, 6 February 1908; Whitney to Whitney, 29 January 1908, Whitney Papers, MU 3124, PAO, Toronto.

65 Fleming, *Railway King*, 134.

66 Hopkins, ed., *Canadian Annual Review* (1908), 97–8. For further discussion, see Christopher Armstrong and H.V. Nelles, *Monopoly's Moment: The Organization and Regulation of Canadian Utilities, 1830–1930* (Philadelphia: Temple University Press, 1986).

67 Quoted in W.R. Lawson, *Canada and the Empire* (London: William Blackwood and Sons, 1911), 263.

68 B.E. Walker, *Canadian Credit and Enterprise* (Toronto: S.N. 1908), 7.

69 Ibid., 2.

70 Ibid., 6.

71 J. Castell Hopkins, ed., *Canadian Annual Review of Public Affairs – 1908* (Toronto: The Annual Review Publishing Company, 1909), 298.

72 Ibid., 302.

73 Charles W. Humphries, *Honest Enough to Be Bold: The Life and Times of Sir James Pliny Whitney* (Toronto: University of Toronto Press, 1985), 174.

74 Hopkins, *Canadian Annual Review* (1909): 298.

75 Ibid., 373.

76 Grenfell to Whitney, 17 November 1908, Whitney Papers, MU 3125, PAO, Toronto.

77 Whitney, "Memo re Interview with Financial Times Journalist re Ontario Hydro," 20 November 1908, Whitney Papers, MU 3125, PAO, Toronto.

78 *Outlook*, 13 March 1909.

79 For City attitudes to property rights, see Dilley, "Rules of the Game," 1020–2

80 W.R. Lawson, "Canadian Finance. III: Abolishing Magna Charta in Ontario," Fielding Papers, MG 2/514/48/2805, Public Archives of Nova Scotia, Halifax.

81 J.P. Whitney to E.C. Whitney, 26 March 1909, Whitney Papers, MU 3127, PAO, Toronto.

82 Williams-Taylor to Whitney, 12 May 1909, Whitney Papers, MU 3127, PAO, Toronto.

83 Whitney to Williams-Taylor, 21 May 1909, Whitney Papers, MU 3127, PAO, Toronto.

84 Whitney to Hanna, 24 June 1909, Whitney Papers, MU 3127, PAO, Toronto.

85 Whitney to Hanna, 17 June 1909, Whitney Papers, MU 3127, PAO, Toronto

86 Whitney to A.J. Dawson, 7 July 1909, Whitney Papers, MU 3128, PAO, Toronto. See also, Whitney to Dawson, 23 July 1909, Whitney Papers, MU 3128, PAO, Toronto.

87 Dawson to Whitney, 23 July 1909, Whitney Papers, MU 3128, PAO, Toronto.

88 Thorold to Whitney, 22 July 1909; Whitney to Thorold, 4 August 1909, Whitney Papers, MU 3128, PAO, Toronto.
89 Hanna to Whitney, 28 June 1909, Whitney Papers, MU 3127, PAO, Toronto.
90 Whitney to Dawson, 27 July 1909, Whitney Papers, MU 3128, PAO, Toronto.
91 Farrer to Whitney, 1 July 1909; Whitney to Williams-Taylor, 9 August 1909, Whitney Papers, MU 3128, PAO, Toronto.
92 "Sir James Whitney's Statement," *Economist*, 28 August 1909, 413–4.
93 On these moves, see Andrew S. Thompson, *Imperial Britain: The Empire in British Politics, c.1880–1932* (London: Longman, 2000).
94 "Sir James Whitney's Statement," 413–4.
95 J.P. Whitney to E.C. Whitney, 13 September 1909, Whitney Papers, MU 3128, PAO, Toronto. On London press practices, see S.J. Potter, *News and the British world: The Emergence of an Imperial Press System, 1876–1922* (Oxford: Clarendon, 2003), 24.
96 Whitney to Dawson, 1 October 1909, Whitney Papers, MU 3128, PAO, Toronto.
97 Field, *Capital Investments in Canada*, 254–82; I.M. Drummond, "Government Securities on Colonial New Issue Markets: Australia and Canada, 1895–1914," *Yale Economic Essays* 1 (1961): 151.
98 Whitney to Williams-Taylor, 21 May 1909, Whitney Papers, MU 3127, PAO, Toronto.
99 I.M. Drummond, "Capital Markets in Australia and Canada, 1895–1914: A Study in Colonial Economic History" (PhD diss., Yale University, 1959), 58–64, 116.
100 *Canadian Annual Review* (1908), 219.
101 For full discussion, see Dilley, *Finance, Politics, and Imperialism*, 124–5.
102 Editorial, *Financier*, 7 May 1909; "British Capital and Enterprise," *Standard*, 7 May 1909; Editorial, *Statist*, 10 July 1909; Editorial, *Investors' Review*, 11 September 1909; W.R. Lawson, "Canada's Competative Borrowing," *Outlook*, 13 March 1909; all reproduced in A.V. Dicey, *The Credit of Canada: How It Is Affected by the Ontario Power Legislation* (Toronto: Toronto Power Company, 1909), 12–37.
103 Griffith to Laurier, 2 September 1909, Laurier Papers, MG 26G/c880/608/159354, Archives Canada (AC), Ottawa.
104 All quoted in Dicey, *The Credit of Canada*, 4–8.
105 Marshall to Laurier, 14 July 1909, MG 26G/c.877/578/157990, AC, Ottawa.
106 Lord Ridley to W.S. Fielding, 4 May 1909, quoted in Dicey, *Credit of Canada*, 2.
107 Hanna to Whitney, 26 January 1909, Whitney Papers, MU 3127, PAO, Toronto.
108 Walker to Laurier, 5 June 1909, Laurier Papers, MG 26G/c.877/575/156477-8, AC, Ottawa.
109 Blaikie to Laurier, 11 June 1909, Laurier Papers, MG 26G/c887/575/15686-9, AC, Ottawa.

110 Ibid.

111 Their power was highlighted by their defection from Laurier over reciprocity in 1911. See R. Cuff, "The Toronto Eighteen and the Election of 1911," *Ontario History* 57 (1965): 189–203.

112 *Weekly Sun*, 1 September 1909, quoted in Dicey, *Credit of Canada*, 52.

113 Baker, Ayling and Co. to Whitney, 26 December 1907, Whitney Papers, MU3123, PAO, Toronto.

114 Baker, Ayling and Co. to Laurier, 23 June 1909, MG 26G/c877/575/157267; Vanderlip to Laurier, 22 November 1909, Laurier Papers, MG 26/c883/599/ 16256204; N.W. Harriss and Co. to Laurier 29 May 1909, reproduced in Dicey, *Credit of Canada*, 253.

115 Walter D. Beadmore to Governor-General [1909], MG 2/514/48/2804 (W.S. Fielding Papers), Provincial Archives of Nova Scotia.

116 Only one American extract appeared in the EDC compilation of protests published as petitions were submitted for disallowance. See Dicey, *Credit of Canada*, 253.

117 Laurier to Walker, 11 June 1909, Laurier Papers, MG 26G/c877/575/156482, AC, Ottawa. Laurier made similar points to Blaikie and Wood, see Laurier to Wood, 19 June 1909; Laurier to Blaikie, 14 June 1909, Laurier Papers, MG 26G. c887/575/157061 and 156870, AC, Ottawa.

118 D. Owen Carrigan, *Canadian Party Platforms, 1867–1968* (Urbana: University of Illinois Press, 1968), 49.

119 Lyon to Laurier, 16 October 1909, Laurier Papers, MG 26G/c881/593/160980, AC, Ottawa.

120 Carrigan, *Canadian Party Platforms*, 49.

121 Hopkins, *Canadian Annual Review* (1909), 403.

122 Brodser to Whitney, 24 December 1909, Whitney Papers, MU 2138, PAO, Toronto.

123 Kerr to Laurier, 23 November 1909; Laurier to Kerr, 26 November 1909, Laurier Papers, MG 26G/c881/593/162629 and 152629, AC, Ottawa.

124 They also focused on other constitutional niceties (including the laughable idea that as a *navigable* river Niagara fell under federal jurisdiction). See F.H. Chrysler, *A Question of Disallowance …* (Ottawa, 1909); Nelles, *Politics of Development*, 297.

125 Dicey, *Credit of Canada*.

126 Mavor, *Niagara in Politics*, 160.

127 Laurier to Vanderlip, 24 November 1909, Laurier Papers, MG 26/c883/599/ 162564, AC, Ottawa.

128 Nelles, *Politics of Development*, 298–300.

129 "Ontario's Two Victories," *Mail and Empire*, 25 April 1910.

130 Aylesworth to Governor-General in Council, 29 March 1910, Whitney Office
     Records, RG3/2, PAO, Toronto.
131 Cain and Hopkins, *British Imperialism, 1688–2000*, 240.
132 For a reading along these lines, see Kubicek, "Economic Power at the Periphery,"
     124–6.
133 Rodrik, *The Globalization Paradox*, 200–2.
134 Ibid., 238–50.
135 Ibid., 280.

2

"Pulpwood Is the Only Thing We Do Export": The Myth of Provincial Protectionism in Ontario's Forest Industry, 1890–1930

MARK KUHLBERG

Ha-Joon Chang and Dani Rodrik demonstrate the degree to which conscious decisions to pursue the policy of "smart" or "selective" globalization were, in large part, responsible for the prosperity attained by today's First World nations. These countries charted a "middle way" between the extremes of unrestricted free trade and an autarkic system. Instead, these nations retained those barriers to the free movement of workers, capital, and goods that they saw as beneficial and jettisoned others. It is against the retention of such barriers that the neoliberals and World Trade Organization (WTO) have been fighting for years, and one of the more recent battles involved Russia. Beginning in 2007, that country's government began implementing a schedule of steep tariff increases on the export of raw logs in an attempt primarily to stimulate its domestic wood-processing industry; by January 2009, the tax would be a whopping 80 per cent. The WTO made dismantling such nationalist economic measures a condition for Russia's entry into the organization. The perverse irony of such a demand, Chang and Rodrik point out, is that the very nations at the centre of the push for international trade liberalization after the Second World War, the United States and Canada, had earlier used such protectionist policies to foster their own forest industries.[1]

Canada actually led the world in this regard, and its richest province – Ontario – was the first to come up with the idea of enacting a measure that was ostensibly designed to promote the "home manufacture" of its extensive treasure trove of natural resources. Known as the "manufacturing condition" and introduced in 1898, it prohibited the export of unprocessed trees (i.e., pine sawlogs and spruce pulpwood) and minerals (i.e., nickel). Practically from the moment the Ontario government implemented this embargo on these resources, it endeavoured to curry public favour by publicizing its fervent commitment to enforcing the policy, and in terms of the manufacturing condition on pulp-wood, historians have generally accepted the politicians' claims about its ap-plication. In the main, these accounts contend that this trade restriction was the central tool by which provincial governments fostered the birth and growth of the domestic pulp and paper industry at the expense of foreign competitors. H.V. Nelles is most commonly identified with having designed the imprima-tur for this school of thought through his analysis of the situation in Ontario. Other authors stamped their works with the same trademark when they ex-amined the respective provincial government's approach to administering pulpwood in other bailiwicks.[2] And the chronicling of the vigorous campaign waged by some pulp and paper producers in the United States in the early 1900s to eliminate the manufacturing condition on pulpwood speaks volumes about the fear the measure invoked in the minds of forest industry executives south of the border.[3]

The evidence indicates, however, that the situation in Ontario was not as we have heretofore believed. This province's experience with the manufacturing condition on pulpwood between 1890 and 1930 vividly demonstrates how, oc-casionally, it was politically expedient for a government with jurisdiction over natural resources to present merely the impression of being a fervent defender of nationalistic policies. During those years, Ontario handled the manufactur-ing condition on pulpwood in a manner that was never intended to stop the flow of spruce heading south across the international border. Rather, the pro-vincial government aimed the policy squarely at creating the crucial foundation on which it could revitalize its languishing northern colonization program, namely, by creating the best possible market for the trees the northern settlers cut as they cleared their land and nearby tracts controlled by others. Thereafter, those involved in the export trade quickly capitalized on this convenient excuse for its existence in the province to further their enterprises, and the prosper-ity they enjoyed was in no small part attributable to the remarkably tight ties that connected them to the elected officials. The consequence was that both the number of American mills that imported pulpwood from Ontario and the volume of fibre that they procured in the province grew steadily over the next three decades. It will be shown that a succession of provincial governments – of various political stripes – repeatedly reiterated its devout commitment to en-forcing the embargo on spruce, but their actions belied their words. A host of "domestic" considerations thus resulted in the Ontario government facilitating the growth of the province's export trade in pulpwood from just before until long after the turn of the twentieth century, an approach that resulted in On-tario vying for the mantle of Canada's biggest supplier of fibre to the American pulp and paper industry by the eve of the Depression.

To understand how Ontario achieved this position by the 1920s, we need to look at the province's political institutions in earlier decades. The former Canada West entered Confederation in 1867 from a position of strength, boasting roughly half of both the fledgling dominion's population and seats in its House of Commons. It owed its preponderance largely to geography and climate, which had gifted the province's "southern peninsula" with the largest acreage of the newborn country's best farmland. This terrain had attracted vast waves of settlers beginning after the American Civil War, causing the colony's population to roughly double on a decadal basis for the next seventy years. Ontario's leaders were acutely aware that the province's prosperity during this period rested on its successful agricultural sector, and were thus deeply troubled when the province's prime arable land (i.e., in Southern Ontario) had all been settled by the time of Confederation. Their concerns were exacerbated when, during the remainder of the nineteenth century and first decade of the twentieth century, Ontario's population growth slowed considerably. At the same time, the prairies were being settled at a meteoric rate because of the attractiveness of homesteading on the prairies' vast acreage of unbroken grasslands. These developments gave Ontarians every reason to believe that their lack of a new farming frontier was bringing closer the day when the province would be toppled from its position of national ascendancy.

Determined to avoid this fate, Ontario prepared to do battle. It had laid the foundation for taking up the cudgels years earlier through the timber policy that it had implemented. Determined to extend its farming frontier by offering practically free land to would-be settlers who were willing to take on the challenge of clearing a tract of its trees before they could sow food crops, the provincial government had endeavoured first to capitalize on its valuable stands of white and red pine by licensing lumbermen to cut them. It sold them only the privilege of harvesting the trees, however, and not the land on which the pine grew. This allowed the province to generate income from the harvesting of Crown timber *and* expedite the establishment of farms when it handed the settlers the cut-over areas. Moreover, there had been little conflict between the lumbermen and settlers in the province's most southerly reaches because these woodlands were generally composed of hardwoods with only a few scattered large pine trees.

This arrangement created immense problems in the late 1800s when settlers began pushing onto the Canadian Shield in places like the Parry Sound District in which large swathes of pine dominated the landscape, and the government solved the problems in a way that favoured the lumbermen (Map 1). Undeniably, the provincial state's priority was furthering its agricultural agenda, but it also recognized the lifeblood that the lumbermen's stumpage dues represented to the treasury. Between 1890 and 1910, timber revenues from cutting pine constituted roughly one-third of the province's annual income. As a result, the government took steps to protect the timber industry from its greatest threats. At the top of the list was the very real danger posed by pioneers, who were renowned for their proclivity for recklessly employing fire in clearing their land only to have the blazes raze adjacent tracts of pine. A close second was the seemingly ever-expanding ranks of "bogus settlers," who exploited the government's willingness to hand out practically free land to potential homesteaders to acquire stands of timber, fell them, and then abandon them. To address these issues, Ontario reserved practically all the pine on settlers' land for the lumbermen, anticipated the future advance of settlement by selling timber stands to the lumbermen *before* the homesteaders arrived, and protected the province's remaining great pineries by setting them aside as "forest reserves" within which it prohibited settlement.[4]

These measures served the lumbermen's interests well, but they had a detrimental effect on the move to settle Central Ontario and the more accessible southern fringes of Northern Ontario. It was already an uphill battle to try to eke out an existence as a farmer on land that was often defined by shallow and unfavourable soils and a harsh climate, but even before the homesteader could dream of seeding his tract, he had to clear it. When the government denied him access to all but nominal volumes of the only valuable species of tree on his land (i.e., the pine), it had thereby eliminated the opportunity for those occupying the lower rungs of the socio-economic ladder from even considering the prospect of heading north to farm. These would-be settlers could not afford to be self-financing during the land-clearing (i.e., no income) phase of their homesteading experience. In fact, the fires settlers typically set to clear their properties attested to the worthlessness of much of the forest crop on their land.

But then, serendipity smiled on the province's floundering drive to extend its farming frontier. North American paper producers began using wood – specifically spruce – instead of rags in the 1860s. In the next three decades, the patents on the machinery required to make trees into paper expired. This conjunction of circumstances made spruce "pulpwood," which was previously considered a worthless "weed" species, a highly valuable commodity. Fortunately, spruce grew – often in profusion – in the areas in which settlement had heretofore been stalling, and its presence gave the settlers an opportunity to cut and sell it during the trying days of clearing their properties; working to harvest spruce from other nearby tracts would also provide badly needed income. In addition, although Ontario's pulp and paper industry was relatively small prior to the First World War, there were dozens of mills across the border in the

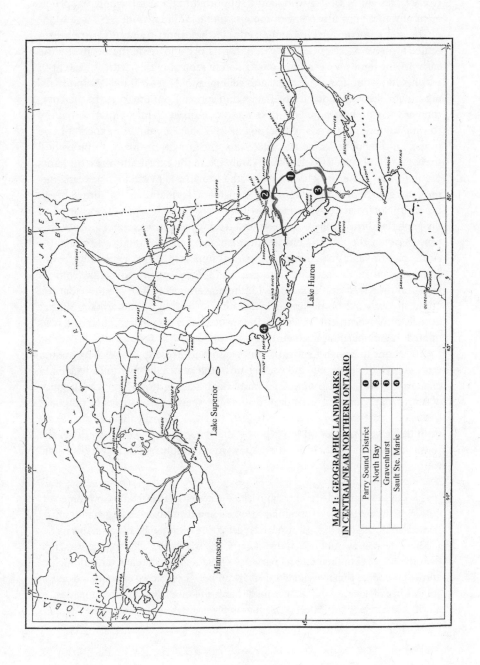

**MAP 1: GEOGRAPHIC LANDMARKS
IN CENTRAL/NEAR NORTHERN ONTARIO**

Parry Sound District	❶
North Bay	❷
Gravenhurst	❸
Sault Ste. Marie	❹

Great Lakes states whose woodlands supported but a scant supply of spruce. Naturally, these producers eagerly sought Ontario's pulpwood.[5]

The government quickly recognized that the export trade in spruce represented – above all else – the salvation for its drive to settle the north. By the early 1890s, senior government officials were reporting that settlers were both cutting pulpwood from their lots and selling it to American buyers and making money during the winter by harvesting spruce from the forest in the environs of their homesteads. For these reasons, Aubrey White, Ontario's deputy commissioner of Crown lands, argued in 1892 that "it would be expedient and proper in the public interest to encourage the growth of this new [pulpwood harvesting] industry (which will no doubt cause the expenditure of large sums of money in the newly settled parts of the Province)." Within a few years, numerous reports were describing the "considerable quantities" of spruce being cut from Northern Ontario and how they were being "every year exported to the paper factories of the United States." And when a new conflict arose at this time between the settlers and lumbermen as a result of pulpwood's rags-to-riches rise in value in Ontario, the critical importance that exporting spruce had assumed in the settlers' lives caused the government to break from its long-standing tradition of siding with the powerful sawmillers in these battles. Thereafter, when a homesteader located his lot within a lumberman's timber licence, the government "reserved" the spruce pulpwood to the settler and prohibited the lumberman from cutting it.[6]

The extent to which exporting pulpwood had become the settlers' manna was made clear during the intense debate in the late 1890s over the advisability of allowing this trade to continue. Milton Carr, a settler from Trout Creek south of North Bay, captured the homesteaders' perspective in a series of poignant letters he wrote to the *Globe* in early 1897 (Map 1). He asked what else – apart from harvesting pulpwood for export – the "poor settlers" could do to get the "basic necessities for their families. They would simply be on the verge of starvation." Carr continued:

> I have lived in this district for twenty years and have seen the Ontario Government feeding the settlers by distributing cornmeal and oatmeal in small quantities to each family through their Crown lands agents here at the public expense. This was before the railway ran through this country, and which now allows the settlers to realize on some of their natural resources of the country, the chief one of which is pulpwood, to gain a livelihood … they can always cut a cord of pulpwood and buy a bag of flour at a day's notice in the hardest of times. But shut off his market, which is naturally the States … and you simply starve the settlers out.[7]

The wrangling over this issue also raised several other critical points about Ontario's export trade in pulpwood. Although on a per family basis the income generated by harvesting and selling pulpwood was relatively tiny, it was crucial to the homesteaders' survival. "Spruce is the poor settler's only asset," Tom Swalwell, who lived near Sault Ste Marie, argued at this time; "it is his winter harvest" (Map 1). Second, Carr pointed out that it would be hypocritical for politicians in Ontario – a province whose economic backbone was based largely on the export of farm products – even to suggest restricting the trade in the hinterland's trees. For settlers living in the north, Carr stressed that "pulpwood is the only thing we do export. I never saw or heard of a car of grain go out of these districts ... An export duty on pulpwood is to the people of these districts the same as an export duty on wheat, beef, pork, butter, cheese, etc., would be to the settlers of the border counties of Ontario." Finally, Carr underscored the issue's high political profile in the hinterland when he reminded Ontario's ruling party – the Liberals – of the damage they would inflict on their fortunes if they ever curtailed the flow of spruce heading south to the United States. Attesting to the size of Carr's flexed political muscle was the letter-writing campaign that the exporting interests orchestrated at this time, one supported by several notable elected officials from Northern Ontario, to convince the dominion government not to implement a pulpwood embargo.[8]

Obviously, American pulp and paper makers were crucial players in this nascent business, and from the outset, they acted shrewdly. They sought a stable, long-term fibre supply, and also realized that the development of Ontario's pulp and paper industry would both cut into the quantity of fibre available for export as well as create a string of new competitors north of the border. Mills in the United States thus had good reason to establish branch timber operations in the province that could perform several functions. These functions included acting as brokers between the individual settlers and the American buyers and acquiring Crown pulpwood tracts from the Ontario government from which they could harvest the spruce and ship it to the United States. By the early 1890s, the Ontario government was deluged with applications for pulpwood-cutting privileges of this nature.[9]

In an effort to avoid creating a public relations disaster for the Ontario government – exporting unprocessed natural resources was intensely controversial in the context of late nineteenth-century Canada – the Americans established a distinct modus operandi. Most often, they offered financial support to Ontarians who would cooperate with them in arranging access to the province's spruce on at least a semi-permanent basis. To provide their operations with an acceptable façade, the Americans traditionally incorporated subsidiaries to which they gave names that bore no resemblance to the American parent company and instead identified the new enterprises with a leading local son or landmark. To head the newly created "local" firm, they hired either the area's most prominent businessmen or politicians, who were often one and the same. This arrangement gave the exporting business the appearance of having the blessing of the northern region in which it operated and provided the prominent clique of native denizens involved in the venture with a vested interest in ensuring the continued flow of pulpwood barges and railcars across the border.

The inaugural cast of characters – ignominiously christened the "Timber Barons" by one author – who functioned in this capacity was legendary. James Conmee personified Ontario's pioneering pulpwood exporters. He sat as the Liberal member of Provincial Parliament (MPP) from Northern Ontario for most of the late 1800s and early 1900s, and he and James Whalen, his son-in-law, obtained the privilege of cutting prime stands of spruce on several watersheds that drained into Ontario's side of Lake Superior. In the early 1890s, the Port Huron Sulphite Company, with pulp and paper mills in Michigan, incorporated the aptly named North Shore Timber Company in Ontario, and Whalen became its spokesperson in the province. Similarly, transplanted Detroit lawyer Walter H. Russell was another leading figure in the trade at this time and over the next few decades through his eponymous firm. A prominent Conservative, he initially represented Northern Island Pulpwood Company in the province, which purchased and harvested pulpwood for another group of American mills, primarily Detroit Sulphite Pulp and Paper Company. Frank H. Keefer was also a well-known Tory lawyer and principal player in the pulpwood exporting business at the Lakehead in the Thunder Bay District.[10]

Although these entrepreneurs could obtain exportable pulpwood legally by buying it from settlers and obtaining tracts of Crown timber from the government, by the 1890s they had devised several cunning – and far more enticing – schemes for achieving the same aim, the first two of which flourished only because of the provincial government's complicity. In 1892, Conmee succeeded in amending Ontario's mining legislation. Thereafter, only the pine – and not the pulpwood – found on a claim was reserved to the Crown, thereby freeing "bogus miners" to procure spruce at the cost of only a nominal administrative fee. By 1897, Conmee and Whalen had secured dozens of square miles of exportable timber in this manner. The pulpwood exporters also adopted the time-honoured subterfuge of posing as "bogus settlers." It permitted them to gain control over the timber on the virtually free land the government offered potential homesteaders and earned them the epithet "pulpwood pirates." Once they had cleared these tracts of spruce and exported the timber free of Crown dues, they simply abandoned the territory and moved on to new terrain. Finally, the exporters often simply cut spruce illegally, confident that they were operating – just like the lumbermen – in a vast wilderness that was patrolled by but a handful of government officials.[11]

Considering that this was the context within which the Liberals imposed the manufacturing condition on pulpwood in 1900, it is little wonder that they stressed that their aim in doing so was certainly not to put an end to the robust export trade in spruce. Consider a comparison of their approach to applying this embargo with the one they had imposed on pine logs in 1898. At that time, they had vigorously enforced the measure, for example. The Department's[12] *Annual Report* for 1899 boasted that it had hired special agents to patrol Crown woodlands to ensure that the embargo on pine sawlogs was "strictly observed, so that everybody might realise that the policy adopted by the Legislature was one deliberately adopted and was intended to be enforced ... The work entailed considerable expense, but as an object lesson of Ontario's intention it ... had an excellent effect." Furthermore, the embargo on sawlogs was simply the capstone on a series of steps the government had taken to protect the supply of lumbermen's timber in Ontario. Because the government had already enacted statues that prohibited anyone – such as miners and settlers – from cutting pine, the only pine timber available in commercial quantities in Ontario was on Crown lands, and now the government had stipulated that it had to be processed domestically. The upshot was the halt – virtually overnight – to pine sawlogs heading to the United States for manufacture into lumber.[13]

It was a fundamentally different story, however, when the government extended the manufacturing condition to "spruce and other pulpwood" in 1900. The reigning Grits certainly contended that doing so would foster domestic industry, but they never even suggested that it would end the export trade in pulpwood. They devoted no resources to enforcing the statute and, unlike.the embargo on pine, nary a voice was raised in protest against it.[14] Moreover, in explaining their rationale for implementing the restriction, they stressed time and time again how it would aid the settlers because the bulk of the pulpwood heading to the United States was coming from the homesteaders' private lands and the embargo applied only to timber cut on Crown lands. The government had thus carved out a marketplace in which the settlers were theoretically the sole legal sellers of exportable pulpwood in Ontario. In the same breath as the Grits were declaring their fervent belief that it behoved them to push settlement aggressively into the hinterland because this policy was the only way "that the Province could retain its present foremost position in the Dominion," they were explaining that "[u]nder the [manufacturing condition] regulation the settlers were the only persons entitled to export or sell [pulpwood] for export, and the necessary effect must be to greatly improve the conditions for the settler. As the supply was lessened and the American demand increased, the settlers, and they only, would reap the benefit."[15]

Although this theory was the Ontario government's official rationalization for imposing the manufacturing condition on pulpwood, the government was also intent on using the embargo to foster the export trade in spruce in a way that had little to do with pushing farming in the north. For example, the law that had imposed the manufacturing condition on pine in 1898 insisted that this species had to be processed into lumber, whereas the "embargo" on pulpwood declared that it must be made "into merchantable pulp or paper, or into sawn lumber, woodenware, utensils ... or other articles of commerce or merchandise as distinguished from the said spruce or other timber in its raw or unmanufactured state." This significant detail created a potential loophole, which, it will be seen, was easily exploited in due course to allow for the export of pulpwood from Crown land. Likewise, the fact that the legislation insisted that Crown pulpwood be processed in Canada and not Ontario protected American interests such as the largest exporter of spruce from the dominion, International Paper Company (IP). Although IP obtained most of its spruce from Quebec, it had been both harvesting pulpwood on "Indian Reserves" in Ontario's Algoma District north of Sault Ste Marie since the early 1890s and shipping the pulpwood to its mills in New York and New England. If IP were able to obtain Crown timber limits in Ontario, the firm could harvest this pulpwood, ship it to Quebec, and then export it. Even the pro-Liberal *Globe* spoke out against this lacuna in the legislation, declaring that "a Province has no means of following its pulpwood or ore after it has passed to another Province, and there are circumstances under which it could then be exported in violation" of Ontario's embargo.[16]

Most importantly, the new pulpwood legislation spoke to the political pull exercised by the entrepreneurs engaged in exporting spruce. The statute exempted the Crown timber licences held by North Shore Timber – James Whalen's firm – from the interdict's effect. Moreover, just prior to introducing the measure in 1900, the Liberals had granted Whalen a 60-square-mile tract of prime exportable pulpwood on the shore of Lake Superior, which represented for the next fifteen years the largest Crown pulpwood licence in this region. In defending this proviso in the legislation, E.J. Davis, Liberal commissioner of Crown lands, indicated that it had been asked for by both Liberals and "Port Arthur Conservatives, including Mr. Keefer, President of the Conservative Association" (Map 2). The bipartisanship in this instance reflected the crucial link that had developed between the pulpwood exporters and the provincial government. Over at least the next three decades, as the balance of power in the

Ontario Legislature swung between Liberals, Conservatives, and United Farmers and the quantity of pulpwood exported from Ontario steadily rose, control
over this remunerative business was concentrated in the hands of this tightly
knit group based largely at the Lakehead for whom the moniker "the old non-
partisan 'Timber Ring'" was most apt.[17]

And when the government announced a series of initiatives to reinvigorate
its colonization program in Northern Ontario concomitantly with its enactment of the manufacturing condition on pulpwood, it did so in a manner that
demonstrated how facilitating the export trade in spruce was becoming the
dominant force shaping its hinterland settlement policy.[18] To be sure, the ruling Liberals continued to believe and argue – as did most good Ontarians –
that settling the hinterland was both a feasible and highly desirable part of the
province's growth strategy. At the same time, however, the government used
it as a convenient excuse for strengthening the exporters' operations. In 1900,
for example, it funded an investigation into the agricultural potential in a large
part of Northern Ontario. Predictably, the study's report waxed eloquent about
the tens of thousands of square miles – particularly the northern Clay Belt (the
southern Clay Belt was already being settled) – that were "well adapted for cul-
tivation" and how "the climate in this northern district present[ed] no obstacle
to successful agricultural settlement" (Map 2). Also in 1900, the government
established the Colonization Bureau with a mandate to publicize wide and far
Northern Ontario's unlimited agricultural potential. The next year, the Liberals
brought in the Voluntary Land Grant Act, which sought to kick-start the settlement process by rewarding veterans of the Boer War and the Fenian Raids with
160-acre grants of free land in townships that it would set aside in Northern
Ontario specifically for this purpose.[19]

Although this policy was arguably a benign use of Crown resources, and
undoubtedly at least some who qualified for land under this program endeavoured to make a go of it on the hinterland, the statute's details indicated that
its prime intent was to augment the flow of spruce to the United States. The
Liberals had offered virtually free land to potential homesteaders since the time
of Confederation, and there were ample means available to continue doing so.
But singling out the "veterans" enrobed the export of pulpwood from the lands
set aside for them in a cloak that would be nearly impervious to criticism. An
initiative geared towards assisting those who had defended the colony and dominion in their time of need struck a chord that resonated perfectly with the
electorate in "Empire Ontario," which was experiencing an unprecedented desire to celebrate its past military glories. This aegis would not have been needed
had the veterans actually been keen to settle on the hinterland, but they were

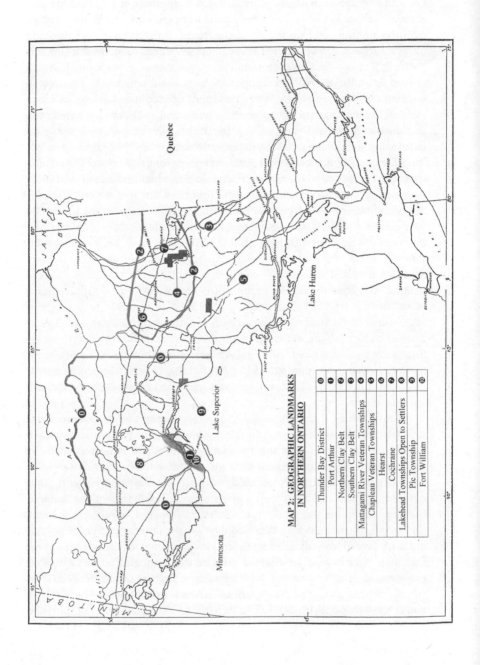

**MAP 2: GEOGRAPHIC LANDMARKS
IN NORTHERN ONTARIO**

⓪	Thunder Bay District
①	Port Arthur
②	Northern Clay Belt
③	Southern Clay Belt
④	Mattagami River Veteran Townships
⑤	Chapleau Veteran Townships
⑥	Hearst
⑦	Cochrane
⑧	Lakehead Townships Open to Settlers
⑨	Pic Township
⑩	Fort William

not. Instead, the overwhelming majority of them chose not to take the government up on its offer of free land but instead to simply apply for "scrip," a voucher entitling them to their lot on the frontier. When they went to sell their interest in their quarter section (most often to a pulpwood exporter), it was only a foolhardy Ontarian who would dare criticize the state for providing the province's war heroes with this type of social assistance.[20]

The eventual scope of the 1901 statute spoke directly to this issue. The Liberals had defined "veteran" in the broadest terms imaginable, and if a particular applicant whose claim to a homesteading tract in Northern Ontario seemed to fall outside even these wide parameters, the government habitually expanded them. The upshot was staggering. Although only a total of 7,368 men from *all* of Canada had enlisted in the Boer War and far fewer had "served" in the clashes with the Fenians, mere months after the legislation had been enacted the commissioner of Crown lands, E.J. Davis, stated the obvious when he declared that the number of applications under the act – 16,000 so far! – had greatly exceeded expectations; he added that they "were continuing to pour in at the rate of 100 [to] 150 a day." Even though he openly admitted that he could not "for a moment imagine" that this number had been on active service, within a few years the Ontario government had processed the paperwork required in doling out nearly 14,000 certificates for lots in the north.[21]

Two other aspects of the Voluntary Land Grant Act reveal how its de facto aim was to assist the export trade in pulpwood. The statute's original terms left the veteran, within ten years of being granted a lot, free to sell its timber except for the pine (i.e., the pulpwood). More significant, however, were the townships the government chose to set aside for the veterans. Experts exhorted the government to investigate carefully soil types and drainage in Northern Ontario's townships to ensure that they would support agriculture before opening them to settlement and to permit settlement to proceed only in areas that were near existing communities and transportation links. Even though the government had heretofore taken this approach in places like Parry Sound and Muskoka, the Liberals discarded it in selecting the townships that the veterans could settle. Granted, a couple of the sites in the Kenora District and one at the Lakehead met these criteria, but the rest – more than twenty – did not. The Liberals (and the Tories later) chose sixteen townships, for example, that bordered much of the east side of the Mattagami River watershed. In the context of early twentieth-century Northern Ontario, these tracts were as far from civilization as one could possibly have imagined; the nearest town was more than 100 miles to the south! Likewise, the six townships that the government set aside in what is now the Chapleau District were only a short distance north of the Canadian Pacific Railway, but they were still literally in the middle of nowhere (Map 2).

As poorly suited as these townships were to supporting commercial farming, however, their rich spruce forests made them ideal for hosting pulpwood harvesting operations.[22]

Finally, the wake that the act created spoke to its ultimate aim. No sooner had the statute become law than a host of interests sprang up to traffic in land "scrip" solely for the purpose of acquiring practically free tracts of prime, exportable spruce. Veterans were already organized into local associations, and prescient entrepreneurs – many of whom held elected office or were closely allied with those who did – endeavoured to profit from tapping into these existing networks to track down eligible parties, or their descendants, and purchase their interest in these land entitlements. Moreover, a political insider later revealed that the government intentionally selected lots for which scrip could be redeemed that were "unfit for farming" but prime for timbering. Within only one year, an especially zealous party at the Lakehead was able to net a Michigan pulp and paper mill thousands of acres of rich spruce timberlands in this way. As a result, just as the Ontario government had outlawed the export of pulpwood cut from Crown land, this act had set aside more than 2 million acres of prime pulpwood on private land that the exporters could exploit now and far into the future, a move that must have assuaged any concerns they entertained about the impact of the province's "embargo" on spruce.[23]

Although there is no official estimate of the quantity of pulpwood exported from Ontario prior to the Liberals' defeat in 1905, a few contemporaries left accounts that paint a graphic picture. B.M. Wylie was one of the Department's officials in the Thunder Bay District. Even before the implementation of the manufacturing condition, he had repeatedly endeavoured to throw a wrench into the machinations of the pulpwood pirates. Outraged by Liberal (and subsequent government) collusion with these schemes, Wylie lamented years later that "long before the advent of the Whitney regime [in 1905] ... the Conmees, Whalens, McCumbers [sic] [a prominent Lakehead lawyer] etc. ... had ... denuded entire townships of the standing timber through manipulations of Fenian Raid Veterans Script and other very questionable procedure[s] to the discredit of honourable and righteous government."[24]

When the Conservatives swept to power in Ontario in 1905, they did so on a reformist platform that promised, among other things, to improve on their predecessors' record of administering the province's timber resources. The Tories were particularly aware that it was politic to present the appearance of strict adherence to the manufacturing condition on pulpwood. In this era of bursting Canadian economic nationalism and optimism, every government in the dominion with jurisdiction over significant quantities of pulpwood placed a manufacturing condition on spruce cut from Crown lands.[25] The Conservatives thus repeatedly reaffirmed their commitment to this measure. Typical was the exchange in 1910 between Sir William Van Horne, one of the period's most vocal defenders of the pulpwood embargo, and James P. Whitney, Ontario's premier. Alarmed at the extensive export of unprocessed spruce from Canada in general and the Thunder Bay District in particular, Van Horne conveyed his anxieties to Whitney. The premier responded by giving the Montreal industrialist a personal pledge. "You may rely upon it," Whitney promised, "that in every way possible we will prevent the exportation of pulpwood."[26]

This rhetoric was the government's official line, but it bore little resemblance to reality. With the dominion government's promotion of the prairies as a land of golden opportunity for grain farmers attracting millions of both overseas immigrants and Canadian migrants to the region, the need for Ontario to transform the north into its own Arcadia acquired an unprecedented level of urgency. In some ways, conditions seemed ripe for realizing the province's aim. Ontario benefited from the construction of several railways into and across its northern reaches, thereby rendering them more accessible. Furthermore, the government continued to receive sage advice on this matter from numerous forestry officials, including Bernhard E. Fernow, the august dean of the provincial forestry school in Toronto. They called not for an end to the campaign to farm on the hinterland, but rather measures to strengthen it, specifically ending the pulpwood exporters' abuse of the settlement legislation and undertaking careful surveys of the territory before encouraging farming there. There was a crying need for this type of study, after all. No one had ever farmed this far north in Ontario where frosts were not uncommon in July, the growing season lasted barely three months, and its heavy soils and swampy terrain provided prima facie evidence that it was best suited to growing spruce and sphagnum moss, not wheat and oats.[27]

The Tories ignored this counsel, however, and more. They excoriated officials like Fernow for casting aspersions on the idea of farming up north and devoted enormous sums to a comprehensive public relations campaign that grossly misrepresented the lifestyle that would be possible in the north. Prominent in the campaign's promotional literature were prosperous farmers proudly standing in fields teeming with bushels of wheat, images that suggested that there was little to choose between taking up a quarter section in Saskatchewan or Ontario's hinterland (Figures 2.1 and 2.2). All the while, the Conservatives – and all other governments in Ontario between at least 1890 and 1930 – knew full well that the survival of nearly all settlers would depend on cutting pulpwood largely for export (there were only seven pulp and paper mills in Ontario prior to 1919, when the Tories left power). Whereas farming out west was, by and large, a full-time, year-round occupation, senior government officials recognized that this would never be the case in places like Hearst and Cochrane (Map 2). "It is, of course, understood that a man cannot be expected to maintain his family by his agricultural operations," a government memorandum on the subject declared in 1919. "The land, however, is ... well wooded with spruce and other woods suitable for pulp. The taking out of pulpwood will afford a considerable income."[28]

During the Tories' fifteen-year reign (1905–19), they demonstrated their wholehearted commitment to the pulpwood exporters in a manner that was truly remarkable. During this period, the value of spruce doubled, and American pulp and paper mills grew in size and became increasingly dependent on Canadian fibre. These factors greatly extended the range within which it was feasible for paper makers in the Great Lakes states to procure pulpwood. The Hammermill Paper Company in Erie, Pennsylvania, for example, had begun procuring spruce from settlers and small contractors in Northeastern Ontario in 1908. Although the provincial politicians would have welcomed this type of activity, the advent of the First World War could have fundamentally altered their views. Hammermill was, after all, owned by German interests, and Canada was swept by a virulent anti-Kaiser fervour during the conflict, a campaign that sought to wipe out all signs of a Prussian presence in the country. The Ontario government did its part by convincing the provincial university in Toronto to fire three of its professors of German heritage. However, when concerned Canadians voiced their concerns over Hammermill being allowed to export spruce from the country, given that the dominion was at war with Germany, the provincial government did not even bat an eyebrow. In fact, Hammermill enlarged its footprint in Ontario at this time, setting up a permanent office in the province to help coordinate its annual purchase of spruce.[29]

What made this period so noteworthy is both the degree to which the Conservatives facilitated the exporters' two favourite ruses – posing as bogus settlers and miners – and how patronage considerations increasingly determined who enjoyed these lucrative privileges. The Lakehead had been the traditional bastion for securing practically free grants of land under the guise of settling them, and W.A. Dowler, a leading local lawyer, provided a front-line account of how the system functioned. In "nearly every riding," he contended, "there is a coterie or clique, which have in the past been close to the Counsels of the member or the party leaders." These "insiders" exploited their connections to learn about townships that the government was about to open for settlement and the location of the best spruce stands within them. "When the public learn that the Township is open," Dowler continued, "they are surprised to find that the best

Figure 2.1. Northern Ontario agricultural propaganda poster, ca 1915

Figure 2.2. Northern Ontario agricultural propaganda poster, ca 1915

locations, particularly the best timbered locations, are already allotted."[30] As a result, by the eve of the First World War, most of the pulpwood in a string of townships that buffered Lake Superior for more than 200 miles rested in the hands of several exporting interests (Map 2). After the construction of railways opened up Northeastern Ontario's Clay Belt to the exporters, they moved in to acquire land set aside for the veterans at a clip that came as a shock even to the premier himself. One enterprise, which had amassed nearly 150 square miles of land in the veterans' townships on the Mattagami River watershed, tried to "flip" its holdings to a Wall Street investment house in 1912. Curious to learn more about the opportunity, the financiers wrote Premier Whitney for information. He replied matter-of-factly that the Americans were being had because the Crown owned the land to which they were referring. The bankers then asked how it could be possible "for any one to offer lands, to the amount of 100,000 acres ... in Fee Simple, as has been done to us, if the same is owned by the Crown and cannot be bought outright, but only leased." The premier was unable to provide an answer because he was clearly unfamiliar with the darker side of his own government's "colonization" scheme.[31]

The Tories also oversaw the dramatic expansion in the staking of bogus mining claims. They permitted, for example, the local representatives of Wisconsin-based Marathon Paper Mills to "stake out" much of Pic Township as its pulpwood domain (Map 2).[32] Although officials in the Department and members of the general public provided the government with evidence of the pseudo-miners' activities, the Tories did nothing to end them; the minister of lands, forests and mines, G. Howard Ferguson, was infamous for laughing incredulous informants out of his office.[33]

The Tories even went so far as to suspend the manufacturing condition on specious grounds when they passed An Act Respecting the Export of Pulpwood in 1914. It declared that it was desperately needed to address the crisis caused by "severe windstorms" that had blown down a large quantity of spruce pulpwood, timber it contended would "be destroyed unless speedily cut." The statute explained that holders of timber licences in the affected area had complained that there was no market in Canada for their pulpwood, prompting them to apply for permission to export it. This may well have been a laudable initiative, but the legislation failed to indicate the location of the windstorms or why this spruce could not be sold in Ontario to any of the province's operating mills. Nevertheless, the legislation granted the affected licensees relief "by temporarily suspending the operation of 'The Manufacturing Condition'" and authorizing the minister to permit wind-thrown pulpwood to be exported "for such period as to him may seem proper within the current season of 1914." Although the Tories denied charges that enacting this legislation undermined their commitment to the embargo on Crown pulpwood, over the next few years the provincial government stood alone in its belief that Northern Ontario had been repeatedly swept by gales that warranted quietly extending the act's provisions until 1918.[34]

The result of the Tories' actions was highly predictable. The Department's "official" records indicate that the quantity of spruce leaving the province annually doubled between 1913 (when the data begin) and 1919, a period that saw more than 1 million cords exported by a host of firms that were growing in size and number (Figure 2.3). Considering the clandestine nature of many of the exporters' activities, it can safely be estimated that they shipped at least twice the official total to the United States during these years.

Like the Tories before them, the United Farmers of Ontario (UFO) promised many things upon their victory in the provincial election of 1919. One was to clean up the administration of Crown forests by putting a stop to the chicanery, including that carried out by pulpwood exporters. They also looked to reinvigorate the push to extend farming in the north, a highly predictable goal from a party that spoke for the province's agricultural interest. The government's aim remained transforming forests into wheat fields in the north in general and the northern Clay Belt in particular, and no politician in Ontario dared suggest that this dream was illusory. During one debate over this issue in 1920, *Hansard* reported that "[e]veryone [in the Legislature] defended the North against any insinuation that it wouldn't produce [agriculturally]."[35]

But in the name of attempting to realize this particular objective, the UFO continued to implement policies that aimed primarily to export pulpwood from both private and Crown lands. In fact, Ernest C. Drury's government did much more than merely permit the American pulp and paper mills and their Ontario subsidiaries to continue abusing the province's settlement and mining legislation to realize their ends.

We can see this in the UFO government's dealings with Russell Timber Company, one of the province's leading pulpwood exporters since the early 1900s. Under the Tories, the company had operated with apparent impunity in procuring spruce from bogus mining claims, settlers' lots, and Crown lands on which it trespassed. When a royal commission learned of the company's illegal activities in early 1920, the Department assigned B.M. Wylie, one of its most experienced field officials, to rein the firm in. For several months, Wylie investigated Russell's operations, compiled an impressive dossier of improprieties, sent his findings to Toronto, and awaited further instructions. Although he was imploring his superiors to authorize him to seize the pulpwood that the firm had recently illegally procured and was preparing to export, W.H. Russell's counsel and partner, F. H. Keefer, lobbied the Farmers to allow Russell

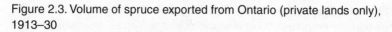

Figure 2.3. Volume of spruce exported from Ontario (private lands only), 1913–30

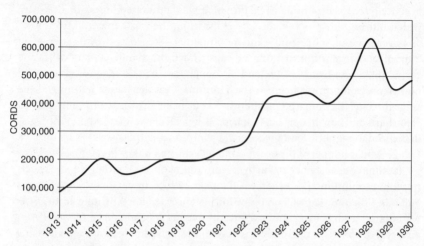

Source: "Regulations Governing the Export of Unmanufactured Timber on Crown Lands in Ontario," table 2, 21 March 1939, RG1-E-10, 19, 1–6-1, vol. 1, Archives of Ontario, Toronto.

to continue exporting. Apparently persuaded by Keefer's case, the government directed Wylie to sit tight. Aghast at this complacency, Wylie declared despairingly to the deputy minister in late July that he was "at a loss to know what to do, as regards this Russell Timber Company, as heretofore any action that I have taken in the protection of your Department, has been cast aside ... through the influence of their solicitor [Keefer] visiting Toronto." Wylie watched helplessly as the firm continued its illicit harvesting in Crown forests and was dumbfounded by its audacity. Despite "all the evidence of the depredations of this man Russell and his employees during the past summer," Wylie dejectedly explained in November 1920, "one would naturally suppose that he would cease his acts of Piracy; but today we find him still plying his trade of rascality in pilfiring [sic] the property of the Crown to his own use and behalf ... I see these thefts being carried on from day to day and I am powerless to do anything to prevent them, other than report them to Toronto, and I must say that too often such reports have been treated with contempt."[36]

Although the Drury government was simply treading down a well-worn path by indulging the exporters' behaviour, it soon made two extraordinary moves on their behalf. The first was its decision to classify "rossed" timber (i.e., wood that had been mechanically debarked) as being "manufactured" under the terms of the embargo on exporting Crown pulpwood. The exporters were practically the only ones in the province who processed wood in this way, which minimized shipping costs by eliminating the waste material from logs. The Farmers took the second – and monumental – step a short while later when they enacted legislation that officially suspended the manufacturing condition on pulpwood cut from Crown land. Although they had done so to create an ad hoc privilege for an exporter in the Timmins area, the statute authorized the cabinet to lift the embargo on pulpwood cut from Crown land in any part of "Northern and North-western Ontario." When Drury was attacked in the legislature for having set "a bad precedent" by introducing this measure, he insisted that he would not permit "pulpwood to be exported in any great quantity."[37]

Nothing could have been further from the truth, as the pulpwood exporting interests in Ontario enhanced their operations under his watch. Detroit Sulphite Pulp and Paper Company, for instance, reflected its long-term plans for obtaining fibre from the province by buying a prime piece of waterfront land in Fort William (Map 2). It used the site as both a location for a rossing plant, which debarked the 20,000 to 40,000 cords of pulpwood it obtained in Ontario each year, and a place for stockpiling the timber before shipping it to the United States. Not surprisingly, the quantity of spruce shipped across the border from Ontario jumped considerably during the Farmers' years in power (1919–23), rising from less than 200,000 cords to more than 400,000 cords, and these figures represented only the pulpwood shipped from private, not Crown, lands (Figure 2.3). Moreover, with the government having vested the power to suspend the manufacturing condition on pulpwood cut from Crown lands in the cabinet's hands, it made this trade more vulnerable than ever before to patronage considerations.[38]

No doubt the Conservative government under G. Howard Ferguson that won power in 1923 saw this as a propitious development, for Ferguson was renowned for his penchant for using his end to justify his means. Ferguson's reign as Ontario's minister of lands and forests in the 1910s proved to be one of the most corrupt periods in the history of the administration of the province's Crown woodlands, and his tenure as premier (1923–30) rivalled his earlier time in elected office in terms of crooked timber dealings. "The Chief," as he was known, oversaw many – if not most – of the transactions that involved the forest tracts that the government controlled to ensure that the supplicants for Crown timber paid the requisite "commissions" to his small coterie of lieutenants, who then ensured that these funds were funnelled to his Conservative allies. Fortunately for the exporters, Ferguson proved most receptive to their activities, and they to paying his tolls.[39]

The story of the deal that the premier personally approved for Ebbs Township provides an object lesson in how these dynamics played out. Consolidated Water Power and Paper in Wisconsin had been exporting pulpwood through Newaygo (Timber) Company, its Ontario subsidiary, since at least the First World War. Thereafter, it had grown increasingly dependent on the province for pulpwood, exporting roughly 100,000 cords per year by the end of the 1920s. However, doing so had caused it to strip the merchantable pulpwood from much of the freehold land it owned in the Thunder Bay District. Desperate to meet its future fibre needs, it had also purchased seven townships worth of freehold timber (nearly 350,000 acres holding roughly 3 million cords of pulpwood) that had originally been part of railway land grants located along the line that ran from Sault Ste Marie north to Hearst. Although not exportable, at least this wood served as an excellent reserve that the firm could hope the Ontario government would one day permit it to ship to the United States for processing (the provincial state soon acquiesced to this wish).[40]

Consolidated sought assistance in meeting its immediate fibre needs – specifically a total of roughly 500,000 cords of spruce – from two of Ferguson's most infamous lieutenants, Major General Donald M. Hogarth and Colonel James A. Little. They were seasoned, prominent businessmen at the Lakehead; Hogarth was the Conservative MPP for Port Arthur almost continuously between 1911 and 1934, and Little was his closest associate. They concocted a scheme that was as Byzantine as it was perfectly executed and rewarding for all involved. Their stratagem saw them acquire geologically deficient and relatively inaccessible mining claims in the Thunder Bay District that comprised roughly 4 square miles and on which – a generous guess would estimate – grew roughly 15,000 cords of pulpwood. Because these claims were within the pulpwood limits that a few local newsprint makers leased from the Ontario government, Hogarth and Little's contacts within the provincial bureaucracy deemed it within "the public interest" to have their owner relinquish them in exchange for land of commensurate value elsewhere in the hinterland. The compensation came in the form of roughly 80 square miles of prime pulpwood forest in Ebbs Township north of Sault Ste Marie, coincidentally adjacent to a railway that ran from the location to Consolidated's mill in Wisconsin. After producing fabricated data to rationalize the transaction, Premier Ferguson ensured that a walking Order in Council was executed to legalize it. Hogarth and Little then sold – for C$500,000 – their interest in the resources to Consolidated, which exported nearly 400,000 cords of spruce from this tract over roughly the next decade. For Hogarth and Little, their rich payday was only slightly diminished by news that they were expected to contribute C$50,000 of their windfall to R.B. Bennett's and the national Conservatives' 1930 local election campaign.

Ferguson's Tories also acted in far more banal ways to help the exporters, most importantly rendering the manufacturing condition on pulpwood a dead letter. In 1927, they oversaw the consolidation of a number of provincial statutes, including those that applied to timber administration. In the process, they incorporated into the new legislation the manufacturing condition on Crown pine, hardwoods (to which the manufacturing condition had been extended in 1924), and "spruce and other pulpwood." Although the Crown Timber Act (1927) was silent on the matters of suspending the prohibition on exporting unprocessed pine and hardwoods from the province, it included the 1920 law that had authorized cabinet to suspend – at its discretion – the embargo on exporting pulpwood from Crown land.[41]

Finally, the Conservatives completed the circle in the late 1920s when they dropped the pretence that had been the original raison d'être for exporting pulpwood from the province. During this period, senior officials from the Department of Lands and Forests began circulating instructions to their field agents that outlined the rules governing the cutting of pulpwood for export by homesteaders. Among other things, these regulations emphasized that cutting the timber efficiently – not clearing the land – was the priority. Moreover, these directives also revealed the double standard the government applied to pulpwood. Whereas it prohibited domestic mills from peeling spruce – even though this arrangement would have reduced shipping costs for those engaged in the practice – because, it was argued, doing so would have created an enormous fire hazard during the warm weather months, settlers were permitted to engage in this practice.[42]

Not surprisingly, Ferguson's reign as premier pushed the exporters' activities to new heights. Yet again, American pulp and paper mills that had long procured pulpwood in Ontario dramatically expanded their operations in the province, and new firms from farther afield also appeared on the scene, most notably the West Virginia Pulp and Paper Company. Shipments of spruce from the province to the American mills rose from more than 400,000 cords immediately upon Ferguson's victory in 1923 to a peak of more than 600,000 cords five years later, and again, the actual figures were probably much higher (Figure 2.3). But it was also the relative importance of the booms and boatloads of wood heading south that deserve attention. Whereas Quebec had traditionally been unrivalled as Canada's leading exporter of pulpwood, by the late 1920s Ontario was battling neck and neck with its eastern neighbour for this distinction (Figure 2.4). This trend had already caught the eye of E.H. Finlayson, the dominion's forester, during his time acting as the secretary to Canada's Royal Commission on Pulpwood in the mid-1920s. Noting that the volume of pulpwood leaving New Brunswick and Quebec for the United States had been steadily declining

since before the First World War, Finlayson observed that, over the same period, "there has been a very decided, and almost continuous, upward trend in
the amount of Ontario exports."[43]

In the early 1930s, at the nadir of the Depression, the debate over the wisdom of exporting spruce was alive and well in Ontario. American interests
that had depended on pulpwood harvested from private lands in the Thunder
Bay District had nearly exhausted these supplies. Moreover, the period's unprecedented unemployment had created pressure for the government to allow
timber to be exported from Crown timber licences as a means of generating
desperately needed jobs. Faced with a steady stream of such requests from timber licensees who conveyed heart-rending stories of the challenges they faced,
Walter C. Cain, Ontario's deputy minister of lands and forests, felt it was time
to put a stop to these maudlin inquiries. "While these individual requests may
appeal to one's sentiment," Cain advised the minister, "I do consider it of rather
doubtful practical ... value ... or even political wisdom to continue this export
practice, which fortunately we have not permitted to any extreme extent." He
thus recommended that the Department "prevent further requests" and "nip in
the bud" this movement by rejecting the applications.[44]

Although this advice may have seemed prudent for anyone unfamiliar with
the inner workings of government policy in Northern Ontario, and notwithstanding the politicians' claims to the contrary, the reality was that they had
never had any intention – neither in the early 1930s nor over the preceding
four decades – to "nip in the bud" the business of exporting pulpwood. Instead,
from the outset the manufacturing condition on this type of Crown timber
had been designed to foster this business in a particular manner that would
help Ontario people its northern hinterland. But the American mills, and the
clique of entrepreneurs they hired in the province to act on their behalf, not
only purchased settlers' timber but also obtained pulpwood through both legal
and illegal means. With their presence in Ontario sanctioned by the provincial
state, they aggressively pushed to expand their business. In short order, the government used the need to support homesteading in the north as the rationalization for facilitating the export of pulpwood in a variety of ways; it concurrently
turned a blind eye to the various stratagems the exporters employed to achieve
their ends. As a result, when Ontario's elected officials legally emasculated the
manufacturing condition on spruce during the 1920s, they merely recognized
in law their decades-old commitment to making the province's pulpwood readily available to American industry.

Ultimately, we are left asking, did it matter? Was the Ontario government's
decision to feign adherence to this particular policy of economic nationalism
good or bad for the province? Undeniably, this strategy was one element in a

Figure 2.4. Total volume of pulpwood exported from Ontario as a percentage of total volume of pulpwood exported from Canada, 1913–30

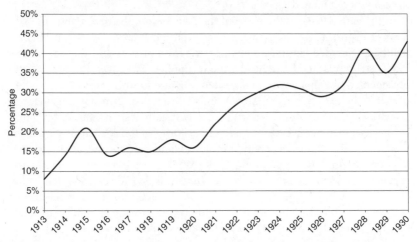

Sources: R. Craig to E.H. Finlayson, table 1, 17 March 1931, RG39, 243, 22490–2, Library and Archives Canada, Ottawa; "Regulations Governing the Export of Unmanufactured Timber on Crown Lands in Ontario," table 2, 21 March 1939, RG1-E-10, 19, 1–6-1, vol. 1, Archives of Ontario, Toronto.

broader plan that helped attach families to Ontario's hinterland; the region's population grew from 55,000 in 1891 to more than seven times that total four decades later. But to credit the provincial state's decision to foster the export of pulpwood with having driven this exponential growth in the north's population is to confound these issues. For during these years, the Ontario government pursued another strategy to create the most robust possible market for settlers' spruce, specifically limiting the volume of fibre it made available to the province's own pulp and paper producers. This approach to allocating timber resources limited the ability of Ontario's newsprint industry to expand in a manner that would have provided stable and well-paid employment both in the province's woodlands *and* its timber-processing plants. Moreover, the government undermined the future prosperity of Ontario's pulp and paper industry by literally giving enormous volumes of the most readily available stands of spruce to the exporters. Although this handicap was not a major factor for the province's mills during the historical period under examination, it would become increasingly so in the years that followed.[45]

Finally, the evidence is unequivocal that, prior to 1930, the Ontario government's handling of the province's pulpwood resources stymied domestic industrial development in very direct and important ways. It was axiomatic that firms interested in exporting raw materials from foreign lands would seek to curry favour with domestic governments by establishing branch plants within the latter's jurisdiction. The hope was that doing so would help convince domestic governments that allowing some portion of their trees to be shipped abroad unprocessed was a prudent quid pro quo for realizing the establishment of a new industry. However, between 1890 and 1930, several leading American pulp and paper producers felt confident enough in the provincial government's commitment to permitting indefinitely raw spruce to be exported from Ontario that they abandoned their branch plants – and plans for such production facilities – in the province. The most notable example involved Hammermill. In the mid-1920s, it set out to endear itself to the provincial government by establishing a mill in Ontario. Although its decision to pursue this strategy was driven in part by its desire to hurdle the tariff wall that protected Canadian producers from foreign competition, Hammermill was also acutely aware that doing so would "serve the purpose of assisting in obtaining our wood supply for some years to come."[46] After the firm invested significant time and money in pursuit of realizing this end (it spent nearly $50,000 to acquire a suitable building site), it abandoned the project by 1929 because of uncertainty surrounding its ability to sell its products north of the border and knowledge that ditching the initiative would not jeopardize its exporting privileges in Ontario; such privileges would remain sacrosanct for roughly another three decades.[47] By that time, the disadvantages accruing from Ontario's decision to take a dissembling approach to the export of unprocessed pulpwood from 1890 to 1930 had already been laid bare for all to see.

NOTES

1 *Globe & Mail*, 13 April 2007, W. Stueck, "Supply Crisis on Wood Industry Horizon," B3; *Wood Resources Quarterly* 3Q/2011, 25; B.P. Resosudarmo and A. A. Yusuf, "Is the Log Export Ban Effective? Revisiting the Issue through the Case of Indonesia" (Economics and Environment Network Working Paper, Australian National University, Canberra, 13 June 2006).

2 H.V. Nelles, *The Politics of Development: Forests, Mines and Hydro-Electric Power in Ontario, 1849-1941* (Hamden, CT: Archon Books, 1974); R.A. Rajala, *Clearcutting the Pacific Rain Forest: Production, Science and Regulation* (Vancouver: University of British Columbia Press, 1998); S. Gray, "The Government's Timber Business:

Forest Policy and Administration in British Columbia, 1912–1928," *BC Studies* 81 (Spring 1989), 24-49; W.M. Parenteau, "Forests and Society in New Brunswick: The Political Economy of Forest Industries, 1918–1932" (PhD diss., University of New Brunswick, Frederiction, 1994); L.A. Sandberg, "Forest Policy in Nova Scotia: The Big Lease, Cape Breton Island, 1899–1960," *Acadiensis* XX, no. 2 (Spring 1991): 105–28; J. Hiller, "The Politics of Newsprint: The Newfoundland Pulp and Paper Industry, 1915–1939," *Acadiensis* XXI, no. 2 (Spring 1990): 3–39.

3 B. Parenteau and L.A. Sandberg, "Conservation and the Gospel of Economic Nationalism: The Canadian Pulpwood Question in Nova Scotia and New Brunswick, 1918–1925," *Environmental History Review* 19, no. 2 (Summer 1995): 55–83.

4 Richard S. Lambert and Paul Pross, *Renewing Nature's Wealth: A Centennial History of the Public Management of Lands, Forests and Wildlife in Ontario, 1763–1967* (Toronto: Department of Lands and Forests, 1967), passim with the citation taken from 132.

5 The numerous authors who have chronicled the history of the pulp and paper companies – and the industry as whole – in the Great Lake states have said very little about how these enterprises conceived of the pulpwood in Northern Ontario as constituting an integral – if not *the* integral – source of fibre for their mills beginning in the 1890s and continuing for roughly the next half-dozen decades. In other words, these American firms' understanding of this region's resources resonated with that presented by John J. Bukowczyk, *Permeable Border: The Great Lakes Basin as Transnational Region, 1650–1990* (Pittsburgh: University of Pittsburgh Press, 2005); the mills in the United States did not view the numerous artificial political borders – international, state, and provincial – that dissected the area as barriers to the free flow of trees across the lakes. As a result, these firms were only too grateful to capitalize on the Ontario government's willingness to facilitate the export of pulpwood from the province. For details, see Mark Kuhlberg, "'Practically Every Mill … in the State Has Been Dependent upon Ontario for Its Supply of Wood for Many Years': The Great Lakes Pulp and Paper Economy and Ontario's Feigned Economic Nationalism, 1890–1960" (unpublished manuscript, 2013).

6 A. White, "Memo re: permits to cut pulpwood," October 1892, RG1-545-1-2, 15017/92, Archives of Ontario (AO), Toronto; *Fourth Report of the Ontario Bureau of Mines, 1895* (Toronto: Warwick Bros. & Rutter, Printers, 1895), 120; A. White, "Rights of Licensees to Timber …," December 1894, RG1-545-1-2, AO, Toronto.

7 *Globe*, 9 April 1897, "Duty on Pulpwood," M. Carr, 9.

8 *Globe*, 20 April 1897, "The Pulpwood War: A Second Letter," M. Carr, 8; ibid., Letter from T. Swalwell, 8;ibid., 17 September 1898, Letter about Export Duty, 9; Petition [form letter by signed by the Reeve, Councillors and MP for Algoma District], 25 January 1897, RG20, A-1, vol. 1149, Library and Archives Canada (LAC), Ottawa.

9 "P," all entries, RG1-546-4-2, AO, Toronto.

10 J.L. McDonald to J.P. Whitney, 29 March 1900, MU3114, March 1900, AO, Toronto; T.J. Tronrud and A.E. Epp, *Thunder Bay: From Rivalry to Unity* (Thunder Bay: Thunder Bay Museum Historical Society, 1996), 207; R.W. Wightman and N.M. Wightman, *The Land Between: Northwestern Ontario Resource Development, 1800 to the 1990s* (Toronto: University of Toronto Press, 1997), 134; *Hansard*, 30 March 1900.

11 *Statutes of Ontario (SO), 1892*, 55 Vict., ch. 9; *Hansard*, 25 February and 6 March, 1897.

12 The name of the department changed over time, from being the Department of Crown Lands (until 1905) to the Department of Lands, Mines and Forests (1906–1920) to the Department of Lands and Forests (1920–1972). For simplicity, in this chapter, we refer to it as the Department.

13 *Ontario Sessional Papers, 1896*, no. 74, passim; *Report of the Commissioner of Crown Lands of the Province of Ontario for the Year 1899* (Toronto: Warwick Bros. & Rutter, Printers, 1900) [hereafter *Annual Report, year*], xi.

14 In contrast, pulpwood exporters in Quebec lobbied vociferously and successfully against the enactment of manufacturing condition legislation in 1900.

15 *SO, 1900*, 63 Vict., ch. 11; *Globe*, 9 January 1900, "Its Export Prohibited," 8; ibid., 16 February 1900; ibid., 19 May 1902, "In New Ontario, Splendid Liberal Meeting Held at Thessalon," 5. Nelles, *The Politics of Development*, ch. 2, argues that the enactment of the manufacturing condition on pulpwood attested to the successful lobby by domestic pulp and paper producers, a view that overestimates their strength and ignores the fact that the export trade expanded after the measure was implemented.

16 RG10, 2366, 73,850, vols. 1 and 2, all documents, LAC, Ottawa;—*Report of the Auditor General for the Year Ended June 30 1900, Part I* (Ottawa: S.E. Dawson, Printer to the Queen's Most Excellent Majesty, 1901), J-162; *Globe*, 27 February 1900, "Provincial Protection," 27 February 1900, 6.

17 *Hansard*, 27 April 1900. The use of the term "the old Tory Timber Ring" by Nelles and others is a misnomer.

18 T.R. Roach, "The Pulpwood Trade and the Settlers of New Ontario," *Journal of Canadian Studies* XXII, no. 3 (Fall 1987): 78–88, argues that the most settlers were bona fide but that they failed as farmers because of environmental factors and their dependence on harvesting pulpwood. This analysis supports the argument that the government's colonization policies promoted the export trade in pulpwood ahead of agriculture.

19 *Report of the Survey and Exploration of Northern Ontario, 1900* (Toronto: L.K. Cameron – Printer to the King's Most Excellent Majesty, 1901), xvii; *SO, 1901*, 1 Edw. VII, ch. 6.

20 C. Berger, *The Sense of Power: Studies in the Ideas of Canadian Imperialism,*
    1867–1914 (Toronto: University of Toronto Press, 1970); E.J. Parnell to A. White,
    11 August 1906, RG1-99-7, AO, Toronto.
21 *Globe*, 24 October 1901, "Mr. Charlton Nominated," 1–2.; RG1-99-7, all docu-
    ments, AO, Toronto.
22 T.W. Crossen, *Nicholson: A Study of Lumbering in North Central Ontario, 1885–*
    1930, with Special Reference to the Austin-Nicholson Company (Cochrane: Ontario
    Ministry of Natural Resources, 1976).
23 "Fenian and South African – Memorandum re: settlement duties," RG1-99-7, AO,
    Toronto; E.J. Parnell to A. White, 11 August 1906, RG1-99-7, AO, Toronto; D.M.
    Hogarth to W.F. Finlayson, 8 July 1932, RG1-246-3, 68397, AO, Toronto; 1902 cor-
    respondence, B22/2/1, Thunder Bay Historical Museum Society (TBHMS), Thun-
    der Bay; G.T. Clarkson to Royal Trust Company, 10 July 1915, B22/2/2, TBHMS,
    Thunder Bay.
24 B.M. Wylie to G.A. Drew, 18 December 1936, MG32-C3, Box 144, File – B.M.
    Wylie, LAC, Ottawa; J. and T. Conlon to Mr. Gibson, ca. 1904, RG4-32, 1904/1759,
    AO, Toronto.
25 The dominion government enacted the manufacturing condition on Crown pulp-
    wood in 1907, Quebec in 1910, New Brunswick in 1911, and British Columbia in
    1913.
26 W. Van Horne to J.P. Whitney, 8 August 1910, MU3130, August 1910, AO, Toronto;
    Whitney to Van Horne, 10 August 1910, MU3130, August 1910, AO, Toronto.
27 *Annual Reports, 1899–1919,* passim; T. Southworth to J.J. Foy, 31 March 1905,
    MU3116, File – 28–31 March 1905, AO, Toronto; A. White, "Memorandum for the
    Minister," 5 May 1905, RG1-99-7, AO, Toronto; M. Kuhlberg, *One Hundred Rings*
    and Counting: Forestry Education and Forestry in Toronto and Canada, 1907–2007
    (Toronto: University of Toronto Press, 2009), 45–47.
28 "Memo for the Minister from Acting Deputy Minister," 25 February 1919,
    RG6-I-2, Box 18, DLF, 1914–32, AO, Toronto; D.E. Pugh, "Ontario's Great Clay
    Belt Hoax," *Canadian Geographical Journal* (January 1975): 19–25; *Annual Report,*
    1910, vi, and *1913,* vi; *Northern Ontario – Its Progress ...,* 1, MU1311, ca. 1914, AO,
    Toronto; Kerry Abel, *Changing Places: History, Community and Identity in North-*
    eastern Ontario (Montreal and Kingston: McGill-Queen's University Press, 2006),
    43–51.
29 M.L. Branch, "The Paper Industry in the Lake States Region, 1834–1947" (PhD
    Diss., University of Wisconsin, Madison, 1954), ch. V; *Canada Lumberman,*
    1 January 1924, 59; Crossen, *Nicholson,* 67–68; Contract between J.H. Pat-
    terson and Hammermill Paper Company, 22 August 1908, RG1-99-7, AO,
    Toronto; J.J. Roberts to Department of Commerce [Canada], 15 March 1917,
    RG13, A-2, 1917/455, LAC, Ottawa; M. Kuhlberg, "An Acute yet Brief Bout of

'Returned-Soldier-It-Is': The University of Toronto's Faculty of Forestry after World War I," in *Cultures, Communities and Conflict: Histories of Canadian Universities in War* (Toronto: University of Toronto Press, 2012), 144; M.J. McQuillen and W.P. Garvey, *The Best Known Name in Paper: Hammermill, A History of the Company* (Erie, PA: Hammermill Paper Company, 1985), 3–81: the authors make no mention of any backlash against the company's operations in Ontario during either world war.

30 Ibid., W.A. Dowler to H. Mills, 26 December 1919, RG1-246-3, 13514. Numerous MPPs were at the helm of exporting enterprises, with Driftwood Lands & Timber Company being a classic example: Company Prospectus and Return for 1914, 9 September 1914, TC44895, Ontario Ministry of Consumer and Corporate Relations – Toronto (OMCCR).

31 A.J. McComber to the Minister, 23 September 1920, RG1-246-3, 3372, vol. 1, AO, Toronto; ibid., Return under the Pulpwood Conservation Act, Newaygo, 31 July 1934, 81701, vol. 1; ibid., F.A. Mulholland to A. White, 28 April 1910, RG1-246-3, F789, 33863/90; ibid., Clinton, Graham & Company to J.P. Whitney, 8 and 13 August 1912, MU3134; ibid., Whitney to Clinton et al., 12 and 15 August 1912.

32 Ibid., R.S. Hyslop to T.F. Boultbee, 10 March 1967, RG1-246-3, 70693. Marathon also apparently held a partial interest in the Pigeon River Lumber Company, which had owned several Crown licences and a sawmill in Port Arthur from around the turn of the century. It had contrived a sly means of circumventing the manufacturing condition. It would harvest pulpwood logs from its licences, cut a slab off either side of them in its mill, and then declare them "manufactured" and ship them across the Great Lakes for processing into pulp and paper: ibid., "Memo for the Minister from A. Grigg," 30 December 1920, 2759.

33 J.P. Bertrand, "Timber Wolves," (unpublished manuscript, author's copy, ca. 1961), 49; *Timber Commission Hearings*, 3836–42, RG18-79, AO, Toronto; ibid., *Timber Commission, First Interim Report, 1920*, 3; ibid., J.A. Oliver to A. Grigg, 30 March 1917, RG1-246-3, 8161, vol. 1; Financial Statement, Russell Timber Company Ltd., 1 March 1918, B22/2/3, TBHMS, Thunder Bay.

34 *SO, 1914*, ch. 12, 4 Geo. V.; E.S. Wigle to Mr. Drury, 26 August 1920, RG3-4, Pulpwood 1920 #1, AO, Toronto; ibid., J.B.C. Memo, 8 May 1916, RG1-246-3, 110A, vol. 1; *PPMC, December 1914*, 676.

35 *Hansard*, 18 March and 9 April 1920.

36 *First Interim Report of the Forestry Commission, 1920*, RG18-79, AO, Toronto; ibid., R.T. Harding to E.C. Drury, 19 August 1920, RG3-4, Pulpwood Russell … 1920; ibid., Evidence re: Russell …, MG27-II-F-7, 24, 24-2; ibid., RG1-246-3, 2759, vols. 1–2, all documents, with the citations taken from B.M. Wylie to A. Grigg, 31 July 1920, and Wylie to G.W. Mason, 15 November 1920.

37 E.E. Johnson to D.C. Everest, 22 January 1920, MSS 279, 10, 22, Wisconsin Historical Society – Madison Archives; *SO, 1920*, ch. 14, 10–11 Geo. V.; *Hansard*, 29 May 1920; RG3-4, Pulpwood #1 1920, all correspondence, AO, Toronto; ibid., F.J. Niven, "Memo for the Premier," 28 May 1920, Pulpwood Report 1920; ibid., RG75-57, OC121/354, and OC154/32; ibid., "Memo for the Minister from Attorney-General," 22 June 1920, RG1-246-3, 13095, vol. 1. Experts felt the government merely explicitly recognized what they had suspected all along, namely, that most of the pulpwood exported from Ontario was coming from Crown, not settlers', lands: C.D. Howe to H.G. Schanche, 14 September 1923, A1975-0025/138(Aa–Al), University of Toronto Archives, Toronto; ibid., E. Wilson to Howe, 9 December 1924, /149(Wia-Wil).

38 Articles about Detroit Sulphite Pulp and Paper, MSS 279, 10, 22, University of Wisconsin at Madison Archives,; *Canada Lumberman*, 1 January 1928, 49–54. The Farmers also legalized the export of Crown poplar pulpwood in 1919: RG1-246-3, 13095, AO, Toronto; ibid., RG3-4, Pulpwood #1, 1920; ibid., RG75-57, 121/354; *SO, 1920*, ch. 14, 10–11 Geo. V.

39 Peter Oliver, *G. Howard Ferguson: Ontario Tory* (Toronto: University of Toronto Press, 1977); even this sympathetic biography admits Ferguson's corrupt tendencies.

40 For the full story, see Mark Kuhlberg, "'Nothing but a Cash Deal': Crown Timber Corruption in Northern Ontario, 1923–1930," *Thunder Bay Historical Museum Society Papers and Records* XXVIII (2000): 3–22. This and the following paragraph are based on this source.

41 *Revised Statutes of Ontario, 1927*, ch. 38.

42 W.C. Cain, "Copy of Instructions Handed Mr. Vincent by Major J.I. Hartt," 31 May 1928, RG1-246-3, 79650, AO, Toronto; ibid., W.C. Cain, "Regulations Governing Cutting of Pulpwood on Settlers' Land," 19 July 1928.

43 RG1-246-3, 18199, all documents, AO, Toronto; N. Gray, "Report – Sudbury," 3 January 1929, St Marys Paper Archives, A-1, 6-6; R. Craig to D.R. Cameron, and attachments, 17 March 1931, RG39, 243, 22490-2, LAC, Ottawa; *Report of the Royal Commission on Pulpwood, Ottawa, July 1924* (Ottawa: Printer to the King's Most Excellent Majesty, 1924), 55.

44 O. Styffe to F.J. Sharpe, 1 August 1941, MG7, 10, 3, Lakehead University Library Archives, Thunder Bay; W.C. Cain to Minister, 16 June 1932, RG1-246-3, 13778, vol. 2, AO, Toronto.

45 These subjects are explored at length in Mark Kuhlberg, *In the Power of the Government: The Rise and Fall of Newsprint in Ontario, 1894–1932* (forthcoming with University of Toronto Press).

46 Canadian Properties – Memoranda and Minutes of Meetings 1927–30, all documents with the citation taken from C.W. Hurtubis, "Memorandum for Woodlands

Department," 15 April 1927, W.F. Bromley Papers, J.M. Lilley Library Archives –
Penn State Erie, The Behrend College, Erie, Pa.

47 Ibid., Port Weller Property 1943–47, all documents especially W.F. Bromley to
W.T. Brust, 8 February 1943, and Brust to Bromley, 10 February 1943, W.T. Brust
Papers; RG1-E-3-B, vol. 1, A-5, all documents, AO, Toronto; ibid., vol. 4, A-17,
A-18, and A-24, all documents; ibid., vol. 5, A-30, all documents; ibid., vol. 7, A-62,
all documents.

3
Managing a War Metal: The International Nickel Company's First World War

DARYL WHITE

In *Understanding Globalization*, Robert Schaeffer states that the practice of selective globalization emerged at the end of the Cold War and the onset of the debt crisis in the developing world.[1] As Smith and Anastakis point out in the introduction to this collection, Canada has long practised a form of smart or selective globalization at odds with the neoliberal teachings embodied in the Washington Consensus. Canada used interventionist and protectionist policies to encourage development and attract foreign capital. Normally, the Canadian economy operates in what William Coleman and Michael Atkinson describe as a "firm-centred industry culture" amenable to business and prone to its influence.[2] However, when the nation state faces an imperative, such as war, that culture shifts, and the existing paradigm of selective globalization is susceptible to change. Indeed, as Smith and Anastakis also remind us, the First World War "shattered" the global economic system of the late nineteenth and early twentieth centuries.

The pressure for change is especially evident when an industry becomes part of the arsenal of a modern state practicing economic warfare. During the First World War, a key Entente strategy (primarily British and by extension Canadian) was the blockade of the Central Powers (primarily Germany). The efficacy of the blockade has been the subject of substantial historical debate. Although the interwar failures of the League of Nations suggested that the blockade had only limited value as a tool of economic warfare, as late as 1957, Marion Siney asserted that "the system of coercion was ultimately a decisive factor in the downfall of the Central Powers."[3] Niall Ferguson's more recent *The Pity of War* suggests that the blockade was far less effective than had been assumed.[4] Of particular importance was the role of neutral states, chiefly the Netherlands, Scandinavia, and, most significant, the United States, in circumventing the blockade and providing raw materials to Germany.

The effort to impose the blockade required governments to modify their approaches to international commerce and to impose them on corporations as required. Examining the economic warfare of the First World War and the blockade in particular reveals how extensively security considerations can modify the economic philosophies of a society, but it also reveals the other considerations that shape the newly selected pattern of globalization. It is thus surprising that the North American nickel industry, producer of a critical war commodity used in the manufacture of bullet jackets and armour plate and which spanned the border between a belligerent and a neutral nation, has not received more attention. It is all the more unusual because the nickel industry breaks with the pattern of open American industrial collaboration outlined by Siney and was connected to one of the most dramatic failures of the blockade during a period of heightened Anglo-American tension in 1916. By the end of the war, new attitudes towards globalization had permanently altered the structure of what was now more strictly the *Canadian* nickel industry.

In 1914, a vertically integrated transborder North American nickel industry existed. The industry's largest producer, Inco, mined and smelted in Canada and refined its product in New Jersey. In the late nineteenth century, despite the National Policy tariffs intended to develop domestic secondary industry, the Canadian government had been receptive to globalization insofar as it brought the American capital and technology necessary to develop Canadian resource wealth. However, attitudes had shifted, and the combination of an American corporation exploiting a militarily significant resource of the British Empire was certain to produce complications with the coming of war. Canadians recognized that the risks of the international economy extended beyond the loss of the economic activity associated with refining. Faced with the danger of Allied soldiers being cut down by bullets jacketed in Canadian nickel, the British and Canadian governments attempted to secretly impose extraterritorial control of the exported nickel and refused to violate that secrecy even when it meant preserving the blockade. Nor was a more restricted internationalism a choice merely for the Canadian government. Inco, forced to choose between its neutral American corporate citizenship and its existing refinery or the need to appease the political will in Canada and Britain, opted for the latter to preserve its competitive advantage.

In 1914, the Canadian nickel industry was still relatively new. Production had only begun in Sudbury, Ontario, in 1886, and Inco had formed only in 1902 with the merger of the Canadian Copper and Orford Copper companies. Inco mined and smelted its ore in Sudbury, but the refining stage in which nickel and copper were separated was performed in Orford's plant in Bayonne, New Jersey. This multinational structure offered some locational advantages beyond the obvious need to mine in Canada (Inco would later identify the ability to dump refinery effluent into the ocean off New Jersey as important), but it is better understood as a defensive integration in the Chandlerian model.[5] Orford faced the loss of its supply of refinable metal if Canadian Copper was successful in developing its own refining process.[6]

The new metal had struggled to find a market until its value in hardening steel armour plate was proved by the United States Navy in 1889. The failure of several 8-inch shells to inflict more than a slight crack and dent meant nickel had a strong future. By the First World War, 90 per cent of the world's nickel was being used for munitions (predominantly armour plate and bullet jackets), and Canada supplied 70 per cent of it. Under cartel arrangements among Inco and the only other significant suppliers, the French firm Société Anonyme Le Nickel and the Mond Nickel Company from Britain (hereafter Le Nickel and Mond), Inco supplied the entire American market and a major share of the European market.[7] Although Mond also mined in Sudbury, it and Le Nickel concentrated on European sales. Inco's significance as a world nickel producer contributed to political activism in Canada, which criticized the company as a "foreign monopolist" and for refining in the United States instead of Canada.

Early on, the Ontario government had actively encouraged American entrepreneurs in their development of provincial resources.[8] However, at the turn of the century, public policy entered what O.W. Main called "the nationalistic phase," and Ontario attempted to address the economic loss caused by Inco's American refining.[9] It had succeeded in forcing the processing of lumber in the province but was limited in what it could do to the mining industry. Forestry companies harvested timber on land leased from the Ontario government. This gave the government an opportunity to periodically revisit its management of those lands. The mining lands had been sold outright. Determined to do what it could, in 1899 Ontario moved to impose export fees on nickel. However, lobbied hard by Inco and other mining companies, the Canadian government intervened. Prime Minister Laurier advised Premier Ross that he might disallow the provincial law, and the export fees were never proclaimed.[10]

Although the Canadian government had supported Inco against the Ross government, there remained the potential for either Canada or Ontario to exercise significant power over the nickel industry. By the second decade of the twentieth century, Canadian nickel dominated global markets, but Inco's success and survival depended on its access to Canadian ore bodies and on the ready transportation of its matte across the Canadian-American border to its New Jersey refinery. The psychic distance across the border was critical. If the Canadian government felt it could no longer allow its nickel to move freely into the United States and blocked the flow of matte, it would temporarily strangle the company and compel it to undertake either the construction of a Canadian refinery or abandon its mines and smelter in Sudbury. Moreover, the governments might, as they were occasionally encouraged to, support rival firms' entry into the market. If the public were sufficiently antagonized, nationalization was a possibility, though it was never given serious consideration in the years leading up to the First World War.

Upon the outbreak of war in 1914, Britain moved very quickly to establish its economic blockade of the Central Powers. Having used the strategy extensively in the eighteenth and nineteenth centuries, the British (and as Ferguson notes, many Germans) were convinced that the Royal Navy could strangle German economic life.[11] Although not a traditional occupation of ports, naval control of the Dover Straits and the North Sea between Norway and the Shetlands would allow the British to effectively restrict traffic.[12] Britain issued its first lists of contraband on 5 August 1914, and eight days later, the Committee on Restriction of Enemy Supply was established.[13]

The outbreak of war in 1914 gave Canadian nickel great significance. Britain declared nickel absolutely contraband by a 29 October 1914 Order in Council.[14] Production would also be an issue; large quantities would be needed for the conflict. Mond moved to expand production to meet the war requirements of the British Empire.[15] However, to the shock of Canadians, Inco announced a shutdown. Stockpiles of metal and market disruptions were the stated reasons. An outraged public posited an alternative: the company was under German control. Although these allegations were of concern, more pressing to both the company and the Canadian government were calls for a ban on the export of nickel from Canada. The public was adamant that Canadian nickel could not leave Canadian control lest it reach Canada's enemies. The Canadian-American border, hitherto a formality, was now a potentially imposing barrier. Senior Inco executives were blunt. W.A. Bostwick asserted that such a move would "destroy" the company. With its refinery on the other side of the border from its smelter, barring the company from exporting matte would leave it without a product to sell. Bostwick urged Canadian prime minister Robert Borden to prevent such rash action. He offered assurances that the company had not supplied nickel to any enemy nations since the outbreak of war and invited the government to inspect the company's books as proof.[16]

Bostwick's offer invited Canadian officials into the United States to supervise an American corporation. Although he may not have appreciated the broader implications of the act (and there is no indication in the correspondence that he did), American neutrality was being transgressed. Woodrow Wilson may have declared that Americans "must be impartial in thought, as well as action,"[17] but Inco had evidently decided it could not afford to assume such a lofty stance; a nickel export embargo would have strangled the company. Inco certainly was not alone among American corporations in recognizing the need to comply with the British. Carnegie Steel, US Steel, a number of US textile manufacturers organized as the Textile Alliance, and American producers of rubber and copper had all concluded private agreements with the British government to restrict their exports to those likely to supply the Central Powers.[18]

For his part, Borden appreciated that an export ban would not only hurt Inco but also significantly impair the British Empire's war effort. Canada had no facilities for refining nickel. If the matte could not be exported, it would deny a supply of nickel to the American and Canadian firms manufacturing arms for the British Empire and its allies. In consultation with Frank Cochrane, his minister of railways and canals, Borden decided to send Graham Bell, the comptroller of Cochrane's department, to examine Inco's records. At first glance, Bell's selection might seem odd. An accounting background was certainly useful for studying corporate records, but Bell's experience in the Department of Railways and Canals seems incongruous with policing a mining company's exports. His selection likely had more to do with his minister's background than his own. Cochrane was Sudbury's MP, and his hardware store did extensive business with Inco. He was thus the most connected, though as his critics pointed out not the most impartial, member of the cabinet in relation to the nickel industry.

Bell's initial visit to Inco's headquarters in October 1914 was satisfactory, and he reported to the prime minister that the company had "taken every precaution to insure that their customers do not reship to our alien enemies."[19] Bell also made recommendations to implement a regular system to control nickel shipments. Inco would notify Bell whenever a quotation was made and provide monthly statements of American shipments. Bell would verify these through a monthly audit at Inco's New York office. If Bell had suspicions about any Canadian shipments, the Dominion Police would investigate. The British authorities would receive copies of Inco's statements to verify European sales. This was intended to satisfy not only the Canadian but also the British government, which acting Canadian high commissioner George Perley related had pledged to assist "in any practical way" to prevent nickel from reaching the enemy.[20]

The one obvious weakness in Bell's control system was nickel sales in the United States. Although Bell could approve of the American firms receiving nickel, he had no way of independently verifying the activities of such firms. In his initial proposals, he had suggested that the British Secret Service monitor companies in the United States, but the Canadian government removed this from the final draft in favour of merely saying steps would be taken, presumably to avoid the appearance that the British were spying on Americans.[21] The entire control system was to be kept secret, so much so that the Canadian government refused to discuss it with Parliament.[22] This was necessary in part to protect Inco. In agreeing to supply Bell with its sales records, Inco was breaching American law, which made it illegal to pass this information to a foreign power.[23]

Both the belief that the arrangement violated the law (obviously this was never actually tested in court) and the supposed need for secrecy are curious. The arrangements that other corporations made with the British have been noted previously. In 1914, William Jennings Bryan, then secretary of state, commented that the American government would consider providing the British with guarantees against the re-exportation of wool.[24] Although the discussions were abandoned, even the suggestion is obviously incompatible with Canadian fears over the nickel arrangements. Why, then, was nickel different?

Nominally, the refined nickel was American, not Canadian, and this may have influenced fears that the American government would be inclined to see it as interference with domestic commerce. The next year, when Lloyd George's new Ministry of Munitions sent its first mission to the United States, it had concerns that American isolationists would accuse the British of coming "to organize American industry in the British interest."[25] When the British had taken over the Eddystone Ammunition Company of Pennsylvania in 1915, they had left the company's leadership intact for fear of arousing American ire.[26] Similarly, the suggestion that British agents monitor American firms was likely thought to make Americans anxious and kept secret for the same reasons the British were reluctant to disclose the activities of the naval intelligence's code-breaking operation, Room 40.[27] Although Kathleen Burk has described the American disposition as "benevolently neutral" in the early years of the First World War, it was certainly ground where the British and, by extension, the Canadians had to tread lightly.[28]

Another strong possibility is that the Canadians were simply unaware of the progress the British had been making with other American firms. The flow of information between Canadian and British officials over nickel export regulation did cause problems during the war. As late as January 1917, the British minister of blockade, Lord Robert Cecil, informed the Canadian high commissioner, George Perley, that he had no documented evidence of the nickel control arrangements.[29] Without knowledge of comparable agreements with other companies, the Canadians may have been more inclined to the safety of secrecy.

The secret control system functioned well for much of the war. Inco provided information to Bell who in turn took appropriate steps to achieve his dual objectives of keeping nickel matte flowing to the New Jersey refinery and preventing nickel from reaching Canada's enemies. Bell's tools were somewhat limited. Some firms were placed on a blacklist, usually on the advice of British officials. In these cases, Bell advised Inco that the Canadian government could not issue export permits for matte to be refined to fill orders for the specific companies. Others were required to post bonds as guarantees of their good behaviour. For example, when the Bayard Company of New York wanted nickel for manufacturing anodes in 1916, Bell asked the firm to put up a US$10,000 bond payable from a British or Canadian guarantee company. The company complied.[30]

Inco's efforts to comply with the control system went beyond its customers to include its suppliers. In August 1916, W.A. Bostwick wrote to Bell to discuss the Eugene Dietzgen Company. The firm appeared on the British blacklist in the United States, but Inco had purchased supplies for its engineering department from the firm's Toronto branch. Bostwick wished to know if Inco should change its purchasing practices. Bell advised that although the British had blacklisted the firm, the Canadian government had not. Inco was therefore free to continue to trade with the Canadian branch of Eugene Dietzgen, though Bell noted that it would be better to trade "with firms who are friendly to the Allies."[31] Bell evidently looked into the practices of the Canadian government regarding Eugene Dietzgen and two weeks later advised Solicitor General Arthur Meighen that a number of government departments were still doing business with the firm.[32]

Certainly, some of the cases that crossed Bell's desk were more unusual than others. In early 1916, Inco reported to Bell that an attorney claiming to represent a firm named the Universal Tool Steel Company and another individual had visited Inco's New York offices seeking to purchase nickel for the Russian government. The pair produced a bank credit for the Universal Tool Steel Company and requested two invoices showing prices of US48¢ and US35.5¢ per pound, respectively. The difference was a commission to be shared with a senior Russian army officer. Inco advised them that it could not conduct European business except through its London agents. A few days later, another representative of the Universal Tool Steel Company, R.I. Henderson, called W.A. Bostwick requesting up to 200 short tons of nickel for the company's Toronto plant. Bostwick advised him that such business had to be conducted in person. Bell had the company investigated and discovered that the Universal Tool Steel Company's "plant" measured only 50 square feet. Moreover, during the investigation, Henderson offered the Canadian government's investigator C$16,000 to help the company secure 400 short tons of nickel.[33]

The Universal Tool Steel Company's scheme was easily thwarted, but others proved far more difficult to control. In early 1915, John Hammar, the managing director general of the Export Association of Sweden, approached Inco in New York about buying up to 1,000 short tons of nickel for delivery to a New York warehouse. Hammar offered guarantees that the nickel would be shipped to consumers in Sweden or some other point until the war was over. Inco officials, doubting Hammar's intentions, notified British authorities (because the customer was European) who expressed concerns. Thus, Inco refused to provide a quote.[34]

Hammar would not be so easily put off. He arranged for various agents in New York to purchase nickel from the Nassau Smelting & Refining Company of New York. Nassau had been an Inco customer before the war and, in February 1915, concluded a contract with Inco for 765 tons of nickel.[35] The contract included a standard clause that the nickel was for the company's own use and would not be resold. Despite this, Nassau transferred several hundred tons of nickel to Sandersen & Porter, Hammar's agents, who held it in a Brooklyn warehouse.

The Canadian and British governments became aware of what had occurred in July 1915. Inco had learned that Nassau was breaching its contract, and when it advised Canadian officials, an investigation led to the warehouse in Brooklyn. At least part of the metal held there was positively identified as nickel pellets that Inco had sold to Nassau.[36] Given this evidence of Nassau's breach, Inco advised that it was suspending shipments to Nassau, leaving 385 of the 765 tons undelivered. However, Nassau would not accept Inco's position. The company denied it had breached the contract and asserted that the material was being stored for its future needs.[37]

This forced the hand of both Inco and the Canadian government. If Inco refused delivery, Nassau might pursue legal action. A lawsuit would inevitably reveal the workings of the Canadian nickel control system, including Inco's breaches of American law and Canada's intelligence-gathering efforts in the United States. The very secrecy designed to protect the system became a liability in this case. The American outrage would presumably be all the greater over revelations of a secret conspiracy to regulate commerce in the United States. The Canadian public would also likely be outraged at learning that the government had failed to police nickel shipments. Canadian officials decided it was preferable to risk the nickel being shipped to Germany than face an angry American government and Canadian public. Bell instructed Inco to resume its shipments to Nassau, and A.P. Sherwood, commissioner of the Dominion Police, made arrangements for Pinkerton's Detective Agency to monitor the

Brooklyn warehouse.[38] The hope was that if any effort was made to ship the nickel, the British would be able to intercept it.

Several months elapsed before the nickel was moved. In May 1916, 280 of the approximately 1,000 tons of nickel from the Brooklyn warehouse was loaded onto train cars and delivered to Baltimore. In June, more than a dozen cars were supposedly sent to various destinations and then diverted to Baltimore en route.[39] However, how the nickel would actually leave the United States remained unclear. Britain's blockade of Germany remained a seemingly insurmountable obstacle to anyone attempting to bring contraband from the United States to Germany. The answer came on 9 July as the submarine *Deutschland* docked at Baltimore harbour.

The *Deustchland* posed an immediate diplomatic conundrum for the American government. Submarines were generally considered warships ineligible to dock in a neutral harbour, but the *Deutschland* was a cargo submarine and carried no armament. The State Department therefore ruled it a merchant vessel and gave it free access to American ports.[40] British intelligence had been aware of the cargo submarines and attempted to persuade the Americans that the *Deutschland* should be considered a military vessel because its crew were members of the German navy. However, *Deutschland* was not a modified military submarine, but a purpose-built vessel conceived by Bremen merchant Frederik Alfred Lohmann. The only firearm the American inspectors discovered was signalling rockets. *Deutschland*'s crew was likely composed of sailors drawn from the navy, but the boat's papers confirmed them as members of the merchant marine.[41] Following its transatlantic voyage, the submarine spent a month in American waters conducting tests and making repairs. On 2 August, the *Deustchland* left harbour under cover of darkness and returned to Germany with 325 tons of nickel.[42]

The public outrage that the Canadian government had hoped to avoid began as soon as the *Deustchland* arrived. Despite Prime Minister Borden's and Ontario minister of mines G. Howard Ferguson's assurances that it was not Canadian nickel that the *Deutschland* was loading, speculation that Canada would move to block nickel exports grew.[43] The Toronto *Globe* called for an immediate embargo "if it is shown that the Deutschland carries any considerable quantity [of nickel] on her return trip to Germany."[44] The Toronto *Star* expressed surprise that the American government had no knowledge of the nickel control system that the Canadian government had insisted was in place.[45] Despite efforts by Robert Borden to persuade several newspaper editors of his government's case, the public outrage could not be quieted.

The *Deutschland* incident came at a precarious time in Anglo-American relations. On 18 July 1916, only a week after the *Deutschland*'s arrival in Baltimore, the British released the first version of the blacklist (those firms with which British citizens were barred from trade), which included American companies.[46] With the submarine's arrival, the British threatened to extend the blacklist. The American government protested against this apparent British prohibition on transactions within the neutral United States. American exporters urged Congress to embargo the sale of munitions.[47] Britain's ambassador to the United States, Cecil Spring Rice, was instructed to assure the Americans that Britain had no intention of interfering with neutral commerce with those other than British subjects.[48]

By September, A.P. Sherwood had received information that nickel was again being moved from the Brooklyn warehouse. Several hundred tons were moved, presumably in anticipation of the arrival of another cargo submarine. However, the *Deutschland* did not reappear until early November and stayed just ten days to collect a cargo of 360 tons of nickel.[49] This was the *Deutschland*'s final trip to the United States. A third voyage in February 1917 was cancelled amidst rising German-American tensions.

Ultimately, the submarine's strategic impact was negligible. Estimates made by Rear Admiral Montagu W.W.P. Consett in his 1923 *The Triumph of Unarmed Forces* suggest that for nickel Germany depended on Norway to provide approximately 700 tons annually (the British government paid the Norwegians to limit production).[50] After 1917, the sinking of Norwegian ships had led to public demand for an end to these exports because some of the nickel was used in torpedo manufacture. Although Jonathan Clay Randel has favourably compared the *Deutschland* with pre-war cargo ships, its internal hold capacity was merely 740 tons (though it could carry rubber externally) as opposed to upwards of 6,000 tons for the others.[51] At a time when Inco was producing 2,700 tons of nickel per month for the Entente, the approximately 700 tons that the *Deutschland* carried on its two trips still left the Germans significantly outsupplied. Far from being the first step in a successful blockade-running operation, the *Deutschland* was a sign of the effectiveness of the blockade.

Graham Bell, the architect of the nickel control system, felt the public criticism keenly. He had worked to improve the system after the news of the *Deutschland* broke and asked A.P. Sherwood to investigate 122 companies only to be told that the expenditure necessary would be excessive.[52] To Arthur Meighen, then Canada's solicitor general, Bell stressed that this was a failure of the British government far more than the Canadian government. He had urged the use of British intelligence to investigate the American firms receiving nickel and had advised the British authorities of the nickel resold by Nassau, yet nothing had come of this.[53] For their part, the British blamed the Canadian officials. Sir Leonard Llewelyn of the Ministry of Munitions observed that if Bell was "really carrying out his instructions efficiently, it should be impossible for shipments to be made to Germany."[54]

Although the Canadian and British officials blamed each other, neither blamed Inco. In fact, Bell praised the company for providing "every assistance" in keeping nickel out of the hands of Canada's enemies.[55] The public, on the other hand, held Inco largely responsible. For those who had long called for Inco to refine in Canada, the *Deutschland* incident was proof of the perils of letting this "foreign monopolist" exploit Ontario's nickel ores. The public's anger at the idea that Canadian nickel was being used to arm Canada's enemies had sufficiently changed the political climate such that Inco decided to bow to public pressure and revise its international structure. On the same day the news of the *Deutschland* broke, Inco announced that it would open a Canadian refinery. This marked a reversal of the company's historical position that refining in Canada was uneconomical. The new plant would cost C$4 million with an initial capacity of 15 million pounds and was designed to expand.[56] Publicly, Inco maintained that the new refinery would mean economic sacrifice in the interests of "Imperial necessity," but privately the company acknowledged that the move was an effort to silence its critics.[57]

In 1916, public anger posed a much greater threat to the company than ever before. It was not only Inco that seemed to be reconsidering its globalized approach. The years of opposition to Inco had led the Ontario government to organize a Royal Commission on Nickel. Among the questions it was investigating were compulsory refining of nickel in the province and the potential for nationalizing the Ontario nickel industry. Inco's announcement of a new refinery (eventually constructed at Port Colborne, Ontario) pre-empted the commission's work. The move successfully deflated much of the public agitation against the company, and when the commission finally reported, it argued that because nickel was not a necessity of life, there was no compelling argument for public ownership. In any event, it was likely unaffordable; the cost of nationalizing Inco with appropriate compensation was estimated to be C$100 million, equivalent to the paid-up capital stock of every chartered bank in Canada.[58] The commission also recommended new taxes, which Ontario enacted in 1917. The profit tax for the nickel-copper industry was increased from 3 per cent to 5 per cent and graduated, with 5 per cent on the first C$5 million, 6 per cent on the next C$5 million, and an additional 1 per cent on each C$5 million thereafter.[59]

The additional taxation levied by Ontario and the construction of a Canadian nickel refinery did not mean that Inco's working relationship with the Canadian government had suffered. This was evident from the circumstances surrounding the British America Nickel Corporation (hereafter Banco). A group of prominent business figures – including the American engineer Frederick Stark

Pearson; William Mackenzie and Donald Mann, the pair driving the construction of the Canadian Northern Railway; and E.R. Wood, one of the financiers behind Dominion Securities – was behind the venture. Since the early days of the war, the group had worked to launch its project. However, despite the influence of Banco's proprietors, it had difficulty securing the requisite financing. Requests for bond guarantees were rejected by the Canadian government.[60] Frank Cochrane made the case to Borden that Inco had made the Canadian nickel industry a world leader and that for the Canadian government to support Banco would be unfair to those who had pioneered the industry.[61]

Although the Canadian government continued to support Inco and felt no need to revisit its policies towards the industry, the British government felt the need for adjustments, ultimately placing the Canadian government in an embarrassing position. In August 1916, Graham Bell visited Inco's New York offices to finalize the arrangements for the new Canadian refinery. Inco officials confronted him with the rumours that the British government was advancing a large part of the capital for Banco's Canadian refinery and had entered into a contract for a "large proportion" of the company's production.[62] Inco officials reminded Bell of the large expense of their new refinery for a market they now believed had been largely contracted to Banco. Only through "considerable persuasion and pressure" did Bell convince them to proceed. By October, Inco had confirmation that the British had guaranteed a market for Banco's nickel. Inco's president, Ambrose Monell, appealed to Robert Borden to urge the British to reconsider and prevent "this serious injustice to our Company."[63] Borden stressed that the Canadian government had no part in the scheme and would pass the concerns along to the Canadian High Commission in London. In a letter to George Perley, Borden agreed that Inco's complaint had some merit because the government had insisted on the construction of a Canadian refinery, but he also observed that this had not been unreasonable and that the Canadian ore deposits had been "immensely remunerative" for Inco.[64]

Ultimately, Monell's concerns proved exaggerated. Banco's ore deposits were low grade, and this significantly increased its operating costs. Moreover, it had borrowed C$4 million on the security of its contract with the British government. When the war ended, the contract was cancelled. Banco attempted to enter the American market to find an outlet for its production, provoking a price war with Inco, which it ultimately lost. The company collapsed, and Inco acquired its assets.[65]

The Canadian government's struggle to control exported nickel was largely resolved in April 1917 when the Americans entered the war. As new legislation regarding trading with the enemy took effect in the United States, those firms that had put up bonds for the purchase of nickel were released from them.

The synchronization of Canadian and American foreign policy had once again reduced the psychic distance between the countries and, along with it, the significance of the border.

The strategic imperative had certainly motivated extraordinary actions by the British and Canadian governments with respect to international trade. In his classic study of the blockade, Marion Siney stated that "no serious legal arguments could be raised if a belligerent stipulated conditions on the use to which raw materials, manufactured products, or foodstuffs, exported from its own territory, were put by those permitted to receive them."[66] The case of nickel control reinforces the idea that legality was not the chief concern in the strained Anglo-American relationship. From a pre-war state of relatively unfettered commerce, the need for security drove the Canadian and British governments to risk transgressions against the law and the sensibilities of the neutral United States to enforce the blockade and to preserve the confidence of their own publics. Moreover, they were able to use their control of raw materials to compel the complicity of the American multinational Inco.

Nickel was obviously a significant commodity to warrant the risk of the secret control arrangement. Clearly, this was a measured risk, and when the Nassau breach forced them to weigh enforcing the blockade against arousing American anger, they chose to weaken the blockade. Thus, the nickel example demonstrates one of the identified flaws in the British blockade. Where the United States was concerned, it was simply not possible to absolutely enforce it without triggering a political backlash. However, the resulting *Deutschland* incident must be taken as a sign that the blockade was reasonably effective at least as far as the commodities it carried (nickel, rubber, and tin) are concerned. As Ferguson states, naval blockade did not decide the war, but in the case of nickel, it almost certainly hindered Germany's steel makers.[67] If extraordinary measures had been taken to enforce the nickel blockade, at least they had achieved some degree of success

The war compelled both the Canadian and Ontario governments and Inco to revisit the accepted practices of and structures for Canadian resources in the international nickel industry. Although the two governments had steadily embraced a more selective approach leading up to the war, the war had proved the tipping point. Security concerns required Canadian nickel to be refined domestically. Of course, even this historic reversal still represented a limited response. Nationalization was ruled out, as was supporting the British-backed competitor Banco. Thus, the governments were still comfortable enough with globalization to allow an American corporation to dominate the Canadian nickel industry. This obviously had a great deal to do with Inco's own revised international strategy, which included violating the laws of its home country, America, to satisfy its Canadian host government. After the war, Inco would close its New Jersey refinery and produce entirely within Canada. However, it would not restructure to make Canada its home rather than host country until 1928 and only then to avoid an impending antitrust suit.

NOTES

1 Robert Schaeffer, *Understanding Globalization: The Social Consequences of Political, Economic, and Environmental Change*, 3rd ed. (Oxford: Rowman & Littlefield, 2005), 184.

2 William D. Coleman and Michael Atkinson, *State, Business and Industrial Change in Canada* (Toronto: University of Toronto Press, 1989), 32–3.

3 Marion Siney, *The Allied Blockade of Germany, 1914–1916* (Ann Arbor: University of Michigan Press, 1957), v.

4 Niall Ferguson, *The Pity of War* (New York: Basic Books, 1999), 252.

5 Alfred D. Chandler, *The Visible Hand: The Managerial Revolution In American Business* (Cambridge, MA: Belknap Press, 1977), 363.

6 R.M. Bray, "Nickel-Steel Alloy: The Not-So Stainless Formation of the International Nickel Company of New Jersey, 1902" (Paper presented to the American Business and Economic History Society, Milwaukee, Wisconsin, 24 April 1998).

7 R.M. Bray and Angus Gilbert, "The Mond-International Nickel Merger of 1929: A Case Study in Entrepreneurial Failure," *Canadian Historical Review* 76, no. 1 (1995): 22.

8 H.V. Nelles, *The Politics of Development* (Toronto: MacMillan, 1974), 48.

9 O.W. Main, *The Canadian Nickel Industry: A Study in Market Control and Public Policy* (Toronto: University of Toronto Press, 1955), 53.

10 Nelles, *Politics of Development*, 93–102.

11 Ferguson, *Pity of War*, 252.

12 Jonathan Clay Randel, "Information for Economic Warfare: British Intelligence and the Blockade" (PhD diss., University of North Carolina, 1999), 91.

13 Siney, *Allied Blockade of Germany*, 30.

14 Ibid., 28.

15 Main, *Canadian Nickel Industry*, 82.

16 W.A. Bostwick to R.L. Borden, 5 October 1914, RG25, B-1-f, vol. 540, "London High Commissioner. 242. Nickel Exported from Canada 1914–1916," National Archives of Canada (NAC).

17 Woodrow Wilson, "Message to Congress," 63rd Congress, 2nd Session, Senate Document No. 566 (Washington, DC, 1914), 3–4

18 Siney, *Allied Blockade of Germany*, 58.

19 G.A. Bell to R.L. Borden, 30 October 1914, RG43, vol. 1736, File 1-177, NAC.

20 G. Perley to R.L. Borden, 21 October 1914, RG25, B-1-f, vol. 540, "London High Commissioner. 242. Nickel Exported from Canada 1914–1916," NAC.

21 G.A. Bell to A. Meighen, 5 March 1917, MG26 H, vol. 106, NAC.

22 L.C. Christie, "Memorandum Respecting the Control of the Exportation of Nickel," 27 February 1916, MG26 H, vol. 106, NAC.

23 Philip K. Smith, *Harvest from the Rock: A History of Mining in Ontario* (Toronto: Macmillan of Canada, 1986), 208.

24 Siney, *Allied Blockade of Germany*, 57.

25 Kathleen Burk, *Britain, America and the Sinews of War, 1914–1918* (Boston: G. Allen & Unwin, 1985), 31.

26 Ibid., 42.

27 Kathleen Burk, *Old World, New World: Great Britain and America from the Beginning* (New York: Grove Press, 2007), 452.

28 Burk, *Sinews of War*, 4.

29 Lord R. Cecil to G. Perley, 29 January 1917, RG25, B-1-f, vol. 540, "London High Commissioner 243. Nickel Exported from Canada 1916–1920," NAC.

30 G.A. Bell to D.K. Hill of the Bayard Company, New York, 20 November 1916, RG43, vol. 1738, File 783-966, NAC.

31 G.A. Bell to W.A. Bostwick, 7 September 1916, RG43, vol. 1737, File 645-782, NAC.

32 G.A. Bell to A. Meighen, 22 September 1916, in Ibid.

33 G.A. Bell to R.L. Borden, 28 February 1916, RG25, B-1-f, vol. 540, "London High Commissioner. 243. Nickel Exported from Canada 1916–1920," NAC.

34 W.A. Bostwick to H. Gardner, 4 March 1915, MG26 H, vol. 107, NAC.

35 G.A. Bell to A. Meighen, 5 March 1917, MG26 H, vol. 106, NAC.

36 Memorandum, n.d., RG43, vol. 1736, File 326-423, NAC.

37 Ibid.

38 Bostwick to Bell, 9 August 1915, and Pinkerton's National Detective Agency to A.P. Sherwood, 13 August 1915, RG43, vol. 1736, File 326-423, NAC.

39 War Trade Intelligence Department, "Purchases of Nickel &c in the U.S.A. for German Account," 19 December 1916, MUN, 4, File 2100, Public Record Office (PRO), London.

40 "'Diving' Deutschland Crosses Ocean Carries Cargo, Not Torpedoes," *Globe* (Toronto), 10 July 1916, 1.

41 Randel, "Information for Economic Warfare," 271–2.

42 Estimates vary between 325 and 400 tons.

43 Press Statement, 11 July 1916, MG26 H, vol. 36, NAC; "No Ontario Nickel for German 'Subs,'" *Globe* (Toronto), 11 July 1916, 9.

44 "Notes and Comments," *Globe* (Toronto), 13 July 1916, 4.

45 "Notes and Comments," *Daily Star* (Toronto), 13 July 1916, 6.
46 Siney, *Allied Blockade of Germany*, 146.
47 Burk, *Sinews of War*, 40.
48 Siney, *Allied Blockade of Germany*, 146–7.
49 T. Terry Champion, "Memorandum," 21 October 1916, RG25, B-1-f, vol. 540, "London High Commissioner 243. Nickel Exported from Canada 1916–1920," NAC.
50 M.W.W.P. Consett, *The Triumph of Unarmed Forces (1914–1918): An Account of the Transactions by Which Germany during the Great War Was Able to Obtain Supplies Prior to Her Collapse under the Pressure of Economic Forces* (London: Williams and Norgate, 1923), 198–200.
51 Randel, "Information for Economic Warfare," 270.
52 G.A. Bell to A.P. Sherwood, 25 July 1916, RG43, vol. 1737, File 536-644, NAC.
53 G.A. Bell to A. Meighen, 15 November 1916, RG43, vol. 1737, File 645-782, NAC.
54 L. Llewelyn to Sir Frederick Black, Director General of Munitions Supply, 9 February 1917, MUN, 4, File 2100, PRO, London.
55 G.A. Bell to R.L. Borden, 10 February 1917, RG43, vol. 1738, File 967-1141, NAC.
56 E.F. Wood to R.L. Borden, 20 July 1916, RG25, B-1-f, vol. 540, "London High Commissioner 243. Nickel Exported from Canada 1916–1920," NAC.
57 A. Monell to R.L. Borden, 7 January 1916, RG25, B-1-f, vol. 540, "London High Commissioner 243. Nickel Exported from Canada 1916–1920," NAC; Bray and Gilbert, "Mond-International Nickel Merger," 24.
58 Main, *Canadian Nickel Industry*, 86.
59 Ibid., 87.
60 R.L. Borden to E.R. Wood, 5 January 1915, MG26 H, vol. 106, NAC.
61 F. Cochrane to R.L. Borden, 29 April 1915, MG26 H, vol. 107, NAC.
62 G.A. Bell to A. Meighen, 5 March 1917, MG26 H, vol. 106, NAC.
63 A. Monell to R.L. Borden, 31 October 1916, RG25, B-1-f, vol. 540, "London High Commissioner 243. Nickel Exported from Canada 1916–1920," NAC.
64 R.L. Borden to G. Perley, 8 November 1916, RG25, B-1-f, vol. 540, "London High Commissioner 243. Nickel Exported from Canada 1916–1920," NAC.
65 Main, *Canadian Nickel Industry*, 95–98.
66 Siney, *Allied Blockade of Germany*, 157.
67 Ferguson, *Pity of War*, 253.

4

Natural Resource Exports and Development in Settler Economies during the First Great Globalization Era: Northwestern Ontario and South Australia, 1905–15

LIVIO DI MATTEO, J.C. HERBERT EMERY, AND MARTIN P. SHANAHAN

The nineteenth-century drop in transportation costs fuelled trade expansion and a wave of globalization rooted in the demand for primary product exports that were inputs into the urbanizing industrial centres of the Atlantic economy. During this era of globalization, the successful development of many of the high-income countries of today, such as Canada, the United States, Australia, and New Zealand, was based on the exploitation and export of abundant natural resources, such as fish, fur, timber, gold, grain, coal, and oil.[1] In contrast to this historical experience, resource-abundant economies during the recent era of globalization remain dependent on their resource sectors and have had slower growth than resource-scarce economies.[2] The negative correlation between natural resource exports and growth during the recent era of globalization has been dubbed the "curse of resources" and has triggered a sizeable literature that seeks to explain this surprising outcome. As Sachs and Warner note, the resource curse is a surprising phenomenon given the expectation that

Martin Shanahan acknowledges the assistance of an Australian Research Council Grant in supporting this research and thanks John Wilson for research assistance. Livio Di Matteo acknowledges the support of the Social Sciences and Humanities Research Council of Canada. Herb Emery acknowledges the support from the School of Commerce, University of South Australia, which allowed him to visit the School in August 2003, which resulted in this collaboration. The authors thank participants at the Canadian Network for Economic History Conference at Kingston, Ontario, April 2005 for comments.

natural resource exports resulting from rising world demand would be a cata-
lyst for development as historical experience seems to demonstrate.[3]

Sachs and Warner dismiss the relevance of historical successful resource-
based development cases for understanding the resource curse.[4] First, they
argue that these countries developed in a world of relatively high transportation
costs that encouraged manufacturing and processing industries to locate near
available resource endowments, such as coal, and that they never had as intensive exploitation of natural resources compared to resource-dependent economies of the mid- to late twentieth century. This view neglects that in the absence
of protectionist policies, countries like the Canada, Australia, and New Zealand
primarily exported raw, or unprocessed, natural resources and imported much
of the manufacturing needs from the distant British market. Crafts notes "that
the United States was a high tariff country throughout its rise [to] world economic leadership."[5] If the abundance of local power sources and resources for
inputs into manufacturing was the key determinant of industrialization, then
the failure of much of the US Northeast and Northern Ontario in Canada to
industrialize and develop stands as an important historical counter-example. If
we consider the resource intensity of Canada and the United States just prior to
their creation as nation states, then we see their successful development began
as resource-based economies.[6] Finally, Auty argues that there is nothing deter-
ministic about resource abundance and successful development and sustained
growth. He notes that many resource-abundant economies grew rapidly between 1870 and 1913 and between 1950 and 1973. The growth collapses of the
late 1970s and early 1980s of resource-dependent economies is ironic, he says,
because the collapse was the result of resource-dependent economies trying
to reduce their resource dependence.[7] As discussed in the introduction of this
collection, Rodrik's view is that after the 1970s the capacity of nation states to
manage their degree of integration into the global economy was undermined.

Counter to the view of Sachs and Warner, it could be that the explanation
for the "resource curse" may be found in an understanding of why successful
natural resource-based development has occurred historically but not recently.
In turn, these insights may be useful for determining how the more recent era
of globalization compares to the earlier era in terms of opportunities for natural
resource–based development. To that end, we examine the level, distribution,
and composition of wealth of probated decedents in the Thunder Bay District
(TBD), Ontario, and in South Australia (SA) over the period 1905 to 1915. We
are interested in examining how much wealth accumulated during these wheat
export booms, how much of that wealth was invested in the local economy, and
how much was held in assets external to the local economy. Wealth is in many
ways a superior variable to income for our purposes because it can capture

the long-term impacts of the effect of natural resource exports on economic development.[8] We interpret the accumulation of wealth in a resource-based economy as symptomatic of a successful development episode.

A comparison of wealth accumulation in the Lakehead region and in SA allows us to infer the determinants behind successful and unsuccessful development from natural resource exports. We look at the effects of a common resource for export, wheat, in the same decade, 1905 to 1915, in two British settler economies. Institutional quality in these two economies should be comparable even if the institutions are different.

There are differences between the two regions that may be informative for identifying the ways in which natural resource exports influence economic development. SA benefited from earlier resource export episodes, including copper in the 1840s, wheat and wool in the 1850s, and wheat again in the 1870s. On the other hand, the economy of TBD and its port towns of Port Arthur and Fort William was really a new economy in 1905. Finally, recent work by Gallup, Sachs and Mellinger, and Rappaport and Sachs highlights the positive correlation between coastal locations and income levels but does not provide a satisfactory explanation for why the correlation exists.[9] The grain production in the SA economy was for the most part contained within 60 miles of coast, whereas Port Arthur/Fort William was an intermediate terminus on the Canadian transportation system, with grain being transferred from Great Lakes freighters to ocean-going vessels on the way to market. Our comparison of wealth accumulation in these two economies, therefore, may be able to inform us as to why coastal locations are beneficial for economic development.[10]

Perhaps the most interesting aspect of our comparison of the SA and TBD economies during a period of rising wheat exports is that SA represented an economy where transportation, production, and handling of wheat was carried out by local owners of capital so that the capital's share of income was retained locally. TBD in contrast, was akin to a resource-exporting country where production and transportation functions were controlled by external capital and that income did not remain in the local economy. SA was an economy with the capacity to manage its integration with the global economy and practise what Rodrik refers to as "smart" or "selective" globalization through its ability to set tariffs and control the ownership of the state's railways. In contrast, TBD lacked the capability to manage its degree of integration into the global economy as it relied on external capital and had no power to erect barriers to international trade, especially tariffs, or restrictions on external capital flows and external ownership of productive capacity.

What we learn from the changes in wealth levels in the two locations is that although average wealth levels in SA were substantially higher than in TBD, between 1905 and 1915, the rate of increase in average wealth levels was equivalent in SA and the TBD. The volume of wheat passing through the Lakehead was substantially greater than the quantity of wheat produced in SA, but SA appropriated more linkages from the boom enabling it to match the Lakehead's growth. The higher wealth levels in SA relative to the TBD during the 1905–15 period are rooted in the fact that SA was a region of older settlement and that over time earlier wealth accumulation was able to compound into higher levels relative to the more newly settled TBD. Long-term economic development from natural resources is therefore a function of the ability to retain linkages from the resource activity as well as the passage of time necessary for linkages to develop and wealth to accumulate. Our comparison of TBD and SA highlights the importance of "selective globalization" as a path to successful long-run development.

Wheat Exports from Two Settler Economies

The years 1905 to 1913 were an important period for the economic development of the TBD and the South Australian economy. For TBD, this was the period of substantial initial development, while for SA the period saw the return of prosperous economic conditions following more than a decade of economic stagnation.

Although European settlement of the TBD began during the fur trade when it was home to Fort William, the inland headquarters of the Northwest Company of Montreal, it was the coming of the transcontinental railway in the 1880s linked the region to the prairie wheat economy and central Canada and spurred the region's development. The TBD was uniquely juxtaposed between the prairie wheat economy, from which it would benefit by having its major metropolitan centre serve as entrepôt, and central Canada, where it was part of Canada's wealthiest province. The northwestern portion of the province, along with the TBD, was directly tied to the prairie wheat boom via the grain port function of the twin cities of Fort William and Port Arthur, known collectively as "the Lakehead."[11] Moreover, a portion of the economy was rooted in local manufacturing development, resource extraction, and agricultural development.[12]

The population of the district grew rapidly with the greatest expansion between 1901 and 1911 when the population nearly tripled to approximately 40,000. Most of the population growth during the boom period occurred at the Lakehead as the result of high in-migration, and by 1921 more than 70 per cent of the district's population was at the Lakehead. The economic boom at the Lakehead ended with the onset of the First World War. The increase in interest rates in 1913 tightened farm credit and halted the expansion of the wheat boom that was then followed by the disruption of the war and the reduction in immigrant flows to the west. The opening of the Panama Canal in 1914 may have also redirected some of the flow of wheat and commerce away from the Lakehead and to the west coast. The value of building permits in Fort William rose steadily from 1907 and peaked in 1912 at just over C$4 million and then fell dramatically for the next four years to reach C$0.6 million by 1916. At least a dozen major employers shut down from 1914 to 1922, and the size of the labour force declined. Recovery did not begin until the construction of the first pulp mill in 1917.[13]

The European settlement of SA had been underway for seventy years in 1905. SA had a rural based economy founded under a system of "systematic colonization" to produce a self-supporting system financed by land sales aimed at avoiding the financial and social crises of other Australian colonies or the problems related to penal colonies. Despite initial difficulties, within twenty years of settlement the colony boasted a population of 85,000, and more than 160,000 acres of wheat were sown, with a large portion being used to feed the gold rushes in the neighbouring colony of Victoria.[14] Indeed, so successful was SA in agricultural pursuits that in the 1870s it was regarded as "the granary of the continent."[15] By 1901, the first year of Australian Federation, the population of the new state of SA was 359,000, with 162,000 or just over 42 per cent living in the capital Adelaide.[16] A decade later, the state's population reached almost 410,000, with Adelaide accounting for around 50 per cent of the population.[17]

SA was geographically distant from the Atlantic economy, but culturally and historically linked to England. Although distant from the centre of world financial markets in London and the newly emerging industrial strength of North America, it was still a part of the modern industrial world. Changes in transportation affected the state's external trade. The great circle route (south from England until the "roaring 40s" below South Africa, west to Australia, and then after leaving Australia, back to 40° south and around the Cape of Good Hope) meant that in the 1870s clippers took eighty days to get to England. The opening of the Suez Canal in 1869 and the rise of steamships changed the technology of shipping, although by 1883 still only one-third of cargo returned to the United Kingdom via the Suez. Not until 1911 did steamers replace clippers in the wheat trade.[18]

Despite SA's early expansion in wheat exports (and lead in the use of agricultural machinery), it took some time for farmers to understand their environment. From the mid-1850s, average yields declined in SA until a slight upturn in the late 1860s. Offsetting the decline was the expansion of acreage. Despite considerable research into the topic, it was not until new varieties of wheat were developed and planted in the late 1890s, and these were combined with more effective use of fallowing and fertilizers, that average yields per acre again increased.

A major factor impacting on the South Australian economy was out of the control of settlers: drought. Droughts of differing levels of severity occurred in the 1860s and the 1880s, while the combination of the depression in the early 1890s followed by one of the worst droughts ever recorded (from 1895 to 1903) put significant brakes on economic prosperity. A further drought at the end of the First World War slowed economic recovery.[19] The First World War not only made trading agricultural products with Europe difficult but also impacted heavily on the workforce. The period from 1914 to the 1940 was one of relative stagnation of living standards for the whole of Australia, and SA was not an exception.[20]

Apart from remaining pre-eminent in wheat production within Australia until the 1890s, SA also developed a significant pastoral industry. Together, these gave the economy a large agricultural base for wealth accumulation, as well as heavy exposure to the risk of drought. Although no extensive gold deposits were found in SA, copper deposits north of the capital provided an alternative resource export for more than sixty years. Wheat, wool, and copper, together with the benefits of being the nearest capital to the silver and lead deposits at Broken Hill, underpinned Adelaide and SA's growth through the nineteenth century. Compared to the other states of Australia, SA had the advantage of agricultural land that was comparatively close to the capital and relatively easy to clear.[21] This also contributed to development of a network of rail lines, many of which carried wheat to Port Adelaide and, from there, directly to London.[22]

The onset of Australian Federation in 1901 also brought a change to trade arrangements. As a colony, SA had levied its own tariffs and customs prior to 1900. Until 1877 there was a 10 per cent ad valorem duty on imported wheat, while from 1888 until 1900 SA charged 2s. per cental (100 pounds) on wheat. Only Victoria was seen as being seriously protectionist in outlook and practice.[23] Federation removed customs duties between the states, while overall Australia, like Canada, adopted a protectionist regime.[24] Thus, prior to 1900, SA had the unique ability to capture linkages through protectionist policies, but after 1900, it was not able to do this. On the other hand, the TBD was never able to set its own independent tariff policy.

SA benefited not only from the transport of grain via Adelaide but also from the actual production of wheat in the region. In other words, it also earned substantial rents from the land factor, which would not have been available in the case of Thunder Bay. The TBD benefited from transporting prairie grain in a manner described by McCallum – the appropriation of linkages from a staple produced far from the region.[25] In addition, the South Australian wheat boom economy began earlier than the TBD's, was more regionally focused in terms of the economic impact, and had its transport functions centralized via Adelaide.

Although the Lakehead towns were the dominant metropolis of their region, they did not have access to the rich and compact agricultural hinterland that Adelaide did, and their economic growth was largely dependent on their trans-shipment function, which they increasingly had to share with Vancouver, Montreal, and Quebec City. The railways that shipped grain to the Lakehead and the shipping companies that took the grain from the Lakehead represent external capital/businesses for the TBD, and as such, the share of income earned by that capital would not have been retained in the region. Adelaide, on the other hand, was able to create a virtual locational monopoly on grain shipping out of its relatively compact region. The average rail distance that wheat had to be transported by rail in SA was 50 miles. Despite the development of other ports along the coast in the 1870s, Meinig describes the overall design of the rail network as "long extensions deep into the interior, not only to serve the pastoral and mining regions, but also as instruments of grand strategy to capture a major share of the interior trade of neighboring colonies."[26] Moreover, all railways in SA were state owned so that the transportation income was retained in the SA economy.

SA had a substantial head start in terms of economic development. Although 1885 represents the dawn of grain shipping at the Lakehead and the full prairie wheat boom was still more than a decade away, in 1885, SA exported almost 8 million bushels of wheat and flour, and the population of SA was more than 70,000.[27] However, during the period 1905–15, when wheat production boomed in Canada and regained ground after years of drought in SA, the volume of wheat production in Canada far exceeded that of SA (see Table 4.1), and indeed the volume of wheat shipped through the Lakehead was far greater than that through Adelaide. Whereas SA's wheat production and exports during the 1880s were comparable in scale to those of the Ontario economy in the 1850s and 1870s,[28] the 1905 to 1915 period saw wheat shipments through the Lakehead that dwarfed the size of wheat production and exports of SA (see Table 4.1).

Nonetheless, in relative terms, wheat had been extraordinarily important to SA for many years. From 1860 to the mid-1890s, between 60 and 80 per cent

Table 4.1. Wheat production in South Australia and Canada, 1870–1915

Year	Area under Wheat (acres)		
	SA	Australia	Canada
1870	604,761	1,123,839	1,647,000
1880	1,733,542	3,052,617	2,367,000
1890	1,673,573	3,228,535	2,701,000
1900	1,913,247	5,666,614	4,225,000
1910	2,104,719	7,372,456	8,865,000
1915	2,739,214	12,484,512	15,109,000

Year	Wheat Production (bushel per acre)	
	SA	Canada
1870	11.50	10.20
1880	5.00	13.70
1890	5.60	15.60
1900	5.90	13.20
1910	11.60	14.90
1915	12.50	26.00

Sources: Canada-Historical Statistics of Canada; E. Dunsdorfs, *The Australian Wheat-Growing Industry 1788–1948* (Melbourne: The University Press, 1956), appendix; W. Vamplew, E. Richards, D. Jaensch, and J. Hancock, eds., *South Australian Historical Statistics*, Monograph No. 3 (Sydney: University of New South Wales, 1984), AG46–54.

of SA's wheat production was exported, mostly to the United Kingdom.[29] In SA in 1870, the agricultural (12.6%), pastoral (14.48%), and dairy sectors (3.15%) contributed one-third of the colony's GDP, and by 1910, this had fallen slightly to 29 per cent with agriculture (mostly wheat) contributing 17 percentage points.[30] In comparison, in Canada in 1870, the share of GDP from agriculture (all kinds) was 28 per cent, and by 1910, a little more than 20 per cent. Canadian wheat production contributed 4.5 per cent to GNP (0.16 of 28%) in 1870, and by 1910, 4.8 per cent (0.24 of 20%).[31] Despite SA having been overtaken at the end of the nineteenth century as the single largest wheat producer in Australia by Victoria and New South Wales, we estimate that wheat's contribution to the state product had fallen to "only" 6.97 per cent of SA's gross state product (0.41 of 17%).[32]

The Data

We focused on estimates of average wealth over the period as an indicator of the effect of natural resource exports on development. We were interested in examining how much wealth accumulated during these wheat export booms, how much of that wealth was invested in the local economy, and how much was held in assets external to the local economy. We used the inventory of assets for probated decedents in the SA and TBD economies to estimate wealth accumulation over the period 1905–15.

Given that both countries sold on the world wheat market, from 1905 to 1915, the Canadian grain economy should have generated income at the Lakehead many times larger than that seen in SA. There are two ways in which these differences could be apparent: in the overall increase of the economy and population, and to the extent that linkages are retained/captured in wealth estimates. Chambers and Gordon devised a simple, yet elegant, model of the Canadian economy to demonstrate why natural resource exports in periods of resource booms cannot be a source of sustained growth in per capita income.[33] The mechanism behind this strong conclusion is the high elasticity of factor supply in a small open economy – in other words, the free flow of labour and financial capital into and out of the economy. The high rates of capital and labour inflow in response to increases in resource prices are indicative of the factor price arbitrage process that in the long run returns per capita incomes back to where they were before the resource boom occurred. In the Chambers and Gordon model, the only long-run effects of a resource boom are high "land rents" (incomes to the fixed factor) and a larger economy. Other than the natural resource rents, the long-run effect of the resource boom is a larger economy, as measured by GDP, but not necessarily a richer economy as measured by per capita GDP.[34]

The South Australian data were derived from probate and succession duty documents constructed after the death of an individual. Essential to the legal transfer of assets, these represent consistent, well-monitored information on personal wealth. Probate records contain papers filed to the court by the administrators of an estate, including a copy of the testator's will, the executor's oath, correspondence with the court, and so forth. The records contain information on the testator's name, address, and occupation, as well as a sworn estimate of gross wealth, but no list of assets, the age of the testator, and other family details. To obtain this information, it was necessary to match the probate records with two other sources: the individual's death certificate and succession duty records. The death certificate contained information on the testator's age and cause of death and provided a cross-check for recorded occupation.

Between 1905 and 1915, the state levied succession duty on all estates, and this process produced a succession file that contained a full inventory of the assets of the deceased, their heirs, and the duty payable on each inheritance. The succession duty process required that an independent appraiser estimate the market value of each individual piece of property, which may have included assets as trivial as salt and pepper shakers or as large as pastoral stations or manufacturing businesses.

Between 1905 and 1915, a total of 12,475 people were probated in SA. The top 1 per cent of wealth leavers held approximately 30 per cent of the wealth, and the top 10 per cent, 70 per cent of the wealth. Such a distribution was similar to the distribution of wealth in New Zealand at the same period and to that of the United States in 1860. It was far more equal than the distribution of wealth in the United Kingdom at the same time where probate records suggest the top 1 per cent held two-thirds of all wealth, and the top 10 per cent held 90 per cent of the wealth.[35]

For the purposes of constructing a data set from the probate data, four strata were selected: a 1 per cent sample of estates between £0 and £500; a 2 per cent sample for estates between £501 and £2,500; a 5 per cent sample of estates between £2,501 and £20,000; and the complete population over £20,000. Records of a total of 337 individual estates were recorded; however, the exact date of probate was only available for 307, of which 2 had negative net wealth, leaving 305.

The Ontario data set was constructed from the probate records of the District of Thunder Bay Surrogate Courts from the years 1885 to 1920. Prior to the TBD's creation in 1885, the region's estates were probated in the District of Algoma. Under the Surrogate Courts Act, 1858, a surrogate court with the power to issue grants of probate and administration valid throughout the province was established in each Ontario county, replacing the centralized Court of Probate established in 1793. The inventory was conducted by the executor of the estate (administrator in intestate cases) and legally needed only to be performed in response to a request by a legatee or creditor but in practice was brought in voluntarily without awaiting the compulsory summons.[36]

All estates bearing application dates in the years 1885 to 1920 were examined, but only those 591 estates from 1905 to 1915 were used in this chapter for comparison purposes. Variables recorded include place of residence, occupation, marital status, number of children, date of death, whether they had a will, and the value of the estates. Unfortunately, age at death was not available in these probate records.[37] The inventory provided estimates of wealth grouped into sixteen categories.[38] Like the Australian data, an advantage of this data source was that there were separate estimates of real estate, financial assets, and personal property over a substantial period of time.

Wealth in TBD and SA, 1905–15

After converting the wealth in both data sets into US dollars, the median wealth of SA probated decedents was much greater than the median wealth of probated decedents in the TBD (Figure 4.1). SA wealth levels were higher than TBD in 1905, suggesting that much of that wealth was in place at the start of the period under study as opposed to accumulated over the period. One interpretation is that some of this initial difference in wealth levels reflects SA's development through its earlier copper, wool, and wheat export periods in the nineteenth century. The higher wealth levels for SA also reflect prolonged accumulation and growth over a longer period of time prior to 1905, as well as the possibility that more of the benefits of the wheat economy were retained

Figure 4.1. Median wealth, South Australia and Thunder Bay District, 1905–15

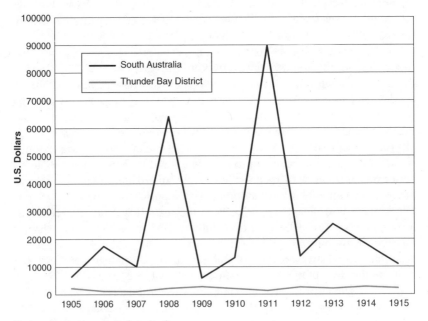

Source: Probate records (see text).

relative to the TBD. In addition, there was inflation in asset values in Australia in the late nineteenth century that could also explain substantially higher levels of wealth.[39] The values of these assets increased during 1870–90, fell somewhat in the mid-1890s, but had high levels by 1905.[40] In addition, some of the difference in wealth levels could also be ascribed to differences in the distribution of ages of the populations in the two regions. The Thunder Bay region was newly settled and therefore likely had a younger average age than SA.

The higher overall levels of wealth of SA can be ascribed to endowments, linkage effects, and timing. A comparison of the changes in wealth levels across the two economies over 1905 to 1915 allows us to identify the conditions and factors that result in natural resource exports developing an economy. If SA's capacity to accumulate wealth exceeds that of Thunder Bay over 1905 to 1915, then the reasons for successful resource export–based development are to be found in factors specific to SA, such as its coastal ports. On the other hand, if there is no difference between the capacities to accumulate wealth across the two economies over the same period, then the reasons for successful resource export–based development are to be found in factors specific to the earlier period, when Ontario was also successfully developed through wheat exports.

As mentioned previously, one of the difficulties that we have encountered in assessing the change in average wealth levels is the relatively high values for SA wealth in 1908 and 1911, which we believe could also partly be the result of having relatively fewer observations for the SA sample in some years. Figure 4.2 adjusts for the impact of outliers on wealth, by removing the top and bottom estate and recalculating the average for each year, and then normalizes the annual value by the average for 1905 to 1915 for the regional economy. This figure suggests that the proportionate changes in wealth levels over the period, particularly from 1905 to the peak value in 1913, are the same.

Table 4.2 shows the proportion of probated decedents reporting financial assets and real estate across the two regions. The differences in the proportion reporting real estate ownership were much smaller across the two regions, whereas there was a very large gap in financial asset ownership. Figure 4.3 shows the value of real estate in each year normalized by the average value of real estate for the period 1905 to 1915. This figure suggests that the value of "local assets" in the two economies had common changes. The common changes in real estate ownership trends and values and the greater importance of financial wealth for the South Australian decedents suggest that members of the South Australian small open economy had the potential to be capital exporters by 1905.[41] The importance of financial assets in the portfolio also suggests that SA is an example of what needs to happen for resource exports to generate sustainable income levels according to Rodriguez and Sachs.[42]

Figure 4.2. Comparison of normalized wealth after adjusting for extreme observations each year*

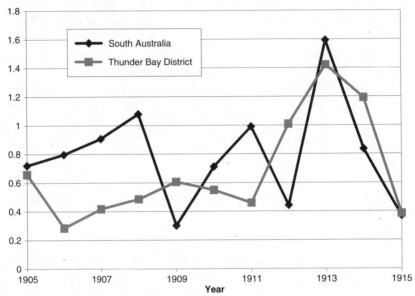

* Bottom and top estate dropped for each year to estimate an outlier-adjusted average wealth for each year. This is normalized by then dividing each year by the average for the whole 1905–15 period.
Source: Probate records (see text).

The fact that the increase in average wealth was common to both economies despite the much greater level of grain trade activity in TBD suggests that there were features of the SA economy that allowed it to capture a greater share of the economic rents/linkages associated with the rural economy. We also suspect, following McCallum, that these characteristics were shared with Southern Ontario from 1840 to 1870.[43] Two potential explanations need to be considered. First is the coastal location of the Port of Adelaide compared to the inland entrepôt location of TBD. To the extent that total resource costs of transporting grain to market were lower in SA than from the prairie grain economy, there was more surplus to be captured by producers and transporters. Second, it may be important who captured the surplus and how they captured it.

Table 4.2. Asset holding proportions, 1905–15

Year	Real Estate		Financial Assets	
	SA	TBD	SA	TBD
1905	0.68	0.87	0.92	0.73
1906	0.85	0.58	0.94	0.67
1907	0.72	0.59	0.84	0.77
1908	0.75	0.62	0.96	0.81
1909	0.79	0.76	0.95	0.71
1910	0.73	0.70	0.95	0.66
1911	0.83	0.72	0.97	0.53
1912	0.82	0.69	0.95	0.64
1913	0.74	0.69	0.97	0.64
1914	0.84	0.74	1.00	0.69
1915	1.00	0.81	0.83	0.68
Average	0.79	0.70	0.95	0.67

Source: Probate records (see text).

Figure 4.3. Comparison of normalized real estate, 1905–15

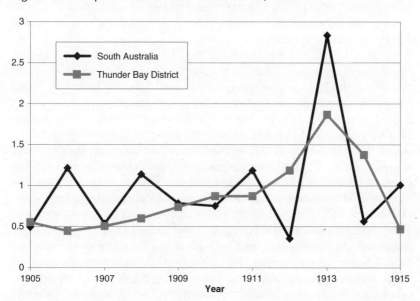

Normalized by dividing each year by the average for the whole 1905–15 period.
Source: Probate records (see text).

To demonstrate the reasons for SA's ability to generate the same average change in wealth as the TBD, despite having total bushels of wheat produced that represented at most 4 per cent of total bushels of wheat shipped through the Lakehead, we provide the following exercise. The role of the TBD in the Canadian grain trade was to handle enormous quantities of grain arriving by rail from western Canada. The grain was transferred from rail cars, weighed, inspected, and stored in terminal elevators before being transferred to a lake freighter. The costs of doing these functions were on the order of 1.5¢ to 2¢ per bushel.[44] As much of the elevator capacity at the Lakehead (80 per cent in 1905 and 60 per cent in 1915) was owned by the railways, a large portion of this income was not retained by the Lakehead region. Only the Paterson Elevators had its private owners based in the Lakehead. In addition, the income of farmers from wheat production accrued to the Prairie Provinces, not the TBD. The income earned by the railways that brought the grain to the Lakehead, other than the wage payments to locally based employees, accrued to the location of the railway's head office in the east of the country, as would the income earned by the companies that owned the ships that plied the great lakes. We estimate the income from the wheat activities at the Lakehead District as the number of bushels of wheat shipped from the Lakehead each year shown in Figure 4.4, multiplied by 1.5¢ per bushel for the years 1905 to 1915.

For the South Australian economy, we are looking at a situation where production, transportation to the ocean port, and handling were all carried out in the SA economy. As we noted earlier, the SA rail network was state owned. Under the strong assumption that the income for these activities was completely captured by local producers, shippers, and handlers, we approximated the income from a bushel of wheat for the South Australian economy by the price of wheat in England less the cost of ocean transportation from Australia. The average market price of an imperial bushel of wheat at Port Adelaide was £0.19 for 1905 to 1914.[45] If we value the pound in US dollars (an average of approximately US$4.85 over the years 1905–1915), the price per bushel of wheat was roughly equivalent to 90¢.[46] The total wheat income for SA is thus approximated as the annual number of bushels of wheat produced times 90¢ per bushel.[47]

Figure 4.5 demonstrates that despite a vast difference in the quantities of grain produced, transported, and traded, wheat exports generated substantially higher income in SA than TBD before 1910, and the convergence in grain trade incomes only took place after 1910 when grain shipments through the Lakehead increased substantially. Our estimates of wheat incomes for the two economies provide a clear explanation for the higher average wealth levels in SA relative to TBD, and the changes in wheat incomes generally reflect the

Figure 4.4. Total grain shipments from the Lakehead, 1905–29

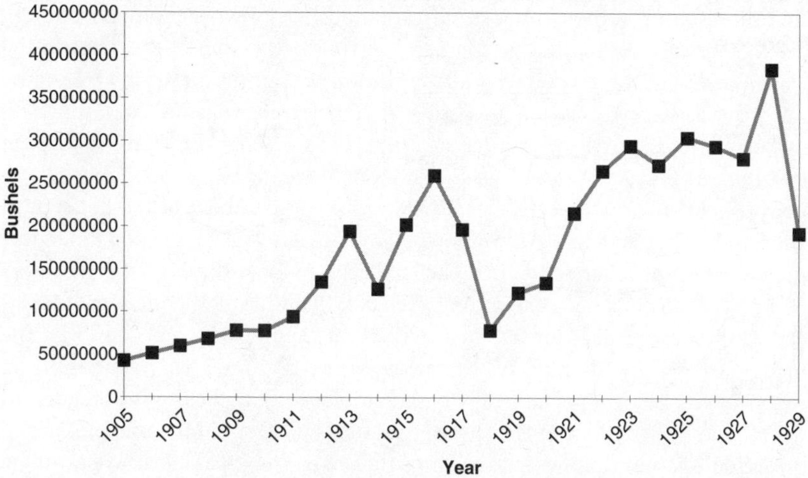

Sources: For the years 1919–1929: (1) Canal Statistics. Dominion Bureau of Statistics, Statistics Canada, Catalogue No. 54–201. Ottawa, Canada. (2) Annual Report of the Department of Railways and Canals, Sessional Papers. Ottawa. Canada. For the years 1905–1918, Canada Year Book. Dominion Bureau of Statistics, Canada (Statistics Canada, http://www66.statcan.gc.ca/acyb_000-eng.htm).

changes we demonstrate in average wealth in the two economies over 1905 to 1915. For the TBD, this estimated income from the wheat trade shows the same approximate pattern as the average wealth estimates in Figure 4.2.

This comparison highlights the key determinants for successful development from the export of natural resources: the ability to retain linkages associated with the resource exports. One way to think of our comparison of these two wheat exporting economies is that SA represents an economy where transportation, production, and handling of wheat is carried out by local owners of capital so that the capital's share of income is retained locally. TBD, in contrast, is akin to a resource exporting country where production and transportation functions are controlled by external capital and income does not remain in the local economy.[48] Although wheat exports would have increased the incomes of farmers, transportation companies, and other sectors across Canada, the regional benefits of the grain trade would have been distributed according to the home address of the head offices and the owners of capital. As a consequence, much of the income and wealth generated by the resource exports did little for the TBD economy.

Figure 4.5. Estimated gross incomes from wheat production, transportation, and trade, the Lakehead and South Australia, 1905–15

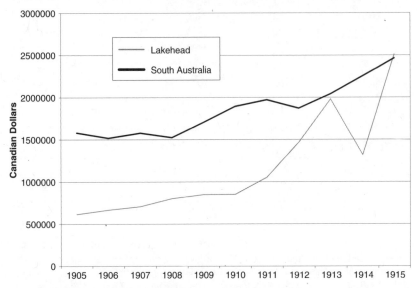

Source: Authors' calculations (see text).

Conclusion

This comparison of SA and TBD highlights the importance of "selective global-ization" as a determinant for successful development from the export of natural resources because the ability to manage the degree of integration into the global economy determines the local economy's ability to retain linkages associated with the resource exports. In this chapter, we have found that natural resources can result in successful economic development in both the short run and the long run. The wheat boom of the early twentieth century during the first era of globalization led to similar changes in wealth in the TBD and in SA, suggesting successful short-term impacts of the wheat boom across regions. At the same time, the level of wealth was substantially higher in SA than the TBD, suggest-ing that the wheat boom certainly generated successful long-term economic development in SA.

There are important differences between the two regions. SA benefited from earlier resource export episodes, including copper in the 1840s, wheat and wool in the 1850s, and wheat again in the 1870s; whereas in 1905, the Lakehead was really a new economy. Adelaide, SA, is a coastal port that, for much of the latter nineteenth century was a direct gateway to the world grain market, whereas the Port Arthur/Fort William port was an intermediate terminus on the Canadian transportation system because grain would have to have been transferred from Great Lakes freighters to ocean-going vessels on the way to market. Adelaide managed to maintain more of a hold on its hinterland region than did the Lakehead, which faced substantial competition from other ports. Nevertheless, the Lakehead experienced similar growth rates in wealth because of the much higher volume of grain produced in Canada and shipped through the Lakehead relative to Adelaide.

Although average wealth levels in SA were substantially higher in SA than in TBD, between 1905 and 1915, the increase in average wealth levels was equivalent in SA and the Lakehead district. The volume of wheat passing through the Lakehead was substantially greater than that produced in SA, but SA was able to appropriate more linkages from grain production. The higher wealth levels in SA relative to the TBD during the 1905–15 period were rooted in the fact that SA was a region of older settlement, and over time, earlier wealth accumulation was able to compound into higher levels relative to the more newly settled TBD. Moreover, SA had greater control over its institutions, especially prior to 1901 when it was actually able to pursue its own tariff and commercial policy.

Long-term economic development from natural resources is therefore a function of the ability to retain linkages from the resource activity as well as the passage of time necessary for linkages to develop and wealth to accumulate. The failure of the TBD by the late twentieth century to have successfully developed self-sustaining long-run economic growth and export capital as SA began to do in the early twentieth century was rooted in the key differences in linkage generation and retention between the two regions. Our comparison suggests that an understanding of the apparent poor performance of resource-abundant economies has little to do with intrinsic properties of natural resources and more to do with the sources and ownership of capital used to produce and transport the natural resources to market. Oil-producing nations would be least likely to succeed given the combination of capital-intensive production and transportation of the commodity along with the traditional reliance on external (most often US) capital.

NOTES

1 The staples approach with its focus on natural resource exports has served as an explanatory framework for nineteenth-century Canadian and Australian economic history. A comparative study of the success of staples in Canada, Australia, and Argentina is provided in J. Fogarty, "Economic History and the Limits of

Staple Theory," in *Clio's Craft*, ed. T. Crowley (Toronto: Copp Clark Pitman, 1988), 179–194. For a comparison of Canada and Australia, see R. Pomfret, "The Staple Theory as an Approach to Canadian and Australian Economic Development," *Australian Economic History Review* XXI (1981): 133–46. Since the late nineteenth century, Canada and Australia have developed more diversified economies, giving rise to the argument that staples are no longer an important force, but they remain small, open economies dependent on a variety of export products – including natural resources – for growth and well-being. For the role of natural resources in US development, see Gavin Wright and Jesse Czelusta, "Why Economies Slow: The Myth of the Resource Curse," *Challenge* 47 (2004): 6–38. For a recent synthesis of the literature on export-led development in nineteenth-century North America and Australasia, see James Belich, *Replenishing the Earth: The Settler Revolution and the Rise of the Anglo-world, 1783–1939* (Oxford: Oxford University Press, 2009).

2 Jeffrey D. Sachs and Andrew M. Warner, "Natural Resources and Economic Development: The Curse of Natural Resources," *European Economic Review* 45 (2001): 827–38; J.D. Sachs and A.M. Warner, "The Big Push, Natural Resource Booms and Growth," *Journal of Development Economics* 59 (1999): 43–76; J.D. Sachs and A.M. Warner, "Natural Resource Abundance and Economic Growth" (NBER Working Paper 5398, 1995), 54.

3 The economic development of resource-abundant, sparsely populated regions has been explained by the classic "staples approach" or models of export-led development as originally set out in the work of H. A. Innis who followed earlier work by G.S. Callender and W.A. Mackintosh. The classic works on Canadian staples by Innis are *The Fur Trade in Canada* and *The Cod Fisheries*. Modern versions of staple theory see economic development as a process of diversification around an export base. For relevant literature, see the papers by Baldwin, Watkins, and Caves. "Staples" (natural resources for export) approaches to economic development describe a process by which "linkages" associated with the natural resource production encourage industrialization provided the linkages are strong enough, and the income associated with them is retained in the domestic economy. See G.S. Callender, "The Early Transportation and Banking Enterprises of the States in Relation to the Growth of corporations," *Quarterly Journal of Economics* XVII (1902): 111–62; G.S. Callender, *Selections from the Economic History of the United States, 1765–1860* (New York: Augustus M. Kelley, 1965[1909]). On Mackintosh, see "Economic Factors in Canadian History," *Canadian Historical Review* IV (1923): 12–25. On Innis, see his *The Fur Trade in Canada: An Introduction to Canadian Economic History* (Toronto: University of Toronto Press, 1984[1930]) and *The Cod Fisheries: The History of an International Economy* (Toronto: University of Toronto Press, 1978[1940]). R.E. Baldwin, "Patterns of Development in Newly Settled Regions," *Manchester School of Economic and Social Studies* XXIV (1956): 161–79; M.H.

Watkins, "A Staple Theory of Economic Growth," *Canadian Journal of Economics and Political Science* XXIX (1963): 141–58; R.E. Caves, "'Vent for surplus' models of trade and growth," in *Trade, Growth and the Balance of Payments: Essays in Honor of Gottfried Haberler*, ed. R.E. Baldwin. (Chicago: Rand McNally), 95–115; R.E. Caves, "Export-led Growth and the New Economic History," in *Trade, Balance of Payments and Growth*, eds. J.N. Bhagwati, R.W. Jones, R.A. Mundell, and J. Vanek. (Amsterdam: North Holland, 1971), 403–42.

4 Sachs and Warner, "Natural Resource Abundance and Economic Growth."

5 Nicholas Crafts, "Globalisation and Economic Growth: A Historical Perspective," *World Economy* (2004): 45–58, 54.

6 In their *American Economic History*, 4th ed. (New York: Harper Collins, 1994), 30, Johnathan Hughes and Louis P. Cain show that in the colonial economy of the 1700s, nine-tenths of the population was employed in agriculture, fishing, timbering, and mining. In *Unequal Beginnings: Agricultural and Economic Development in Quebec and Ontario until 1870* (Toronto: University of Toronto Press, 1980), John McCallum shows that in mid-nineteenth-century Ontario, Canada's industrial heartland today, two-thirds of its population was engaged in farming with substantial cash sales generated from wheat production and 80 per cent of wheat production exported. A comparison of export to GDP ratios for nation states can be misleading at any point in history, and particularly misleading when comparing across time. Comparing large countries like the United States and Canada where there are several identifiable regional economies engaged in interregional, as well as international, trade with smaller, single-region nations like Kuwait is misleading. While the Canadian and US national economies may not be as resource intensive as some of the resource-abundant economies of today, some subnational economies were and are intensive exporters of natural resources. For example, for the provinces of Alberta and Saskatchewan, natural resource (international) exports in 1984 were 35 per cent of provincial GDP, which is higher than Nigeria, Venezuela, and Iran in 1970 as shown in Sachs and Warner's "Natural Resources and Economic Development," figure 1.

7 Richard M. Auty, "The Political Economy of Resource-Driven Growth," *European Economic Review* 45, no. 4–6 (2001): 839–46.

8 Chambers and Gordon show that the effect of natural resource exports on long-run per capita income growth will reflect the increase in the value of "land," the fixed factor in natural resource exploitation. See Hartwick, and Francisco Rodriguez and Jeffrey D. Sachs, "Why Do Resource-Abundant Economies Grow More Slowly?" *Journal of Economic Growth* 4 (1999): 277–303, for the reasons why resource exporting economies need to save and invest resource rents in order to sustain consumption levels experienced during the resource boom. E.J. Chambers and D.F. Gordon, "Primary Products and Economic Growth: An Empirical Measurement,"

Journal of Political Economy 74 (1966): 315–31; J. Hartwick, "Investment of Rents from Exhaustible Resources and Intergenerational Equity," *American Economic Review* 67, no. 5 (1977): 972–4.

9 John Luke Gallup, Jeffrey D. Sachs, and Andrew D. Mellinger, "Geography and Economic Development" (NBER Working Paper Series, Working Paper 6849, 1998); Jordan Rappaport and Jeffrey D. Sachs, "The United States as a Coastal Nation," *Journal of Economic Growth* 8 (2003): 5–46.

10 See Rappaport and Sachs, "United States as a Coastal Nation."

11 L. Di Matteo, "The Economic Development of the Lakehead during the Wheat Boom Era: 1900–1914," *Ontario History* LXXXIII (1991): 297–316; L. Di Matteo, "Evidence on Lakehead Economic Activity from the Fort William Building Permit Registers, 1907–1969," Papers and Records, Thunder Bay Historical Museum Society, XX (1992): 37–49; L. Di Matteo, "Booming Sector Models, Economic Base Analysis, and Export-Led Development: Regional Evidence from the Lakehead," *Social Science History* 17, no. 4 (1993): 593–617.

12 Gross regional product in the absence of the wheat boom at the Lakehead would have been 42 per cent smaller. In addition, by 1921, there were 1,534 farms supporting a rural population of 7,397 around the Lakehead. Forestry also employed thousands, in extraction, at sawmills, and at the three pulp mills either operating or under construction by 1921. See Di Matteo, "Booming Sector Models," 611–14.

13 J. Stafford, "A Century of Growth at the Lakehead" in *Thunder Bay: From Rivalry to Unity*, ed. T. Tronrud and A.E. Epp (Thunder Bay: Thunder Bay Historical Museum Society, 1995); and Di Matteo, "Evidence on Lakehead Economic Activity."

14 T. Stevenson, "Population Statistics," in *South Australian Historical Statistics*, Monograph No. 3, ed. W. Vamplew, E. Richards, D. Jaensch, and J. Hancock (Sydney: University of New South Wales, 1984), tables 1.1, 13.

15 A.G.L. Shaw, *The Story of Australia*. (London: Faber, 1954), 68.

16 J.B. Hirst, *Adelaide and the Country 1870–1917: Their Social and Political Relationship* (Melbourne: Melbourne University Press, 1973), 227–8.

17 In 1911, the population of Adelaide was just under 190,000, representing 46.4 per cent of SA's population. Equivalent figures for 1871, 1881, 1891, and 1901 are 33.8 per cent, 37.6 per cent, 42.2 per cent, and 45.3 per cent, respectively. By 1921, the percentage was 51.6 per cent (Hirst, *Adelaide and the Country*, 227). Ontario had a more dispersed urban settlement pattern. In 1891, Toronto – Ontario's largest city – had a population of 181,000, which represented less than 10 per cent of the province's population. In 1891, only 35 per cent of Ontario's population could be considered urban – that is, living in centers of 1,000 or more.

18 According to E. Dunsdorfs (*The Australian Wheat-Growing Industry 1788–1948* [Melbourne: The University Press, 1956], footnote 12, 172), "Steamships became firmly established in the wheat carrying trade only between 1905 and 1909, or even

1911." The *Official Yearbook for New South Wales* reported for the year 1905–06 (349) that three-fourths of the wheat exported was carried by sailing vessels. For 1911, the same source (438) states that since 1909 sailing vessels had been replaced by steamers: "the proportion of wheat now carried in sailing vessels is very small."

19 For example, in pre-drought 1891, there were 7.6 million sheep in SA; by the end of 1914, there were only 3.6 million. Vamplew et al., *South Australian Historical Statistics*, table 11.9.

20 I. McLean and J.J. Pincus, "Did Australian Living Standards Stagnate between 1890 and 1940?" *Journal of Economic History* 43, no. 1 (March 1983): 193–202.

21 Dunsdorfs, *Australian Wheat-Growing Industry*, 99–106.

22 Until the 1870s, Australia as a whole was not a consistent exporter of wheat, with the colonies of New South Wales, Victoria, and Queensland being net importers until 1867. Against this trend, SA became a net exporter comparatively early, exporting a (then record) 3 million bushels to Great Britain in 1872. Despite large annual fluctuations (that impacted on the local economy), this trade continued through the period of interest (Dunsdorfs, *Australian Wheat-Growing Industry*, 167–8). Note too that in 1870 there were only 133 miles of railway open in SA, while by 1900 there were 1,736 miles – two-thirds of this being built after 1880. N.G. Butlin, *Investment in Australian Economic Development 1861–1900* (Canberra: Department of Economic History, 1964[1976]), 321.

23 This section leans on Dunsdorfs, *Australian Wheat-Growing Industry*, 165–7.

24 R. Pomfret, "Trade Policy in Canada and Australia in the Twentieth Century," *Australian Economic History Review* 40, no. 2 (2000): 114–26, 116. In 1913, Canada had an average tariff of 18 per cent and Australia 17 per cent.

25 McCallum, *Unequal Beginnings*, 1980.

26 D.W. Meinig, *On the Margins of the Good Earth: The South Australian Wheat Frontier 1869–1884* (London: John Murray, 1962), 140. As a further example of the possibilities to "extract more" from wheat production, the 1908 Royal Commission on "The Question of the Marketing of Wheat" in SA found that merchants purchasing wheat from farmers colluded so as to reduce the prices received by farmers by 1d to 2d per bushel. A similar enquiry in Victoria found evidence of "sharp practice" that resulted in wheat bags being systematically underweighed by 1.1 to 3.3 per cent. See Dunsdorfs, *Australian Wheat-Growing Industry*, 223–6.

27 Canada exported 5.2 million bushels of wheat and flour in 1885 (Series M305; F.H. Leacy, ed., *Historical Statistics of Canada*, 2nd ed., Catalogue no. 11-516-X). By 1911, exports of wheat and flour from Canada reached 98 million bushels.

28 See McCallum, *Unequal Beginnings*, table s.3.

29 Dunsdorfs, *Australian Wheat-Growing Industry*, 168.

30 W.A. Sinclair, *The Process of Economic Development in Australia* (Melbourne: Longman Cheshire, 1976).

31 M.C. Urquhart, *Gross National Product, Canada, 1870–1926: The Derivation of the Estimates* (Montreal: McGill-Queen's University Press, 1993); M.C. Urquhart, "New Estimates of Gross National Product, Canada, 1870–1926: Some Implications for Canadian Development," in *NBER Studies in Income and Wealth*, vol. 51, *Long Term Factors in American Economic Growth*, ed. S.L. Engerman and R.E. Gallman (Chicago: University of Chicago Press, 1986), 9–94.

32 This last figure may underestimate wheat's importance to the SA economy. It is calculated by using Butlin's national figures on the contribution of wheat to agricultural output in 1910–11 (41% by value). N.G. Butlin, *Investment in Australian Economic Development 1861–1900* (Canberra: Department of Economic History, ANU, [1964]1976), table 44, 96, Gross Output agriculture 1900–1 to 1938–9.

33 Chambers and Gordon, "Primary Products and Economic Growth."

34 For additional demonstration of the wealth estimates as an indicator of resource boom success, see Hartwick, "Investment of Rents," and Rodriguez and Sachs, "Why Do Resource-Abundant Economies Grow More Slowly?"

35 These comparisons, while all based on probate records, are fraught with danger given differences in the age structure, data coverage, estimation techniques, and so forth. They should be regarded as indicative rather than exact. For a more complete discussion, see M.P. Shanahan, "The distribution of personal wealth in South Australia 1905–1915," *Australian Economic History Review* XXXV, no. 2 (September 1995): 82–111. As a further example, estate multiplier estimates for Wentworth County, Ontario, between 1872 and 1902 show that the top 10 per cent of the distribution owned from 83 to 92 per cent of the wealth. See L. Di Matteo, and P. George, "Canadian Wealth Inequality in the Late Nineteenth Century: A Study of Wentworth County Ontario, 1872–1902," *Canadian Historical Review* 73, no. 4 (1992): 453–83. For SA between 1905 and 1915, multiplier-based estimates of wealth distribution suggest that the top 10 per cent held 70–80 per cent of the wealth.

36 *Statutes of Canada*, 22 Vict., Cap. 93 (1858). According to Howell: "The inventory should contain a statement of all the goods, chattels, wares and merchandize, as well moveable as not moveable, which were of the person deceased at the time of his death within the jurisdiction of the court. A proper inventory should enumerate every item of which the personal estate consisted, and should specify the value of each particular. But unless by order of court, or in obedience to a citation, an inventory does not set forth the goods and chattels in detail." A. Howell, *The Law and Practice as to Probate, Administration and Guardianship in Surrogate Courts* (Toronto: Carswell, 1880), 325–6. Probate instructions do not specify how asset value was assigned. For real estate, livestock, and personal property, the evidence suggests that it was market value. Sometimes, property was sold and its selling

price recorded in the inventory, whereas more often it was an estimate of what the property would fetch if sold. Financial assets by their nature were precisely recorded. Mortgages held, the amount of insurance payments, and bank account balances were precise amounts. In addition, real estate was usually recorded net of any mortgages outstanding.

37 Some data on age could be acquired by census linkage, but only three census years (1881, 1891, and 1901) are currently available.

38 The inventory categories were as follows: (1) household goods and furniture, (2) farm implements, (3) stock in trade, (4) horses, (5) cattle, (6) sheep and swine, (7) book debts and promissory notes, (8) moneys secured by mortgage, (9) life insurance, (10) bank stocks and other shares, (11) securities, (12) cash on hand, (13) cash in bank (14) farm produce, (15) real estate, and (16) other personal property. For further discussion of probate records used in Ontario, 1892 data, see Di Matteo, "Determinants of Wealth" and "Wealth Accumulation," and Di Matteo and George, "Canadian Wealth Inequality" and "Patterns and determinants." For an evaluation of probate sources, see Elliot, "*Sources of bias*"; B.S. Osborne, "Wills and Inventories: Records of Life and Death in a Developing Society," *Families* 19, no. 4 (1980): 235–47; and P. Wagg, "The Bias of Probate: Using Deeds to Transfer Estates in Nineteenth-Century Nova Scotia," *Nova Scotia Historical Review* 10, no. 1 (1990): 74–87.

39 B.L. Bentick, "Foreign Borrowing and Wealth Consumption: Victoria 1873–93," *Economic Record* 45, no. 111 (1969): 415–31; I. McLean, "Saving in Settler Economies: Australian and North American Comparisons," *Explorations in Economic History* 31, no. 4 (1994): 432–52.

40 Another possibility is that differences in extraction methods have resulted in quite different samples being taken from the probate records. For Thunder Bay District, all estates probated between 1905 and 1915 have been included. In the case of SA, we have a stratified random sample being used. Although selecting estates over £20,000, the process also identified those leaving little wealth. While there may be differences in the proportion of estates of different sizes between the two samples, there is no obvious bias of either data set to its relative population.

41 See McLean, "Saving in Settler Economies," figure 4.

42 Rodriguez and Sachs, "Why Do Resource-Abundant Economies Grow More Slowly?"

43 McCallum, *Unequal Beginnings*.

44 Based on estimated costs of moving a bushel of wheat from Saskatchewan to Liverpool in 1925, plate 19, "The Grain Handling System," *Historical Atlas of Canada*. Rutter provides a similar estimate for 1900–10. W.P. Rutter, *Wheat Growing in Canada, the United States & the Argentina* (London: Adam and Charles Black, 1911).

45 The price of wheat in Port Adelaide was £0.33 in 1915, substantially higher than any other price over the period. The average price of a bushel of wheat in Port Adelaide is £0.2 if this 1915 observation is included.
46 This is the US dollar value of one UK pound for the period 1905 to 1915 from the calculator available at EH.net (http://www.measuringworth.com/datasets/exchangeglobal/result.php).
47 The issue of the level of freight rates or prices received by farmers is not relevant to this calculation so long as wheat production is not too supply elastic. Those rates and prices pertain to the distribution of the wheat income across activities and agents involved in the production and trade of wheat. So long as all of these agents reside in the domestic economy, the price of wheat at the port represents the income per unit of quantity for the domestic economy.
48 It should be noted that this characterization is still relevant today with the region referred to as a resource extraction colony. See J. Ibbitson, "A New Province Called Mantario?" *Globe and Mail*, 9 August 2006, A4.

5

Infant Industry Protection and the Growth of Canada's Cotton Mills: A Test of the Chang Hypothesis

MICHAEL N.A. HINTON ·

[I]nfant industry protection ... has been the key to the development of most nations ... Preventing the developing countries from adopting these policies constitutes a serious constraint on their capacity to generate economic development.

– Ha-Joon Chang, *Kicking Away the Ladder: Development Strategy in Historical Perspective* (2002)

Chang's book is provocative and interesting, but falls short of persuading. Perhaps the biggest disappointment is Chang's extremely superficial treatment of the historical experience of the now developed countries.

– Douglas Irwin, *Review of Kicking Away the Ladder*, EH.NET (April 2004)

Canadian Cotton Textiles and the Chang Hypothesis

At first glance, the growth of Canada's cotton mills in the nineteenth century would appear to provide little if any support for Ha-Joon Chang's "provocative" hypothesis, as Douglas Irwin has called it, that infant industry protection is the way the West grew rich. After all, the traditional view is that Canada's cotton mills grew largely because of the National Policy tariff of 1879, and the cotton mills never outgrew their need for protection, remaining instead high cost and inefficient.[1] Little hard evidence, however, has been presented to back up this claim, inefficiency being largely inferred from the fact that the cotton mills were protected. The presence or absence of tariffs tells us very little about the efficiency of an industry except in the classic case of a small, open-economy competitive industry, and Canada's cotton mills were most likely monopolistic firms supplying the lion's share of the domestic market by the early 1880s and exporting as well.[2]

In this chapter, I present new quantitative and qualitative evidence that suggests that far from being an unsuccessful infant industry the Canadian cotton mills are actually a classic case of successful infant industry protection and Chang's hypothesis is supported.[3]

Seven measures of the success of cotton textile manufacturing are examined: (1) the testimony expert contemporary opinion, (2) the timing of its first appearance, (3) the speed of its growth, (4) its size, (5) the modernness of its machinery, (6) exports, and (7) the total factor productivity (TFP) of its mills. But first let us take a closer look at the reasons why historians have been so ready to accept the notion that the manufacture of Canadian cotton textiles was inefficient.

The Assumption of Inefficiency

Canadian manufacturing in the nineteenth century traditionally has been viewed as inefficient.[4] Because manufacturing was inefficient, historians say, it could not compete with imports from the United States, Britain, Germany, and other large industrial countries without substantial tariff protection. But for most of the century, the story goes, little growth took place in manufacturing largely because tariff policy was dictated by Britain's desire, both as a mercantilist and a free trader, to keep domestic tariffs low in what is now Canada and the need for successive Canadian governments, before and after Confederation, to rely primarily on the tariff for revenue. In the late 1870s, however, a favourable "conjuncture of interests" made possible the advent of the National Policy tariff of 1879, which gave manufacturing substantial protection.[5] And, as a result, eventually, manufacturing grew rapidly; however, manufacturing never outgrew its need for protection. On the contrary, protection appears to have made the problem worse.

"[T]ariffs ...," wrote Professors Norrie, Owram, and Emeryin in Canada's leading economic history text, "created not just a secondary manufacturing sector in Canada but a high cost, inefficient one as well."[6] "[T]he tariff," wrote Professor Bliss in Canada's leading business history, "was the mother of a fragmented, inefficient manufacturing sector, slow to modernize and non-competitive outside the Canadian market."[7]

Of course, other explanations have been offered in addition to the tariff to explain the weakness of Canadian manufacturing: a colonial mentality, the strengths and weaknesses of the natural resource base, the small size of the domestic market, entrepreneurial failure, and the closeness of the much larger American economy, to name but a few. A large literature has grownup around debating the relative importance of these explanations as causal factors. Over the past ten-odd years, however, a brave band of revisionist economists and economic historians writing in the cliometric tradition have argued that historians have been wrestling with an illusion.[8] Canadian manufacturing, they claim, may have been far more efficient than historians have traditionally believed.

The idea that manufacturing was weak, they observe, rests on remarkably little hard evidence. Most of the hard evidence comes from studies of the efficiency of Canadian manufacturing in the 1950s and 1960s. Two of the most influential of these studies are John Dales's finding that on average labour productivity in Canadian manufacturing between 1926 and 1955 was 20 per cent less than American[9] and Fullerton and Hampson's 1957 finding that labour productivity in Canadian manufacturing in the single year 1953 was 40 per cent less than American.[10] As far as I am aware, only one study has presented quantitative evidence for the nineteenth century: Broadberry's wide-ranging study of the labour-productivity performance of British manufacturing confirming the traditional view that Canadian manufacturing was on average 12 to 20 per cent less productive than British and 60 per cent less than American in the four census years 1870, 1880, 1890, and 1900.[11] But this evidence is not as damning as it might at first appear.

Labour productivity, the revisionists observe, can be a misleading measure of efficiency. The consensus view among economists is that TFP is a better measure of productivity thbecause it measures efficiency in the use of all inputs not just labour input.

Indeed, the initial findings of these newer studies based on measures of TFP suggest that the traditional view is mistaken. For example, Inwood and Keay compared the TFP performance of thousands of individual Canadian and American manufacturing establishments in the census year 1870 for Canada with that of the census year 1869 for the United States and found "only a small T.F.P. advantage enjoyed by the average U.S. manufacturer."[12] Keay found that for a much smaller selected sample of thirty-nine Canadian and thirty-nine American manufacturing firms covering nine industries over most of the twentieth century, 1907 to 1990: "there is virtually no evidence of consistent and substantial relative technical inefficiency on behalf of the Canadian manufacturers."[13] In addition, Baldwin and Green found for a much more comprehensive matched sample of fifty-one Canadian and American manufacturing industries in the single year 1929 no substantial difference in relative productivity, the median relative TFP of the Canadian industries compared to the American being between 0.89 and 0.96.[14]

But these newer findings, intriguing though they are, still leave many questions unanswered: How did the old-school economists and economic historians get Canadian manufacturing so wrong? How well do these findings apply to the critical years after 1870 and before 1913, the years in which the problem allegedly began? What can we say more directly about productivity in particular industries within the manufacturing sector?

Lessons from the Cotton Mills

Historians do not always have the luxury of judging the efficiency of an industry by measures of its productivity. It is customary when data is scarce to use other less trustworthy indicators of the industry's strength or weakness, such as the opinion of contemporaries, the industry's early or late appearance, whether it grew fast or slow, its large or small size, or whether it used the most up-to-date machinery. Before looking at TFP in the Canadian cotton mills, let us see what can be learned by looking at these other indicators.

Today, historians seem convinced that the pre–First World War Canadian cotton industry was inefficient. "At all times the cotton manufacturers," wrote Michael Bliss, "kept a close eye on the tariff, for any significant reduction in the National Policy rates could doom the Canadian industry. There was little hope that the twenty-odd cotton mills scattered from Yarmouth to Hamilton, many more than the Dominion needed, many equipped with obsolete machinery and second-rate managers, could ever mature into a truly competitive industry."[15]

Some contemporaries, however, thought highly of the efficiency of the late nineteenth-century Canadian cotton textile industry. "It is gratifying to find Canadian grey cottons successfully competing with English made goods," said H. Beaumont Small in 1868.[16] "I believe," said George Parkin in 1895, "coarse cottons or woolens ... can be produced in Eastern Canada to-day and placed upon the [domestic] market as cheaply as those from Manchester or Yorkshire."[17] Speaking in the House of Commons in 1893, James D. Edgar said, "The Canadian mills can successfully compete in the outside world with England and the United States without any protection."[18]

Finally, consider this story that dates to the turn of the twentieth century. Like most jokes from another age, this one is not likely to be a knee-slapper for the modern reader, but we can learn quite a bit about contemporaries' assumptions about and attitudes towards the Canadian cotton mills and their managers as they were over a century ago. The anecdote is to be found in T.M. Young's *The American Cotton Industry*, written in 1902, about "which," he says, "although true as stories go, has in this connection some of the significance of a parable":

> The story is this: A Canadian manager, visiting an American mill, was taken by
> the superintendent to see a certain machine at work, and inquired what weekly

production was obtained from it. The American, with a fine air of candour, named a quantity which, although it seemed sufficiently precise to be accurate, the Canadian knew from his own experience to be an exaggeration. But he did not betray the slightest surprise. "Ah," said he, "I thought it would be that, or perhaps a shade more. We have the same machine at our place, and we get off" – here he named a figure slightly in excess of the American's. There the matter dropped. But in the evening the departmental manager of the mill came to meet the Canadian at his hotel, and said.

"Look here, what have you been telling our boss about that new machine? He has been complaining to me that we are not getting nearly enough work out of it."

"I think," said the Canadian, "that you had better ask your boss what he has been telling me."

Visitors to America are seldom heard to complain, like the Queen of Sheba, that the half has not been told them. Some Americans, as a friend of mine put it, have a way of telling rather more than the half.[19]

At least three features of this story are worth underlining. First, it is the American who is the butt of the joke, which is not surprising given Young was a British journalist who had travelled to America to investigate the economic basis for the American "invasion" of British markets. Second, the Canadian is the trickster, which to modern readers may be somewhat surprising and, for the joke to work, also somewhat surprising for contemporaries. Third, and this is the payoff for economic and business historians, the story suggests that all cotton industries in the developed world probably had about the same level of capital or machinery productivity. This is not what Canadian historians such as Bliss and Naylor tell us, but when you think about it, it makes more sense. A machine is what it is in Montreal, Fall River, or Manchester. The idea that Canadians used outdated machinery and were poor managers is hard to swallow, particularly because Canadians had easy access to British and American machinery export markets and many of the managers of Canadian mills were brought in from Britain and the United States.

Opinion, however expert and however interesting, is a poor substitute for evidence, even if it is free from bias, which is far from certain. (Edgar, for example, was an anti-protectionist politician and as such was willing to believe the cotton industry could do without tariff protection. And sometimes a story is just a story.) Let us turn now to examine the evidence on the industry's operation directly, unmediated by expert opinion or our own speculations.

When Did Cotton Mills Come to Canada?

It is not surprising that a cotton textile industry grew up in Canada in the nineteenth century. As Clark points out: "Cotton textiles seemed the path to industrialization ... before World War I. There was a ready local market for textile products everywhere and also a huge, open international market. Textile mills were not capital intensive. And the optimal mill size was small compared even to market sizes in the smallest countries. ... The technology was readily available internationally, at moderate prices, through exports of machinery by British engineering firms. Unskilled labor accounted for the majority of production costs in countries such as England."[20] W. Arthur Lewis says much the same thing.[21] What is surprising is that given these characteristics cotton mills appeared so late. Elsewhere, cotton mills appeared soon after the invention of factory-based cotton textile production. Selecting Arkwright's 1771 water-powered cotton spinning mill at Cromford, England, as the world's first modern mill, Clark presents data on the speed of the diffusion of the cotton mill in twelve other countries around the world. Supplementing his data with the dates for the appearance of the first mills in Canada and six other countries missing from his table, the following pattern emerges: Canada's first mill appeared in 1844 (a lag of 73 years), which was well-behind sixteen countries – among them the United States (20 years), France (7 years), Germany (13 years), and Italy (37 years) – and ahead of only three countries, Brazil (75 years), Denmark (119–128 years), and possibly Portugal.[22]

The relatively late appearance of Canadian cotton mills, however, probably better reflects the openness of British North American markets to British exports of cotton yarn and cloth in the first half of the nineteenth century, as well as the greater ability with which the British were able to prevent both the export of new cotton machinery for spinning and weaving and emigration of skilled workers before the 1840s under the old colonial system to their own colonies, than it does the failure of Canadian entrepreneurs to exploit opportunities to make a profit by investing in cotton mills.

How Fast?

Once planted, the cotton textiles grew rapidly in Canada. Measuring growth by imports of raw cotton, a widely used measure of the real value or quantity of production, Canadian cotton textiles grew at an astounding rate of 15 per cent a year from 1870 to 1890 (Table 5.1), the output of the industry

Table 5.1. Growth of raw cotton imports or consumption of the world's cotton mills (%, year)

Country	1870–90	1890–1910	1870–1910
United Kingdom	2.2	1.0	1.0
United States	5.2	4.6	3.9
Germany	3.8	3.6	3.7
Russia	6.0	3.6	4.8
France	1.2	3.9	2.6
India	10.0*	3.5*	6.4*
Austro-Hungary	4.3	3.3	3.8
Italy	10.1	3.4	6.7
Japan	19.2*	12.8	14.5
Spain	4.6	1.6	3.0
Belgium	3.5	4.0	3.7
Switzerland	−1.8	−0.4	−1.1
Canada	15.0	4.2	9.5
Portugal	8.2	3.8	5.8
Netherlands	4.5	4.3	4.4
Finland	5.5	2.9	4.1

* Spindle growth
Sources: US data from US Bureau of the Census, *Historical Statistics of the United States, Colonial Times to 1970* (New York: Basic Books, 1976), series P228; European data from B.R. Mitchell, *European Historical Statistics, 1750–1970* (New York: Columbia University Press, 1975), tables E14 and E15; data on India from B.R. Mitchell, *International Historical Statistics: Africa and Asia* (New York: New York University Press,1982), table E 19; and data on Japan from Sung Jae Koh, *Stages of Industrial Development in Asia: A Comparative History of the Cotton Industry in Japan, India, China, and Korea* (Philadelphia: University of Pennsylvannia Press, 1966), appendix table 1.

doubling every five years. Looking around the world at cotton mills in the sixteen other main countries in which modern factory-based cotton mills were to be found, only the Japanese mills smoking at 19 per cent grew faster. The Italian mills growing at 10 per cent a year came in a distant third. The cotton mills of Britain and the United States, the oldest and the largest centres of modern cotton textile production, not surprisingly, trailed far behind at 2 and 5 per cent, respectively.

Studying the growth of industries in five major industrial countries, Kuznets found that "the simple logistic and the simple Gompertz curves ... chiefly the logistic, yielded suitable descriptions of the long-time movements in production" and, over periods of thirty to forty years, "the tendency of industries to exhibit a declining rate of growth."[23] According to Rostow, the British cotton mills in the Industrial Revolution grew "explosively" at 9.2 per cent a year between 1775 and 1800, less than half of the rate achieved by the Canadian and Japanese industries a century later. "This," he said, "is what a case of increasing returns ... looks like in real life."[24]

In the last quarter of the nineteenth century, real Canadian GNP grew at 2.9 per cent (1870–90) and 4.8 per cent (1890–1910), which would suggest that Canadian cotton textiles turned in a highly creditable performance.[25]

Yet Canadian business and economic historians have had little good to say about the nineteenth-century Canadian cotton mills. This was partly, and undeservedly, because the Canadian mills, as did almost every other national cotton industry, depended on British and American machinery makers for machinery; partly, and perhaps more deservedly, because of their reputation as harsh, monopolistic, exploitive employers of labour; and partly, and probably most importantly as far as historians are concerned, because it is believed that the industry grew largely, some say wholly, because of the National Policy tariff of 1879, the deep-rooted idea that the National Policy was indispensable to the rapid growth of the cotton mills.[26]

But the speed of the Canadian industry's growth in output, and indeed any industry's growth, can give a misleading impression of success because both demand and cost conditions are at work. If an industry grows largely because demand is growing, its growth has little to tell us about its efficiency. Demand conditions are thought by the industry's historians to be a particularly strong influence on the industry's growth. According to the literature,[27] the 1879 tariff is the single most important causal factor in the industry's history, explaining the lion's share of the cotton industry's nineteenth-century growth. As far as I am aware, only one other student of the industry besides myself, Kieran Furlong, has disputed the importance of the tariff. Furlong argued that the business cycle was the dominant force driving the industry's growth. His work, however, is a curious mix of institutionalism and political economy.[28] The fundamental flaw in his argument is that he does not test the importance of the business relative to other causal factors and fails to see that the industry's growth did not accelerate after 1879, as one would expect given the literature's position; rather, it grew extremely rapidly from 1850 to 1883 and then decelerated sharply and grew at a much more moderate rate from 1883 to 1913. It is difficult to see how the business cycle would determine this pattern.

Moreover, the way in which the industry is said to have grown is troubling. The tariff protection introduced in 1879, it is said, stimulated such rapid "hothouse" growth – a "cotton orgy" the *Monetary Times* called it – that the industry was plunged into depression.[29] It is also said that the overproduction crisis stimulated a cartel and then a merger movement, which resulted in a sharp decline in competition. If the industry's historians are correct, it would seem that one can infer very little about changes in efficiency from the rapidity of the industry's growth.

But it seems likely that the industry's historians are not correct. Consider Figure 5.1 showing the rate of growth of the industry between 1850 and 1913. In this figure, the slope of the line indicates the industry's annual rate of growth. The dotted line marks the year 1879, which the literature claims to be a decisive turning point in the growth of the cotton mills. In Conan Doyle's Sherlock Holmes story "Silver Blaze," the curious event of the dog in the night is that it did not bark; and the curious movement of the curve of growth in 1879 is that it did not move, proceeding along at a well-established and rapid rate of 15 to 19 per cent a year.[30] When did the curve of growth first move upward decisively? The figure suggests it was sometime in the late 1850s, some thirty years before the coming of the National Policy tariff and also at about the same time as the introduction of the "incidentally" protective Galt tariff of 1859 in what is now Ontario and Quebec, which increased protection to the

Figure 5.1. The growth of Canada's cotton mills, 1850–1913

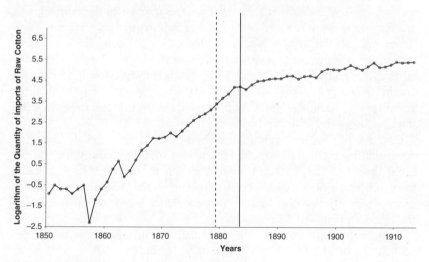

(Log of imports of raw cotton into what is now Canada)

cotton mills on the conversion of raw cotton into cotton cloth from 20 to 25 per cent to between 40 and 68 per cent. The solid line in the figure marks the year 1883, and here as we would expect given the onset of a major recession (1883–9) in cotton textiles in Canada, the United States, and Britain, the curve bends downward, indicating negative growth. A 2012 working paper[31] found that productivity growth explains most of the extremely rapid rate of growth of output in the industry. But this finding tells us only that the cotton mills made great strides forward; it tells us nothing about how efficient the mills actually were. For that we need to measure the mills' productivity relative to some other national industry, which is discussed in a subsequent section (see "Measuring Productivity").

How Large?

By 1910, the cotton textiles industry was a large Canadian manufacturing industry. The census of that year reported that manufacturing's gross value of product was C$1.2 billion, breaking down the sector into 15 large industry groups. Textiles ranked third largest of these groups with a gross value of output of C$135.9 million (11.7 per cent of the total). Only 2 groups, food products and timber and lumber, were larger. Cotton textiles, or cottons as it was called, was the largest industry in the textiles group, accounting for C$24.6 million in output, representing an 18.1 per cent share of textiles. Cotton textiles was also one of Canada's larger manufacturing industries if we look at it in comparison with the 211 smaller kinds of industries into which the census broke manufacturing below the level of the 15 large industry groups. Cotton textiles, for example, was larger than many other industries that historians are used to thinking of as important domestic industries, such as agricultural implements, railroad cars and car works, paper, and tobacco and cigarettes. Above it, but not that far above it, in the C$30 million to C$40 million range, were such important players as lumber products, butter and cheese, iron and steel products, smelting, boots and shoes, and railroad car repairs.

If we accept that the cotton industry was large relative to other Canadian manufacturing industries, what does this tell us about its efficiency? The answer is very little. As is the case with the rate of growth, the industry's large size relative to other Canadian industries may simply reflect the good fortune of greater demand rather than it does superior entrepreneurship and wiser management and or investment discipline.

More importantly, though, the Canadian cotton industry is better described as a small industry in a large world market. The number of spindles installed is a widely used measure of both capacity output and fixed capital in the cotton textile industry. Robson estimated that in 1913 the total number of spinning spindles installed in the world's thirty-five national cotton industries was 143.5 million.[32] In the same year, the Canadian industry had about 0.9 million spindles installed, which is about 0.6 per cent of world capacity.

Is this small? One way to see is to ask what effect an industry of this size could have had on the world price of cotton yarn or cloth. Now, say Canada doubled its output, increasing its output by 100 per cent, by how much would the world price have fallen? The answer depends on the elasticity of demand facing the Canadian industry on the world market (Ec). As is well known, this elasticity can be written as follows:

$$Ec = 1/s \cdot Ew - (1/s - 1) \cdot Es$$

where Ew is the elasticity of world demand, s is the Canadian industry's share of the world market, and Es is the elasticity of supply by the world's other cotton industries. Assuming, not unreasonably, that Ew is equal to -1 and Es to 1, and setting s equal to 0.006, Ec is equal to -332. With this elasticity, a 100 per cent increase in Canadian output would have reduced the world price by less than one half of 1 per cent. The Canadian industry, therefore, was so small as to be insignificant. This, however, tells us nothing about its efficiency.

How Modern Was the Machinery?

The extent to which an industry uses the most modern machinery is often used as an index of an industry's efficiency. As was the case with most other national cotton industries, Canada had no cotton textile machine-building industry.[33] However, the industry could easily have purchased modern machinery at reasonable prices from British and American machinery makers. And it would appear that the Canadian industry was using fairly up-to-date modern equipment. One of the new technologies that spread rapidly in the second half of the nineteenth century in the cotton textile industry was ring spinning. If we look around the world in 1910 (see Table 5.2), the Canadian industry, although behind the American industry, was on the leading edge in terms of mechanization and the shift to rings.

Canada performed creditably in this race, but as the large literature on Britain's lag behind the United States suggests, the faster adoption of ring spinning

Table 5.2. Machinery in the world's cotton industries in 1910

Country or Region	Machines per Worker (index)	Ring Spindles per Worker (number)
New England	1.55	902
Southern United States	1.44	770
Canada	1.41	750
Britain	1.00	625
France	0.81	500
Russia	0.77	450
Mexico	0.77	540
Italy	0.76	436
Spain	0.73	450
Switzerland	0.70	450
Austro-Hungary	0.65	403
Germany	0.63	327
Japan	0.52	190

Source: Gregory Clark, "Why Isn't the Whole World Developed? Lessons from the Cotton Mills," *Journal of Economic History* 47, no. 1 (1987): 152.

in Canada than Britain may say more about differences in Canadian relative prices for labour and capital than it does about efficiency.

What about Exports?

The fact that an industry exports is often looked on by economists as a sign that the industry is efficient, but this is not always the case. Exports present an interesting puzzle. It is a fact that Canada was routinely exporting small amounts of cotton goods, typically to the United States, from the 1850s onwards, but there is little doubt that this was largely a convenience trade in excess cotton waste, produced as a by-product of the production of yarn by domestic cotton mills. As such, this represents neither evidence that Canadian cotton mills had a comparative advantage in cotton textiles nor that they were monopolists, routinely dumping product abroad to keep prices up in the domestic market. Looking at the long-term trend, cottons exports rose on average from less than C$5,000 a year in the 1850s and 1860s to under C$10,000 a year in the 1870s, then for the first time to more than C$20,000 in 1884–5, and pushing dramatically up to more than C$100,000 a year in 1887–8. Most of these exports were cloth and yarn, only C$30,000 of which were cotton waste. At its height in 1905–6, the export trade in Canadian cottons reached more than C$1.3 million. Was this trade simply the "sporadic" dumping of excess production, as Bliss claimed, or was there something more systematic going on? At this point, we cannot say. But this seems to be a more complex problem than anyone has been willing to admit. In the late 1880s, in keeping with Bliss's claims, 87 per cent of the cotton mills' exports went to the United States. But by the early 1900s, when the trade was reaching its peak, less than 15 per cent of exports were sent to the United States. Just over 20 per cent went to Latin America and Northern Europe, but the majority, 55 per cent, went to China, Australia, New Zealand, and elsewhere in Asia. This may have been dumping, but it is also likely to be evidence that Canadian mills were far more productive than the current literature assumes. The export trade in cottons did fall off sharply after 1905–6. By 1912–13, it had fallen to C$124,551, which was down substantially from its peak of C$1,331,712 in 1905–6 and under the exports of 1889–90 when C$155,777 was exported. According to the literature, this sharp decline in exports was attributable to the negative shock of the Boxer Rebellion. It is more likely, however, that exports fell off for a less dramatic reason: with the rapid growth in Canadian GNP of the wheat boom years of 6 per cent a year, Canadian demand grew rapidly, absorbing most of the output of the Canadian mills.

Measuring Productivity

In the absence of better measures, economic historians typically measure productivity by labour productivity, total output divided by total labour input; however, TFP – the rate at which cotton mills can transform all inputs (raw cotton, labour, and capital) into cotton goods such as yarn and cloth – is the best measure of efficiency. To make this a stiff test of the Canadian industry's efficiency, I have measured the TFP for Canadian cotton textiles between 1870 and 1910 relative to the cotton textile industry in the United States, which together with the British industry dominated the world market for cotton textiles and led the world in inventiveness and efficiency.[34]

I have made the usual assumptions that cotton industry output (Q) in both countries can be represented by a standard textbook production function with three factors of production, capital (K), labour (L), and raw materials (C) – that is, $Q = F(K, L, C; A)$ where A is the TFP index. Assuming a Cobb-Douglas technology in both countries – constant returns to scale, unitary elasticity of substitution, and factor-neutral technical change – and that competition takes place in all markets, the percentage rate of growth in TFP ($A^* = \Delta A / A \times 100$) can be written as follows:

$$A^* = (Q^* - L^*) - sk(K^* - L^*) - sc(C^* - L^*)$$

where sk and sc are the output elasticities of capital and raw materials, which are equal, here, to the shares of capital and raw materials in total output. $Q^* - L^*$ is the percentage rate of growth in labour productivity, $K^* - L^*$ is the percentage rate of growth in capital per worker, and $C^* - L^*$ is the percentage rate of growth in raw materials per worker. Note that these starred variables can be interpreted either as percentage changes over time for either the Canadian or US industries or as percentage differences between the Canadian and US cotton industries at a single point in time.

Estimates for A^* are constructed for the Canadian cotton industry in the Canadian census years 1870, 1890, and 1910 and for the United States cotton industry in the American census years 1869, 1889, and 1909. The Canadian and American industries are compared in terms of their productivity performances at three points in time (Canada in 1870, 1890, and 1910 with the United States in 1869, 1889, and 1909) and between censuses (Canada 1870–90 and 1890–1910 with the United States 1869–89 and 1889–1909).

In constructing the estimates, inevitably, a large number of decisions needed to be made. As far as possible, physical measures of the required variables were used rather than value- or money-based measures. Output was measured by estimates of pounds of raw cotton imported (Canada) or consumed by mills (United States). The weight of output, pounds of cloth or yarn, is generally considered a good measure of output. Assuming that the weight lost in spinning and weaving is constant, the pounds of raw cotton consumed will serve as a good index of output. David found this was so for Massachusetts mills from 1825 to 1860.[35] Raw cotton data, available annually, was taken for Canada from the Canadian *Tables of Trade and Navigation* and for the United States from the US censuses. Labour was measured simply by the number of workers as reported in the Canadian and US censuses. Capital input was measured by the number of spindles installed, a commonly used physical measure of capital in the industry. Spindlage data matched as closely as possible to census years was drawn from textile directories and the business press for Canada and for the United States from the US censuses. The cost shares for capital and raw materials used were taken from the censuses of the two countries.

Table 5.3 shows estimates of the rate of change of productivity over time for the Canadian and US industries in the years 1869/70–1889/90 and 1889/90–1909/10. Table 5.4 shows the relative difference in the productivity of the

Table 5.3. Productivity growth in the Canadian and US cotton industries before the First World War

| | 1869/70–1889/90 | | 1889/90–1909/10 | |
	United States	Canada	United States	Canada
$Q^* - L^*$	0.0280	0.0193	0.0374	0.0196
$K^* - L^*$	0.0101	0.0295	0.0102	0.0001
$C^* - L^*$	0.0280	0.0193	0.0374	0.0196
sk	0.1631	0.2485	0.1869	0.2442
sc	0.6038	0.5444	0.5843	0.5333
A^*	0.0094	0.0015	0.0136	0.0269

Source: See text.

Table 5.4. Relative productivity in the Canadian and US cotton industries

	1869–70	1889–90	1909–10
(Canadian – US)/US			
$Q^* - L^*$	−0.0576	−0.2042	−0.0256
$K^* - L^*$	−0.3741	−0.0824	−0.1637
$C^* - L^*$	−0.0576	−0.2042	−0.0256
sk	0.1971	0.2145	0.2166
sc	0.6102	0.5380	0.5795
A^*	0.0508	−0.0766	0.0247

Source: See text.

Canadian and US industries for the years 1869–70, 1889–90, and 1909–10. The cost shares used in each set of calculations are shown in the tables.

Remarkably, given the literature's harping on the cotton mills' failings, these measures suggest that the Canadian industry outperformed the American industry in 1869–70 and again in 1909–10. In 1869–70, I found that the Canadian cotton industry was 5.1 per cent more efficient than the American industry, and in 1909/10 it was 2.5 per cent greater.

Only in 1889–90, at the end of an extremely turbulent decade in the industry's history, was the Canadian industry outperformed by the American industry.[36] Note also that the Canadian industry's lower labour productivity is in line with Dales's finding of a 20 per cent gap in Canadian and American labour productivity, and when corrected for the effects of greater American capital and materials intensity, it is in line with the newer TFP findings for the twentieth century. Overall, the performance of the Canadian industry appears to be much stronger in the later period, 1889–90 to 1909–10, than it was in the earlier period, 1869–70 to 1889–90. The Canadian industry's stronger performance after 1890 may be in part a result of the mergers of 1890, 1905, and 1910, which created much larger firms and a more concentrated market structure in the Canadian industry.

Conclusion

The Canadian cotton industry is traditionally seen as a failed infant industry, a classic example of what was wrong with Canadian manufacturing – weak, high cost, and non-inventive. The evidence presented here, however, says otherwise. In particular, the modernity of the cotton mills' machinery, the large size, and the speed of the cotton mills' growth being driven by productivity change, combined with the strong relative productivity performance of the Canadian cotton mills in comparison with the American cotton mills in 1870 and 1910, suggests that the traditional wisdom on the weakness of Canadian manufacturing before the First World War is in need of revision. It is unusual for a mainstream neoclassical economist such as myself to admit that Chang may be right, but it must be said. Far from being a drag on Canada's per capita growth, industries such as cotton textiles that were granted infant industry protection in the 1850s may have been one of the reasons why Canada was able to make the leap to modern economic growth and become a rich country in the nineteenth century.

NOTES

1 Royal Commission on the Textile Industry, *Report* (Ottawa: King's Printer, 1938); Michael Bliss, *Northern Enterprise: Five Centuries of Canadian Business* (Toronto: McClelland and Stewart, 1987); A.B. McCullough, *The Primary Textile Industry in Canada: History and Heritage* (Ottawa: National Historic Sites, Park Canada, Environment Canada, 1991); Richard W.T. Pomfret, *Diverse Paths of Economic Development* (New York: Harvester Wheatsheaf, 1992).

2 Michael N.A. Hinton, "Cotton Lords: In Pursuit of Monopoly Rents, 1883–1913" (Paper presented at the Fourteenth Conference on the Use of Quantitative Methods in Canadian Economic History, L'Ecole des Hautes Etudes Commerciales, Montreal, 1985); M.N.A. Hinton, "Cottons' False Start in the 1840s" (Paper

presented at the Annual Meetings of the Canadian Economics Association, University of Montreal, Montreal, 1994); M.N.A. Hinton, "The Civil War and the Growth of the Canadian Cotton Industry"(Paper presented at the Fourth Conference on Canadian Business History, Trent University, Peterborough, Ontario, 1994); M.N.A. Hinton, "Corporate Concentration in the Cotton Industry," *Historical Atlas of Canada*, vol. III (Toronto, University of Toronto Press, 1990), plate 7, "The Changing Structure of Manufacturing"; M.N.A. Hinton and T. Barbiero, "Does the National Policy Explain the Growth of Canada's Cotton Mills?" (Paper presented at the 2012 Annual Conference of the Canadian Economics Association, University of Calgary, 2012).

3 The author would like to thank Tom Barbiero, Ian Parker, and Al Tossanyi for their questions and comments on earlier versions of this paper presented at the economics workshop at Ryerson University and as a 2010 Rimini Centre for Economic Analysis Working Paper.

4 J.H. Dales, *The Protective Tariff in Canada's Development* (Toronto: University of Toronto Press, 1966); L.R. Macdonald, "Merchants against Industry: An Idea and Its Origins," *Canadian Historical Review* 15, no. 3 (1975): 263–81; Glenn Williams, "The National Policy Tariffs: Industrial Underdevelopment through Import Substitution," *Canadian Journal of Political Science* 12, no. 2 (1979): 333–68; Neil Bradford and Glenn Williams, "What Went Wrong? Explaining Canadian Industrialization," in *The New Canadian Political Economy*, ed. Wallace Clement and Glenn Williams (Montreal: McGill-Queen's University Press, 1989), 54–76.

5 See Ben Forster, "The Coming of the National Policy: Business, Government and the Tariff," *Journal of Canadian Studies* 14, no. 3 (1979): 39–49, and his *A Conjuncture of Interests: Business, Politics, and Tariffs, 1825–1879* (Toronto: University of Toronto Press, 1986).

6 Kenneth Norrie, Douglas Owram, and J.C. Herbert Emery, *A History of the Canadian Economy*, 4th ed. (Toronto: Thomson-Nelson, 2008), 277.

7 Bliss, *Northern Enterprise*, 14.

8 P. Wylie, "Technological Adaptation in Canadian Manufacturing, 1900–29," *Journal of Economic History* 49 (1989): 569–91; Ian Keay, "Canadian Manufacturers' Relative Productivity Performance, 1907–1990," *Canadian Journal of Economics* 33, no. 3 (2000): 1049–68; Kris Inwood and Ian Keay, "Bigger Establishments in Thicker Markets: Can We Explain Early Productivity Differentials," *Canadian Journal of Economics* 38, no. 4 (2005): 1327–63; J. Baldwin and A. Green, "The Productivity Differential between the Canadian and US Manufacturing Sectors: A Perspective Drawn from the Early 20th Century," *Canadian Productivity Review* 15-206, no. 22 (2008): 4–35; Hinton and Barbiero, "Does the National Policy Explain the Growth of Canada's Cotton Mills?"

9 Dales, *The Protective Tariff in Canada's Development*.

10 D.H. Fullerton and H.A. Hampson, *Canadian Secondary Manufacturing* (Ottawa: Royal Commission on Canada's Economic Prospects, 1957).

11 Stephen Broadberry, *The Productivity Race: British Manufacturing in International Perspective, 1850–1990* (Cambridge: Cambridge University Press, 1997), 53.

12 Inwood and Keay, "Bigger Establishments in Thicker Markets," 1328–32.

13 Keay, "Canadian Manufacturers' Relative Productivity Performance, 1907–1990," 1049–51.

14 Baldwin and Green, "The Productivity Differential between the Canadian and US Manufacturing Sectors."

15 Bliss, *Northern Enterprise*, 305.

16 H. Beaumont Small, *The Products and Manufactures of the New Dominion* (Ottawa: G.E. Desbarats, 1868), 143.

17 George R. Parkin, *The Great Dominion: Studies of Canada* (London: Macmillan, 1895), 205.

18 Canada, Parliament, House of Commons, *Official Report of the Debates of the House of Commons of the Dominion of Canada* (Ottawa: MacLean, Roger, 1894), 17 February 1893, 811.

19 T.M. Young, *The American Cotton Industry* (London: Methuen and Charles Scribner's, 1902), 110–11.

20 Greg Clark, *A Farewell to Alms: A Brief Economic History of the World* (Princeton, NJ: Princeton University Press, 2007), 337.

21 W. Arthur Lewis, *The Evolution of the International Economic Order* (Princeton, NJ: Princeton University Press, 1978), 7–8.

22 Clark, *Farewell to Alms*, 304.

23 Simon S. Kuznets, *Secular Movements in Production and Prices: Their Nature and Their Bearing upon Cyclical Fluctuations*(New York: Augustus M. Kelley, [1930]1967), 324–5.

24 W.W. Rostow, *How It All Began: Origins of the Modern Economy* (New York: McGraw-Hill, 1975), 160.

25 A.G. Green and M.C. Urquhart, "New Estimates of Output Growth in Canada: Measurement and Interpretation," in *Perspectives on Canadian History*, ed. D. McCalla (Toronto: Copp Clark Pitman, 1987), 324–5.

26 See Hinton and Barbiero, "Does the National Policy Explain the Growth of Canada's Cotton Mills?"

27 For an extensive survey, see McCullough, *The Primary Textile Industry in Canada*.

28 Kieran Furlong, "Economic Fluctuations in Canada, 1867–97" (PhD diss., University of Toronto, 1997).

29 Bliss, *Northern Enterprise*, 304–5; R.T. Naylor, *Canada in the European Age, 1453–1914* (Vancouver: New Star Books, 1987), 443–5.

30 Hinton and Barbiero, "Does the National Policy Explain the Growth of Canada's Cotton Mills?"

31 See Michael Hinton and Thomas Barbiero, "Is Protection Good or Bad for Growth? Lessons from Canada's Cotton Textile Mills" (Ryerson University Department of Economics Working Paper, 2012).

32 Robert Robson, *The Cotton Industry in Britain* (London: Macmillan, 1957), 333, 354–5.

33 W.A. Graham Clark, *Cotton Textiles in Canada*, Special Agents Series, No. 69 (Washington, DC: US Bureau of Foreign and Domestic Commerce, 1913).

34 Gregory Clark, "Why Isn't the Whole World Developed? Lessons from the Cotton Mills," *Journal of Economic History* 47, no. 1 (1987): 167.

35 Paul A. David, "Learning By Doing and Tariff Protection: A Reconsideration of the Case of the Ante-Bellum United States Cotton Textile Industry," *Journal of Economic History* 30, no. 3 (1970), 547.

36 T.W. Acheson, "The National Policy and the Industrialization of the Maritimes," *Acadiensis* 1, no. 2 (1972): 1–28; Michael Bliss, "Canadianizing American Business: The Roots of the Branch Plant," in *Close the 49th Parallel etc: The Americanization of Canada*, ed. Ian Lumsden (Toronto: University of Toronto Press, 1970), 27–42.

6

Imperialism, Continentalism, and Multilateralism: The Making of a Modern Canadian Automotive Industry

GREIG MORDUE

The implementation of the Canada-US Automotive Products Trade Agreement (Auto Pact) in 1965 recast the Canadian automotive industry, providing a framework for new sources of growth, the reverberations of which persist to the present.[1] This chapter considers the conditions and events predating its execution and argues that the growth and development of the automotive manufacturing industry subsequent to 1965 emerged from policy decisions and principles established decades before the first volume automobile producer began operating in Canada. During the period, Canada's domestic policies, particularly its policies with respect to tariffs and trade, were shaped by three often competing preoccupations – imperialism, multilateralism, and continentalism – the relative significance of each ascending and descending over the years.

The purpose of this chapter is not to explore in detail or isolation each of the singular events, characters, or companies that helped define specific events or periods within the Canadian automotive manufacturing industry. Rather, the aim here is to delve more deeply to reveal long-standing trends and influences – particularly the competing forces of imperialism and continentalism – and explore them through the lens of the Canadian automotive industry. Specifically, it will demonstrate how these forces shaped domestic policy in Canada and how those public policy decisions affected the Canadian auto industry. Ultimately, all these influences culminated in the appointment of Vincent Bladen to conduct a Royal Commission on the Canadian industry in 1960.[2] Bladen's study provoked a paradigmatic change that led to the negotiation of the Auto Pact in 1965. The conditions leading to his appointment merit further review because Bladen's appointment marked the transition of the Canadian auto industry from one balancing both continental and imperial connections to one that was almost exclusively continentalist in nature. The dynamics leading to Bladen's appointment provide a valuable illustration of the interplay between industrial strategy, monetary policy, imperial connections, and geographical expediency over a prolonged period. In following such inquiry, this chapter offers research heretofore not incorporated into studies of the Canadian auto industry regarding aspects such as the role of the exchange rate starting in the early 1950s.

Moreover, I will argue that that the most influential and disruptive phenomena on the policy framework and manufacturing environment have been globalization-related forces, especially rising import market shares. This chapter will review how this condition arose in the 1920s and again in the 1950s in the Canadian automotive industry, resulting in new information on the conditions leading to Bladen's appointment in 1960 and a fresh perspective on the change manifested in the Auto Pact five years later. The result is a case study of how one sector – the Canadian automotive manufacturing industry – evolved and grew in the face of shifting trends and attitudes with respect to the competing pulls of imperialism, multilateralism, and continentalism. Indeed, the strategies deployed by Canadian policymakers over several decades with respect to the development of its auto industry represent an excellent example of the application of Rodrik's "selective globalization."

From Elgin-Marcy Reciprocity to National Policy

In March 1879, when John A. Macdonald's finance minister, Sir Leonard Tilley, released his first budget following his party's electoral victory of 1878, there was no doubting that tariffs would be the government's economic the centrepiece. During his years in the Opposition (1873–8), Tilley's Conservative Party had made its views on tariffs clear. For example, in the House of Commons on 10 March 1876, Macdonald had stated that "the United States should be dealt with as they deal with us and we would be craven if from fear of offending our neighbours we took any other alternative. If they do not grant us reciprocity in trade we should give them reciprocity in tariff."[3] Whether for political expedience or retribution, Canada was turning economically inward.

Macdonald's stance can be traced to the collapse of the Elgin-Marcy Reciprocity Treaty. Forged in 1854, the treaty provided for the free passage of a variety of commodities between the United States and Canada. Editorial writers greeted its passage with optimism on both sides of the border. For example, the *Toronto Examiner* predicted that "[t]he advantages to both countries will be immense as every approach in a free and unrestricted interchange of the products and manufactures of nations must be."[4] Across the border, the *Rochester Union* forecast that "[t]he confirmation of the Reciprocity Treaty by the Senate of the United States opens a prosperous future to us. If we are true in ourselves, if we labor in this new channel of enterprise with our old native energy, there is in store a future almost without limit."[5]

The Elgin-Marcy Treaty remained in place for twelve years, and despite the disturbance of the American Civil War, trade flourished, rising from C$20 million annually in 1853 to $68 million by 1864.[6] When the US Congress abrogated the agreement in 1866, it did so as a rebuke to the British for their support of the US South during the Civil War and to appease Northern US manufacturers and farmers.[7]

In Canada, the end of Elgin-Marcy lent support to the cause of Confederation. The *Hamilton Evening Times* stated, "Recent events are sweeping away the last elements of opposition to the scheme, and when Confederation is at last complete, we cannot refuse to our American friends the thanks that are their due for having so unilaterally contributed to its success."[8] The *Canadian News* echoed this view: "People begin to see that the very existence of the country depends upon our becoming united, and not only for purposes of mutual defence but also for the arrangement of new commercial treaties with foreign nationals as well as for facilitating intercolonial trade."[9] Macdonald attempted on several occasions to revive open trading relationships with the United States – an effort to detach his new nation from the binds of imperialism – but was regularly rebuffed. Indeed, his pursuit of open trade was entirely consistent with the approach of that of the United Kingdom, arguably the nineteenth century's strongest advocate of free and open trade. But even as Macdonald pursued a more multilateral/continental strategy in the years immediately following Confederation, he faced a US Congress that was progressively increasing tariffs. Eventually, Macdonald was forced to change course. After 1878, his remedy came in the form of the National Policy, a policy framework that shaped and influenced the Canadian automotive industry for nearly a century. The National Policy contained three primary elements. First, it unified the country physically by way of a transportation policy, the already under construction Canadian National Railway. Second, it encouraged immigration. Third, it strengthened domestic manufacturing through higher tariffs, a position with which manufacturers and processors fervently agreed. However, as Lanigan reminds us, in establishing a high tariff regime, Macdonald's motives went beyond retribution against US protectionism. Macdonald also realized that Canada's future prosperity would be based not simply on the export of raw materials, but also on higher value-added processing.[10]

Certainly, the National Policy – and particularly the elements dealing with tariffs – was not without its detractors. Macdonald came under heavy criticism at home and abroad. For example, Britain, the world's only superpower, advocated an extension of free trade. Consequently, its newspapers were scathing: "The action of the Canadian government is very pitiable. *The Times* cannot approve of the tariff. It thinks it unwise, and is thoroughly convinced that it will disappoint the Canadians, proving an injury instead of a benefit to them … Since the Canadians wish to have this tariff they must have it and go their own way; but the result is none the less deplorable."[11] The *Pall Mall Gazette* declared: "The Budget realizes the worst fears entertained as to the late election. A heavy blow has been struck at British trade."[12] And the Manchester *Guardian* held: "In England there is a feeling of profound amazement and sorrow at the great retrograde fiscal movement of a people so closely allied to Great Britain by ties of kindred social intercourse."[13] Canada was taking a bold if not precarious position: it was abandoning the long-held policy direction of its imperial cousin, as well as potentially isolating itself both economically and symbolically from that same partner.

In Canada, Opposition Liberals derided the high tariff policy and its impact, predicting a variety of damaging consequences. Sir R.J. Cartwright, finance minister in the previous Liberal administration, was scathing: "I have no doubt the honourable gentleman has fostered some industries – for instance the industry of smuggling, which was depressed some years ago, and is rapidly reviving under the fostering influence of the honourable gentleman."[14] He also claimed:

A large number of the best of our manufacturers are fully convinced that this policy is of a great injury to them. They find that the cost of the raw material has increased, that in addition they will have to raise the wages of their workmen; while, on the other hand, they find that the power to buy of the customers with whom they deal has diminished under the effect of the Tariff. They find they cannot raise their home prices sufficiently to compensate them for the increased taxation, and that they fight at a disadvantage in the struggle for foreign markets.[15]

Despite the opposition, Macdonald's high tariff policy took hold. It resulted in a 35 per cent tariff being established on carriages, a rate later extended to automobiles, thereby prompting the establishment of foreign owned automotive manufacturing in Canada in the early twentieth century. Some pioneering firms endured and became the bedrock of the industry that exists in Canada today. Therefore, the 1879 policy framework initiated in 1879, stirred by events that can be traced as far back as 1854, has impacted automotive manufacturing in Canada to this day. Indeed, by rejecting the forces of imperialism and continentalism in the 1870s, the seeds were planted for the emergence of a globally competitive, albeit foreign-dominated, Canadian automotive industry more than a century later.

Canada's Emergence as an Auto-producing Nation

Canadian automotive manufacturing at the turn of the twentieth century was not unlike that of other nations. Entrepreneurs from across the country – but particularly Southern Ontario and Quebec – entered the fray. Many started operations and quickly closed. These efforts are well documented by Dykes and include a number of firms that independently sought to establish manufacturing operations in Ontario cities and towns like Toronto, Orillia, Galt, Brockville, Brantford, Chatham, and Berlin (now Kitchener), where Canada's first production-model automobile was built in 1899.[16] All were emphatically non-global in nature.

Sustained success did not occur until the latter part of the first decade of the twentieth century. During this time, the principles of isolationism, continentalism, and imperialism – three apparently contradictory impulses about Canada's relationship with the rest of world – intersected when well-capitalized Canadian carriage makers forged relationships with already established American operations.[17] By aligning themselves with American producers, Canadian firms gained access to the technology and design capabilities of their continental partners. In return, the larger American firms gained access not just to the protected Canadian market, but also much of the British Empire.[18]

When Gordon McGregor of Walkerville, Ontario, established a relationship with Henry Ford in 1904, the Ford Motor Company of Detroit had been manufacturing vehicles for just over a year. McGregor recognized that his small carriage business would find it difficult to survive the advent of the automobile. Automobiles and the automobile industry were in their nascent stage, particularly in Canada where sales were much lower than in the United States. In 1903, for example, just 178 passenger cars were registered in the entire Dominion of Canada, and by 1910, only 5,890 vehicles were registered.[19] In the towns and regions beyond the major cities, proliferation was even slower. As late as 1911, for example, the purchase of a new automobile still passed as news in the Eastern Ontario lumber town of Renfrew where the arrival of the community's second vehicle was reported on page two of the local newspaper.[20] In the United States, by contrast, 8,000 passenger cars were registered as early as 1900, growing to 458,377 by 1910.[21] However, as early as 1904, McGregor recognized that the trend to motorized vehicles was clear with US sales presaging the impending trend in Canada.

McGregor's approach to Ford in 1904 would appear to be a masterstroke, but the fact of the matter is that at the time McGregor approached him, linking oneself to the automotive industry in general and Henry Ford in particular was not without risk. Ford had already overseen the collapse of two automotive ventures and was just one of dozens of entrepreneurs in the United States seeking their fortune in the emerging field.[22]

The deal signed with McGregor in August 1904 was not Ford's first foray beyond US borders. In fact, the sixth Model A that Ford manufactured was sent to Canada in August 1903.[23] Moreover, the Canadian Cycle and Motor Company had already been appointed the company's agent in Canada. However, Canadian sales were struggling. The 35 per cent tariff meant that Ford's American-made cars were considerably more expensive in Canada than in the United States, partially explaining the slower proliferation of the automobile in Canada. A vehicle priced at $800 in the US cost almost $1,100 in Canada with the addition of the duty. Ford recognized that gaining a toehold in Canada could best be achieved by establishing operations in that country, and so McGregor's approach was timely.

The experience of Sam McLaughlin and General Motors (GM) in many ways parallels that of Gordon McGregor and Ford. Like McGregor, McLaughlin recognized that the long-term viability of his family's successful carriage business was threatened by the advent of the automobile. At the time, McLaughlin was the largest carriage manufacturer in the British Empire, with branch offices across the country and sales agents in South America and Australia. In 1908, after researching potential American partners, McLaughlin negotiated a contract with William Durant, who had started out as carriage maker. The fifteen-year agreement provided the McLaughlin Carriage Company with rights to purchase Durant's Buick engines and other parts.[24] By the late 1910s, however, McLaughlin perceived that it was unlikely that GM would be willing to extend the agreement and that going it alone was not a viable option; hence, the decision he made to sell the business to GM in 1918. His firm was the last Canadian-owned volume auto maker.

Meanwhile, the 35 per cent tariff persisted in Canada until 1926 (as shown in Table 6.1). At 35 per cent, it was lower than the rate assigned by the United States and France, but higher than that of Great Britain. During the period, production in Canada grew steadily, and the industry gradually shifted from one where many small firms sought to establish themselves to dominance by just four companies: GM, Ford, Studebaker, and Chrysler. In fact, by 1923, Canada had become the fourth-largest auto-manufacturing nation in the world.[25] So, whether by carefully designed "smart globalization" or mere happenstance,

Table 6.1. General preferential tariff rates on automobiles

Dates	Duty Rates (%)		
	< $1,200	$1,200–$2,100	> $2,100
To April 1926	35	35	35
April 1926 to June 1931	20	27.5	27.5
June 1931 to December 1935	20	30	40
January 1936 to May 1936	17.5	22.5	30
May 1936 to June 1962	17.5	17.5	17.5
June 1962 to March 1963 (temporary surcharge)	27.5	27.5	27.5

Source: Canada, Queen's Printer and Controller of Stationary, Royal Commission on the Automotive Industry (Ottawa: Queen's Printer, 1961); Canada, Minister of Supply and Service, *The Canadian Automotive Industry: Performance and Proposals for Progress*, Royal Commission on the Automotive Industry (Ottawa: Queen's Printer Canada, 1978), 20–2.

Canada had accomplished a deft feat. It had leveraged three seemingly incompatible policy levers to build an industry of global scale: first, the high tariff barriers it had erected for one industry were being used to protect an emergent industry; second, and paradoxically, it used duty-free access to its imperial cousins' markets to gain volume economies; and finally, it built those economies by leveraging technology from US-based corporations.

Certainly, Canada's 35 per cent tariff represented an incentive to manufacture in Canada. A further attraction was the preferential access Canada represented to US manufacturers as a gateway to its imperial connections. This advantage was recognized as early as 1904 when Gordon McGregor conducted his negotiations with Henry Ford. McGregor not only won the right to manufacture and sell Ford products in Canada but was also extended these privileges to the rest of the British Empire. In fact, McGregor's first export sale was made in 1905 when a Model C was shipped to Calcutta.[26]

Canadian auto makers' access to British imperial markets ensured that its automotive assembly industry grew to a size beyond what the domestic market alone could support. In the five-year period before 1926, when the government of Canada overhauled automotive tariffs, imports averaged 10,900 per year, whereas exports averaged 49,900, or 4.6 times more (Table 6.2). The production-to-sales ratio stood at 1.19:1. In the absence of exports, the production-to-sales ratio would have dipped to 0.7:1. Certainly, with exports representing 40 per cent of production, productivity was improved in consequence of economies of scale. As well, without favourable market access agreements, smaller manufacturers may not have produced in Canada, electing when possible to sell into the country and absorb the 35 per cent tariff.

Table 6.2. Average annual sales, production, and trade: Completed vehicles, 1904–65

Year	Passenger Cars Exp.	Imp.	Commercial Exp.	Imp.	Average Total Exp.	Imp.	Overall Balance	Dom. Prod.	Dom. Sales	Imp. Market Share	Exp. as % of Prod.
1904–10	161	596	*	*	161	596	–435	NA	NA	NA	NA
1911–15	3,566	5,930	*	*	3,566	5,930	–2,365	NA	NA	NA	NA
1916–20	14,961	9,980	1,659	813	16,619	10,793	5,826	NA	NA	NA	NA
1921–5	40,814	9,864	9,068	1,055	49,882	10,919	38,963	121,800	NA	NA	41.0
1926	53,628	26,345	20,696	2,199	74,324	28,544	45,780	204,727	NA	NA	36.3
1926–30	48,593	31,705	22,885	4,403	71,478	36,108	35,370	208,294	NA	NA	34.3
1931–5	22,555	2,973	8,134	831	30,690	3,804	26,886	99,786	66,505	5.7	30.8
1936–40	36,646	14,147	27,734	2,116	64,380	16,263	48,117	182,829	124,844	13.0	35.2
1941–5	3,575	825	144,502	1,119	148,077	1,943	146,134	193,446	37,851	5.1	76.5
1946–50	26,766	37,653	26,034	4,936	52,801	42,588	10,212	275,198	257,527	16.5	19.2
1951–5	25,216	43,506	17,798	5,941	43,014	49,447	–6,433	428,154	419,451	11.8	10.0
1956–60	14,144	115,155	3,450	10,994	17,594	126,149	–108,555	400,639	485,761	26.0	4.4
1961–5	30,608	98,028	10,601	8,180	41,209	106,208	–64,999	608,213	661,710	16.1	6.8

* Included with passenger cars.

Notes: Until 1932, the Dominion Bureau of Statistics did not collect automotive retail sales data. Dom., domestic; Exp., export; Imp., import; NA, not available; Prod., production.

Sources: Trade data to 1960 from *Facts and Figures of the Automotive Industry, 1961 Edition,* 37; trade data from 1960 on from *Facts and Figures of the Automotive Industry, 1968 Edition,* 18; domestic production to 1926 from *Facts and Figures of the Automotive Industry, 1968 Edition,* 14; domestic production from 1926 to 1960 from *Facts and Figures of the Automotive Industry, 1961 Edition,* 3; domestic production from 1961 on from *Facts and Figures of the Automotive Industry, 1968 Edition,* 14; sales data to 1960 from *Facts and Figures of the Automotive Industry, 1961 Edition,* 13; sales data from 1960 on from *Facts and Figures of the Automotive Industry, 1968 Edition,* 22.

The arrangements made by McGregor and McLaughlin with American companies in the early years of the twentieth century laid the foundations for the Canadian automobile industry. The tariff regime put in place by Macdonald following his return to power in 1878, including the 35 per cent tariff on carriages, undoubtedly lent impetus to manufacturing in Canada. Thus, a policy of isolationism at the national public level activated deeper continental ties at the level of the firm. Those continental ties, in turn, were validated and extended by leveraging Canada's lingering ties to its imperial cousins – ironic indeed.

Tariff Modifications: 1926–36

By 1926, the automobile industry in Canada was producing 205,000 vehicles per year, and exports had reached 74,000 vehicles. Employment in the industry, not counting those employed in parts and materials, was 12,000.[27] As the industry grew, pressure mounted on the government to ease tariff rates. There were several reasons for this pressure. To begin with, the minority government of Mackenzie King was largely dependent on the pro–free trade Progressive Party for its survival beyond the 1926 election.[28] Second, the industry had coalesced in the area around Southern Ontario, and the continued protection of the booming southern part of the province had become increasingly difficult to justify. Third, Canadian consumers were becoming increasingly unconvinced that the gap in automobile prices between Canada and the United States was attributable to the small size of the domestic marketplace.[29] Dykes reports that on 15 April 1926, Finance Minister James Robb announced, "There is a pronounced sentiment throughout Canada that the automobile industry enjoys more protection than is needed to maintain it on a reasonably profitable basis, and in deference to that sentiment we propose a downward readjustment of automobile, motor truck and motor cycle duties."[30] At this time, then, the 35 per cent General Tariff, which had originally been put in place to protect Canada's carriage industry, was reduced to 20 per cent for vehicles with retail value under $1,200 and to 27.5 per cent for those above $1,200 (Table 6.1). At the same time, the British Preferential Tariff rate was reduced from 22.5 per cent for vehicles valued under $1,200 to 12.5 per cent and to 15 per cent for those valued above the $1,200 threshold.

Not surprisingly, the domestic industry felt aggrieved. In response, it established the Canadian Automobile Chamber of Commerce with the stated purpose of "acting with the Government to promote the manufacture of automobiles in Canada and the development of this business throughout the world but more particularly in the British Empire."[31] The Conservative premier of Ontario, Howard Ferguson, expressed the industry's angst over the

1926 tariff adjustments. In a speech in Midland, Ontario, in August of that year, he declared: "Nothing better illustrated the utter sham of the King Administration than the alleged reduction in the duties on automobiles. In the very first month of the new rate of duty, the importation of automobiles doubled and in the next month, that of May, they had doubled again. Just that many more millions poured into the lap of the United States."[32] The analysis presented by Premier Ferguson was correct. Imports swelled from 14,632 in 1925 to 28,544 in 1926 and 36,630 in 1927, a two-year increase of 250 per cent. However, this period was also an era of rapidly increasing sales. For example, there were 724,000 motor vehicles registered in 1925, climbing to 832,000 one year later; by 1927, 940,000 vehicles were on Canadian roads,[33] an increase of 29.2 per cent in just two years. Yet the essential premise of Ferguson and other opponents to the tariff reductions was correct: imports were taking an increasing share of the market. In 1925, for example, 18.6 per cent of new car registrations were imported; by 1927, 34.1 per cent were made outside of Canada.[34]

The next major round of tariff adjustments occurred in 1936. However, before then, a number of minor changes were enacted. Those changes can be categorized into two types. The first were designed to buttress an industry weakened by the Great Depression, when production fell from 262,000 vehicles in 1929 to 61,000 by 1932. At market, leading Ford of Canada losses grew from $1.4 million in 1931 to $5.2 million in 1932, representing a loss of $118 per vehicle over the two-year period.[35]

The Depression caused nations to act unilaterally and restrict international trade, a development that Ashworth claims simply prevented conditions from further degenerating rather than offering any hope of prolonged improvement.[36] After decades of apparent unilateral defence of free trade, the UK's coalition government launched the Import Duties Act of 1932 including the introduction of duties between 10 and 33 per cent.[37] Kenwood and Lougheed contend that the US Smoot-Hawley Tariff Act of 30 June 1932, which substantially increased American tariffs, severely restricted the capacity of many nations to export manufactured goods and thereby further exacerbated their ability to service debts. In addition, the proliferation of import quotas in the 1930s is cited by Kenwood and Lougheed as further impairing the ability of manufacturing nations to purchase raw materials, precipitating depression in primary producing nations.[38] Clearly, as Rodrik argues, "[W]hen domestic needs clash the requirements of the global economy, domestic needs ultimately emerge victorious."[39]

Canada, like others, also proved unable to avoid the global impulse to shore up tariff walls. To bolster the parts industry, tariff rates were raised on a number of imported parts and components in 1930. In addition, excise taxes on imported parts were introduced in 1931 and then raised in 1932. The assembly industry was supported in 1931 by hiking the General Tariff on imported vehicles valued between $1,200 and $2,100 from 27.5 per cent to 30 per cent and by establishing a third category for tariff classification: a 40 per cent rate for vehicles valued above $2,100 (Table 6.1).

The tariff changes of the early 1930s did not arrest the industry's slide. Production bottomed out in 1932 at just 61,000 units and was 66,000 in 1933 before bouncing back to 117,000 in 1934 (Table 6.3). The tariff barriers may, however, have moderated the depth of the slide. During the five-year period 1926–30, sales of imported vehicles represented 17.3 per cent of Canadian production. From 1931 to 1935, however, that figure dropped to just 3.8 per cent. Dykes also reminds us that the elevated tariff hurdles also coincided with the establishment of the Canadian production operations of Hudson Motors, Graham-Paige, and Packard, potentially presaging even deeper continental ties.[40]

The extent of the slide in the United States was similar to that experienced in Canada, with production dropping from a high of 5.3 million vehicles in 1929 to 1.3 million in 1932, a three-year decline of 75 per cent.[41] The United States did not regain its 1929 levels of production again until 1949. In Canada, record production levels in 1929 of 263,000 declined by 76.8 per cent to 61,000 in 1932 and did not reach 1929 levels again until 1948.

A second and ultimately more important adjustment during this time period came when Canada reverted to its traditional imperial ties. In 1932, a five-way trade pact was tabled in the House of Commons involving Canada, the United Kingdom, South Africa, the Irish Free State, and Southern Rhodesia. The trade pact is significant for two reasons. On a broad basis, it signalled that Canada was bolstering its imperial ties, this at a time when more open ties with its continental partner remained out of bounds. With respect to the automotive industry, the trade pact contributed to the events that resulted in the Auto Pact three decades later. Canada's desire to turn to its British imperial connections was motivated largely by retaliatory impulses resulting from the US Smoot-Hawley Tariff Act, as well a desire to demonstrate tangible success at its hosting of the Imperial Conference of 1932. Among the 223 items the trade pact affected in Canada were British-made vehicles, which could now be imported free of duty. At the time, British firms were not active in the Canadian marketplace, and remarkably, they ignored these new opportunities for almost two decades.

In his 1961 Royal Commission report on the Canadian automotive industry, Vincent Bladen, observed, "[S]o unimportant did this concession appear to be

Table 6.3. Import penetration, 1926–35

Year	Production	Imports – Cars	Imports – Commercial	Total Imports	Imports (% of Production)
1926	204,727	26,345	2,199	28,544	13.9
1927	179,054	32,826	3,804	36,630	20.5
1928	242,054	40,226	7,182	47,408	19.6
1929	262,625	39,446	5,278	44,724	17.0
1930	153,372	19,683	3,550	23,233	15.1
Total: 1926–30	1,041,832	158,526	22,013	180,539	17.3
1931	82,559	7,492	1,246	8,738	10.6
1932	60,789	1,160	289	1,449	2.4
1933	65,852	1,093	683	1,776	2.7
1934	116,852	1,988	917	2,905	2.5
1935	172,877	3,133	978	4,111	2.4
Total: 1931–5	498,929	14,866	4,113	18,979	3.8

Sources: Production data from *Facts and Figures of the Automotive Industry, 1962 Edition*, 8; import data from *Facts and Figures of the Automotive Industry, 1958 Edition*, 37.

for the Canadian automobile industry that little attention was paid to it in the Tariff Board Inquiry of 1936."[42] Since then, Bladen's observation has gained a wider interpretation. For example, Simon Reisman's Royal Commission into the Canadian automotive industry observed, "This concession was considered of little consequence at the time."[43] Bladen and Reisman may have been correct if they had limited their comments to the observation that the changes had little, if any, *impact* at the time.

However, the idea that the tariff reductions generated little *interest* is not accurate. Both the overall tariff reduction program and the aspects dealing with the automotive industry generated much comment in 1932. In remarking on the pact overall, the *Toronto Globe* went so far as to describe it as "staggering in its immensity and absolutely uncircumscribed as to its potentialities."[44] Assessments within the automotive industry were more circumspect. Canadian executives understandably used the occasion to extol the virtues of their own offerings vis-à-vis those of their UK competitors. GM's R.S. McLaughlin declared: "We have spent years in building cars to suit Canadian conditions and the small automobile of British manufacturers could not, in any way, come up to the standards of performance demanded by motorists in the Dominion."[45] T.A. Russell, president of Willys Overland Limited, supported McLaughlin's claim, stating: "English cars have not yet found very much favour in this country. They are so different."[46]

Both Bladen and Reisman correctly observed that the full impacts of the 1932 tariff reforms were not felt for more than two decades. British-made vehicles did not gain significant market share until after the Second World War when passenger car production was resumed and consumer spending regained momentum. By the early 1950s, British manufacturers were earning increasing shares of Canada's growing market. However, it was only towards the end of the decade, when the growth in British imports outstripped the growth in the market, that a major threat to Canada's American-owned auto makers was perceived. Only then did the 1932 tariff come under fire. The inroads made by British manufacturers, in combination with other factors, prompted a series of events that in a few short years changed the face of the industry.

The tariff hikes of the early 1930s obviously ran counter to the consumer interests expressed by Finance Minister Robb when his government lowered tariffs in 1926, and by 1935, the same concerns had resurfaced. With tariffs now standing at between 20 and 40 per cent, Colling argues that Canadians were paying at least $265 more than Americans for the same vehicle.[47] Facing an election within months, in 1935 the Conservative administration of R.B. Bennett turned to the Tariff Board and invited its chairman to thoroughly review the situation and make recommendations. Finance Minister Rhodes's mandate letter to Tariff Board chairman Sedgewick stated:

> It is my thought that such investigation should not be restricted merely to those specific items of the customs or excise schedules which relate to the manufacturing of motor vehicles, but should be general in scope and character ... Such an inquiry should embrace the matter of the relationship of the production of parts to the larger industry, and of both to the general consuming interest: it should have regard for the principles and operations of drawbacks for domestic consumption, as well as for such matters as content and costs of distribution, and it should endeavour to appraise the various factors which determine the prices at which motor vehicles shall be sold.[48]

Even though Bennett's government delivered the mandate to the Tariff Board, the board's recommendations were accepted and implemented by the new administration of William Lyon Mackenzie King in the 1936 budget. Indeed, King had campaigned on the notion that the absence of trade would prolong the Depression, a position that by then had started to galvanize around the world. In the United States, for example, the election of Democrat Franklin D. Roosevelt in 1932 had opened the door to dismantling of some of the trade barriers that had been erected at the start of the decade. Indeed, Canada would exploit the new openness of the US administration when it signed a reciprocal trade agreement with the United States in 1935. The 1935 agreement saw Canada become less reliant on the emotional and historical bonds of the empire and towards the more practical and proximate link of its continental neighbour. This, despite the fact Canada, just three years before, had defaulted to its imperial connections with the signing of the five-way pact.

The new openness that the 1936 automotive tariff regime represented was important to the Canadian automotive industry because it persisted for the next quarter century. A 17.5 per cent Most-Favoured-Nation Tariff on most vehicles was established, and the zero duties set out in 1932 under the British Preferential Tariff were maintained (Table 6.1). Auto dealers were generally pleased. The remarks of A.D. O'Donnell, president of the O'Donnell-Mackie Company, were representative of the dealers: "It means the gap between high and low priced automobiles will now be bridged to a degree that will give the dealer of expensive cars more of a chance to do business."[49] Canadian auto makers were less sanguine, however. Harry Carmichael, vice president and general manager of GM of Canada, pointed to the 20,000 American-made vehicles imported into Canada in 1937 and claimed that if a higher tariff was applied, an additional 10,000 workers could be hired: "What a fallacy it is to accuse our industry of hiding behind tariff walls ... As a result of the present low tariff, one company discontinued Canadian operations last year, a second company with considerably larger production has practically ceased to operate in Canada, and a third will cease to manufacture here within the next few months. Only the three major car manufacturing companies will be left in Canada."[50] Carmichael's comments proved prophetic. Graham-Paige, which had established operations in 1931 in Windsor, Ontario, shut down its Canadian production operations in 1935.[51] Meanwhile, the two other American-owned manufacturers, which had set up Canadian operations in the early 1930s to avoid higher tariffs, also closed their doors. Packard, which started Canadian operations in Windsor in 1931, closed its Canadian production facility in 1939.[52] Hudson in nearby Tilbury, Ontario, ceased Canadian operations in 1941.[53] Dykes concludes that these companies' Canadian production facilities were rendered uneconomical because they were low-volume producers, which were only viable with tariffs between 20 and 40 per cent.[54]

Despite the challenges presented by the new, lower duty, the Canadian industry continued to expand, attributable in large part to exports to its imperial connections. Between 1935 and 1939, export markets accounted for more than 35 per cent of Canadian production (Table 6.2). The advent of war, however, changed the profile of the Canadian automotive industry considerably, as passenger vehicle production was largely diverted to the war effort and new vehicle sales had dropped to just 4,800 by 1943. Yet so great was the surge in new forms of production that the total number of employees in the automotive industry grew from 14,400 in 1939 to 24,300 in 1943. Ford's Canadian plants focused on casting and machining components, as well as assembling trucks, armoured vehicles, and heavy-duty artillery tractors. Chrysler produced combat units, water-purifying units, and tanks, as well as gun parts and special motors. GM's contributions included specialty trucks, armoured cars, and mobile offices, as well as gun parts, anti-tank gun carriages, and bomber fuselages.[55]

When the country and its economy emerged from war, it faced a new set of challenges. Tariff policies introduced years earlier coupled with changing economic conditions resulted in fundamental shifts in the structure of the Canadian automotive industry. These factors eventually sparked the appointment of Vincent Bladen to review the automotive industry in Canada, a study that eventually resulted in the Auto Pact.

The Bladen Royal Commission

Despite the challenges, the 1936 Tariff Board adjustments persisted for the next twenty-five years. In 1960, University of Toronto economist Vinçent Bladen was appointed as royal commissioner charged with assessing the Canadian automotive industry and its future. Bladen's appointment and his report, published in June 1961, provoked a series of policy adjustments that led to the signing in 1965 of the Auto Pact. Those writing about the history of the Canadian automotive industry have focused considerable energies explaining the nuances of the Auto Pact. Some have dug more deeply, scrutinizing the progression of events and policy adjustments that predated the Auto Pact's negotiations beginning with the Bladen report of 1961. They have also explained the policy adjustments that Bladen inspired, such as changes to excise taxes and the implementation of various content-related schemes enacted in 1962 and 1963.

Only occasionally do those writing about the industry or the Auto Pact refer to the conditions leading to Bladen's appointment, and even then, their comments are limited to broad generalizations about the challenges facing the industry in 1960. Emphasis is given to the increasing market share of foreign manufacturers, primarily from the United Kingdom. However, no satisfactory account exists of the complexities or competing priorities that existed prior to Bladen's appointment. This chapter more deeply explores those aspects and provides a new perspective on how the Auto Pact emerged by focusing on events of the 1950s rather than picking up the story, as most have done, with Bladen's appointment in 1960. It places the domestic policy adjustments that influenced these trends in the context of Canada's priorities vis-à-vis international trade. It demonstrates that in post-war Canada, political exigencies, industrial policies and global events came together to create the conditions for a unique and ultimately effective form of selective globalization.

The formation of the Royal Commission was prompted by perceived difficulties that vehicle makers believed could only be mitigated through government intervention. The sales side of the industry had been growing for several years, but healthy sales had served to mask a creeping decay on the manufacturing side. Average annual sales were 257,000 per year in the five-year period 1946–50. They climbed by 63.4 per cent to 419,000 per year from 1951 to 1955, and from 1956 to 1960, they climbed another 15.7 per cent to reach an annual average of 486,000. In fact, sales reached the half-million mark for the first time in 1959, a floor below which the industry never dipped again (Table 6.2). By 1960, however, concerns were being expressed about the long-term viability of domestic manufacturing. This section traces the factors contributing to those concerns and places them in the context of Canada's place in relation to the equilibrium its policymakers sought in terms of maximizing its imperial connections while leveraging relations with its continental partner. Finally, it describes how these factors coalesced in the establishment of the Bladen Commission.

The first factor contributing to the establishment of the Royal Commission was the fact that imports were on the rise, particularly in the passenger car area. Imports had previously occupied more than 20 per cent of Canadian automotive sales only once (in 1950) but had jumped to 25.5 per cent, 32.9 per cent, and then 34.9 per cent in 1958, 1959, and 1960, respectively. At 34.9 per cent, imports now represented more than 180,000 units annually (Table 6.2).

Second, by 1960, the Canadian automotive industry had completed a full reversal of the pattern established in earlier eras when executives like Gordon McGregor had strengthened his company through export sales to imperial partners. In the years prior to the war, exports regularly accounted for more than 30 per cent of Canadian production. By 1960, however, the governments of these imperial partners had come to recognize the importance of automotive assembly as an economic development tool. High tariffs and/or local content restrictions had impelled manufacturers to establish local assembly. By 1961, Ford of Canada had six manufacturing and assembly subsidiaries in Australia and one each in New Zealand, Malaya, Rhodesia, and South Africa.[56] Ford of Canada, for example, which in 1904 had secured the sales rights for Ford products throughout the British Empire, had in the early years filled international demand largely through Canadian production, aided by preferential tariff regimes in overseas (primarily Commonwealth) jurisdictions. In the years before and immediately after the war, Ford of Canada alone regularly exported more than 40,000 vehicles annually to its foreign subsidiaries and was usually responsible for more than 50 per cent of Canada's automotive exports. But by the late 1950s, Ford of Canada had established subsidiary operations in many of these far-flung places, and by 1960, Canadian export sales had dropped to just 11,770.[57] Therefore, by 1960, Canada, which had produced a positive balance of trade in completed vehicles every year from 1919 to 1949, was now experiencing a significant and growing deficit. The 183,000 foreign-built vehicles that Canadians purchased in 1960 were offset by exports of just 21,000, a ratio of almost nine to one (Table 6.2). A policy of counting on preferential imperial connections to help build a domestic auto industry had run its course.

The third area of concern was much less visible but equally compelling. A significant balance of trade deficit had accumulated in the parts portion of the industry. Canada had long experienced a large deficit in parts, related primarily to the fact that low production runs and economies of scale precluded capital intensive parts manufacturing from occurring for certain components. Bladen, for example, acknowledged that optimum economies of scale for automatic transmission production were approximately 400,000 units annually.[58] At the time, total Canadian vehicle production was just 397,000. The 1936 tariff revisions accommodated this reality by establishing the similar duty rate of 17.5 per cent on motor vehicle parts as had been set for vehicles, but only if the imported parts were of a class or kind made in Canada.

Between 1950 and 1959 the Canadian parts industry grew more slowly than did final vehicle sales, although more rapidly than domestic production, which actually declined from 390,000 vehicles in 1950 to 368,000 in 1959, a drop of 7.3 per cent. As Table 6.4 demonstrates, in 1965 dollars, the parts industry did manage to grow its sales by 16.1 per cent in real terms over the ten-year period despite the contraction in demand for Canadian produced vehicles. The result was that local content in Canadian-produced vehicles rose from an average of $779 per vehicle in 1950 (expressed in 1965 dollars) to $960 per vehicle (in 1965 dollars), an increase of 23.2 per cent. In addition, throughout the 1950s, vehicles got larger and more expensive. For example, the average retail value of a financed vehicle in 1950 was $2,037. By 1960 it had climbed to $2,879, an increase of $842, or 41.3 per cent, which when adjusted for inflation represented a real increase of 16.4 per cent.[59] Therefore, on the plus side, Canadian parts production and local content had both climbed over the decade. These increases more than compensated for the drop in overall vehicle production in Canada.

Yet the parts industry was not without anxiety. Its leadership perceived that it was missing opportunities and losing ground. As has been explained, European vehicle brands with practically no Canadian content were seizing ever-increasing portions of the Canadian market, a situation that translated into lost sales for the parts industry. "Every time I see a European car drive by, I think

Table 6.4. Automotive parts: Average annual exports, imports, and content levels, 1921–65

Year	1921–5	1926–30	1931–5	1936–40	1941–5	1946–50	1951–5	1956–60	1961–5
Parts exports ($000s)	3,570	3,002	1,871	4,356	106,608	15,876	27,207	144,437	81,821
Parts imports ($000s)	14,610	35,258	16,172	30,880	73,427	111,423	233,973	1,538,276	584,489
Balance ($000s)	-11,040	-32,256	-14,301	-26,524	32640	-95,547	-206,765	-1,393,839	-502,668
Ratio of parts imports to exports	4	12	9	7	1	7	9	11	7
Average consumer price index (1992=100)	11.1	10.9	8.9	9.2	10.6	13.4	16.7	17.9	19.3
Parts exports (in 1965 $000s)	6,550	5,519	4,266	9,400	198,029	24,670	32,567	160,664	83,542
Parts imports (in 1965 $000s)	26,441	64,818	36,533	67,109	138,610	164,101	279,884	1,719,425	602,192
Export of parts as a percentage of imports of domestic parts	24	9	12	14	144	14	12	9	14
Domestic vehicle production (units)	161,970	208,294	99,786	182,829	193,446	275,198	428,154	400,639	609,213
Domestic motor vehicle metal parts production ($000s)	—	—	—	46,857	154,144	152,628	274,355	316,021	**

(Continued)

Table 6.4. (Continued)

Year	1921–5	1926–30	1931–5	1936–40	1941–5	1946–50	1951–5	1956–60	1961–5
Domestic motor vehicle metal parts production (in 1965 $000s)	—	—	—	—	290,733	224,307	328,190	356,470	**
Domestic motor vehicle metal parts per vehicle (in 1965 $s)	—	—	—	—	1,583	830	767	892	**
Imported parts per vehicle (in 1965 $s)	163	311	366	367	717	596	654	851	880

* Calculated on the basis of motor vehicle metal parts production less exports divided by annual production.
** Denotes that new Standard Industrial Classification (SIC) System in 1960 rendered comparisons from prior years irrelevant.

Sources: Export and import data to 1950 from *Facts and Figures of the Automotive Industry, 1961 Edition* (Toronto: Motor Vehicle Manufacturers Association), 37; export and import data from 1951 on from *Facts and Figures of the Automotive Industry, 1966 Edition*, 16; CPI data from Statistics Canada, *CANSIM II*, Series V735319, Table 3260001, "Consumer Price Index (CPI), 2001 Basket Content," available from: http://dc2.chass.utoronto.ca.proxy.lib.uwaterloo.ca/cgi-bin/cansim2/getSeriesData.pl?s+V73; domestic production to 1960 from *Facts and Figures of the Automotive Industry, 1961 Edition*, 3; domestic production from 1961 on from *Facts and Figures of the Automotive Industry, 1968 Edition*, 14; domestic parts production from 1938 to 1948 from *Facts and Figures of the Automotive Industry, 1950 Edition*, 10; domestic parts production from 1948 to 1953 from *Facts and Figures of the Automotive Industry, 1955 Edition*, 10; domestic parts production from 1953 to 1959 from *Facts and Figures of the Automotive Industry, 1961 Edition*, 10.

there goes $10 we should have got, but didn't," grumbled J.S. Munro, general manager of Raybestos Manhattan, a Peterborough, Ontario, manufacturer of brake linings and clutch facings.[60] Furthermore, despite the fact that Canada enjoyed positive net trade balances with all of the major European economies, European–Canadian trade in automotive goods was entirely one way. For example, in 1960, when 92,000 UK-made vehicles captured 17.7 per cent of the Canadian vehicle market, only $167,000 worth of parts was exported from Canada to the United Kingdom. In other words, if spread out over the 1.8 million vehicles produced in the United Kingdom in 1960, Canadian parts content represented slightly less than 11 cents per vehicle.[61] By the end of the 1950s, Canadian parts makers felt they were falling behind. In addition to lost opportunities from imported vehicles with no Canadian content, imported parts had become an increased threat to the industry. Parts imports were growing more rapidly than domestic parts production. Between 1950 and 1959, parts imports had grown in real terms by 60.8 per cent compared to the 16.1 per cent growth in shipments from domestic producers. Combined with slightly lower vehicle production in Canada, this meant that imported parts had climbed from $558 per vehicle in 1965 dollars in 1950 to $966 per vehicle in 1965 dollars by 1959, a jump of 73.1 per cent. By the end of the decade, foreign parts claimed an equal share of automotive value added to that of Canadian parts manufacturers.

During the summer of 1960 – just one month before the appointment of Vincent Bladen to the post of royal commissioner – the parts industry converged on Ottawa to press its case. Meetings were arranged with several key cabinet ministers, including Prime Minister John Diefenbaker. The parts makers' brief implored the government to provide protection against imported cars and parts: "If cars are not produced in Canada, the parts manufacturer has no market for his products. ... Action is urgently needed to save the jobs of Canadians working in the automotive industry. The industry cannot survive without tariff protection."[62]

A fourth source of pressure for government involvement was that by the close of the 1950s, the growing trade imbalance – in vehicles and parts – had begun to affect employment. The total number of employees in the motor vehicle manufacturing and parts industry dropped from a post-war high of 56,570 in 1956 to 47,346 in 1959, a decline of 16.3 per cent.[63] The drop in employment corresponded with a 15.4 per cent decline in domestic vehicle production.[64] Of course, then, as now, the auto industry represented a desirable source of employment, and the government was motivated to maintain employment levels. Average salaries and wages in the motor vehicle industry in 1960 were $5,400 annually, or $103.85 weekly, and in the motor vehicle and metal parts industries, average salaries and wages were $4,800, or an average of $92.31 per week. Meanwhile, national average weekly earnings stood at $72.22.[65]

A fifth reason for establishing the Bladen Commission was related to the competitive positioning of the North American–owned manufacturers. The Big Three (General Motors, Ford, and Chrysler) had tried to respond to the growing market shares of the Europeans with compact cars of their own, including, for example, the Plymouth Valiant, Chevrolet Corvair, and Ford Falcon. In Canada, the aim was to stem the creeping market share of smaller-sized European vehicles. In the United States, where the vehicles that Canadian subsidiaries would eventually produce and sell were designed, a different phenomenon was underway. There, European imports were of lesser concern because imports occupied a more modest 7.6 per cent of the new car market in 1960.[66] In the United States, the Big Three's sights were set more squarely on the AMC Rambler, which had topped sales of 401,000 in 1959, representing 7.1 per cent of the entire new US passenger car market.[67] In the United States, the smaller cars designed by the Big Three emphatically reflected US tastes. The special features of the Canadian marketplace were not fully understood at the time. Diefenbaker, for example, believed that the new Big Three smaller cars would arrest the decline in Canadian production and pressured the Big Three to build compacts in Canada rather than importing them from the United States.[68] This chapter contends that the failure to fully grasp the unique nature of the Canadian marketplace was demonstrated when the new US compact vehicles failed to do well in Canada. As Table 6.5 indicates, Canadians seeking small cars were being drawn to low-cost European-built vehicles like the Vauxhall (from the United Kingdom) priced at $1,853, the Simca (from France) at $1,845, and the top-selling Volkswagen (from Germany) at $1,595. North American–owned companies were offering their new compacts at an average price of $2,554, a premium of $706, or 38.2 per cent, above the average-priced imported vehicle.

The North American makers were being trumped in their own backyard, and it was naive of policymakers like Diefenbaker to believe that US firms could match the success they enjoyed at home. First, as with all Canadian-made vehicles, low production runs proved to be uneconomic. For example, even when AMC Rambler production in Canada reached 30,000 in 1963, new registrations of the same model in the United States totalled 427,000.[69] In addition, not only were the European vehicles much more reasonably priced, but the North American offerings were priced too close to their companies' larger, standard-sized offerings. At C$2,642, for example, the compact GM Corvair was priced just 7.5 per cent, or C$213, less than the standard-sized Chevrolet.[70] By comparison, in the United States, the gap between the Corvair and the lowest-cost standard-sized Chevrolet (the Biscayne Six) was US$236, or 11.2 per cent.[71]

Table 6.5. Suggested retail prices (Canadian dollars) of small cars, 1960

North American Compacts		Offshore Imports	
Model	Retail Price	Model	Retail Price
Corvair	$2,642	Anglia	$1,504
Falcon	$2,496	Austin A-55	$1,899
Frontenac	$2,510	Consul	$2,079
Lark	$2,586	Hillman	$1,865
Rambler	$2,454	Morris	$1,650
Valiant	$2,636	Morris 850	$1,295
Average	$2,554	Renault	$1,798
		Simca	$1,845
		Triumph	$1,895
		Vanguard	$2,149
		Vauxhall	$1,853
		Volkswagen	$1,595
		Volvo	$2,595
		Average	$1,848

Note: Prices shown are suggested retail prices at Toronto for lowest priced model with heater.
Source: "Compacts Haven't Stalled Yet," *Toronto Star*, 26 March 1960, 10.

Third, the combination of scale economies and tariff policy rendered US-built vehicles more expensive than European imports. For example, even after accounting for exchange rates,[72] in the United States, the Corvair was more than C$700 cheaper than it was in Canada at just US$1,810. Meanwhile, the Vauxhall was available in New York for US$1,957. In the United States, therefore, there was no premium for a Corvair over a Vauxhall. In fact, the Corvair was US$147, or 7.5 per cent, less expensive. By comparison, in Canada, the Corvair came with a premium over the Vauxhall of C$789, or 42.6 per cent. The price differential meant that new compact cars offered by the Big Three in Canada in the 1960 model year captured just 14 per cent of the Canadian market. By contrast, in the United States, compacts regularly accounted for more than 25 per cent of production.[73]

A sixth reason for government pressure to appoint Bladen was that imports were taking an increasing share of the market, the main source of which was the United Kingdom. The market share spike in the late 1950s has been briefly reviewed by Dykes, by Reisman (in his Royal Commission report), by Holmes, and in slightly more detail, by Anastakis.[74] All argue that the root cause was the 1932 treaty that conceded duty-free entry for British vehicles. Although the treaty was contributory, more important was a UK currency devaluation in 1949, which resulted in a reduction in the value of the pound sterling vis-à-vis the Canadian dollar of 19.1 per cent. This action came on top of a 15.5 per cent relative decline that had occurred since the end of the war.[75] In a statement announcing Ford UK's results for 1950, chairman Sir Rowland Smith acknowledged the part that currency devaluation had played in his company's export success: "It is clear that during 1950 the rising level of world-wide economic activity stimulated the demand for motor products. In this country we reaped the benefits of the relatively stable costs and prices of the past few years and sterling devaluation in the latter part of 1949 gave a further price advantage and impetus to export sales."[76] In 1950, import market share jumped to 20 per cent from 13.5 per cent in 1949. Meanwhile, though, Canadian auto sales climbed by 50 per cent to reach 430,000. Therefore, the increase in imports could be ignored as overall sales emerged from the shadows of wartime. In a year-end review of the industry with the *Globe and Mail* newspaper, GM Canada president William Wecker expressed satisfaction with sales and limited his worry list to steel shortages and international currency devaluation. Rather than highlight the impact that international currency devaluations might have on imports to Canada, he expressed concern about the impact it was likely to have on Canadian exports: "Currency restrictions and devaluation will likely continue to bar Canadian auto manufacturers from the once lucrative market overseas for an indefinite period."[77] During a high-profile speech to the Canadian Club in January 1951, Ford's Canadian president Rhys Sale focused his attention on defence spending and inflation, not auto sales in general or increasing imports in particular.[78]

The Canadian executives' initial lack of concern over rising imports existed despite the fact that even though retail sales grew by 50.3 per cent, import sales grew even more. Data from Table 6.2 shows imports jumped from 38,697 units in 1949 to 88,528 in 1950, a one-year rise of 128.8 per cent. However, it was possible to overlook import growth of almost 50,000 when overall sales were up by more than 140,000 and production had swelled almost 100,000. Had more notice been taken, auto executives might have recognized that fully 99 per cent of the rise in imports in 1950 originated from the United Kingdom.[79] In 1946, the 731 motor vehicles that the United Kingdom exported to Canada represented just 3.2 per cent of total automotive imports.[80] By 1949, however, the United Kingdom represented 86.4 per cent of automobile imports to Canada, and by 1950, UK imports reached 82,839 and accounted for 93.6 per cent of all automotive imports. Yet, because the period was one of general stability and growth, and because UK-based imports had gained traction when Canadian production and sales had grown by even more in absolute terms, the rising trend of imports escaped widespread notice for several years.

Even when the size and impact of the UK brands did gain visibility, the chorus of complaints from the Canadian auto makers was generally muted. It is suggested here that the reason Canadian auto makers were quiet was because each of them had relationships with European brands. For example, when import sales reached 166,000 and captured 32.9 per cent of the market in 1959, some of the biggest importers were the North American–owned Big Three. Big Three imports of 69,551 represented 42 per cent of all vehicles imported into Canada that year.[81] Not until the late 1950s, a period when the absolute growth of import sales outstripped the absolute growth in overall sales, did the issue generate significant interest. By then, North American–owned production had started to fall even though overall sales remained on the ascent. From 1957 to 1960, overall sales grew by 65,000. Import sales, however, grew by 100,000 in the same period. Therefore, during a time of relative health, the production portion of the industry – the main generator of employment and value added – was on the decline. Though the Canadian market had jumped by 15.8 per cent to reach annual average sales of 486,000 for 1956–60 over 1951–5, production had dipped by 6.4 per cent between the two periods, from 428,000 to 401,000. Chrysler Canada president Ron Todgham, whose firm's reliance on sales of European made vehicles was significantly lower in both absolute and relative terms than his Big Three competitors,[82] was somewhat freer to be blunt, even contemptuous, in his assessment of the role of imports in the Canadian marketplace. He distributed French- and Italian-made vehicles, which arrived in Canada at a 17.5 per cent rate of duty compared to the GM and Ford Vauxhalls and Fords that were made in the United Kingdom and entered Canada with zero tariffs. In commenting on imported automobiles, he sneered: "[T]hat word, compounded of colonialism and dripping with the essence of snobbery, leads countless Canadian purchasers to betray their country every day in the marketplace."[83]

Against this backdrop, larger issues were at play; issues that in the late 1940s and well into the 1950s allowed Canada and its policymakers to avoid fretting over a trade deficit in a single sector. Despite the large shortfall with the United Kingdom in automotive trade, Canada was experiencing a large trade surplus with the United Kingdom overall. Isolating a single irritant in an otherwise unbalanced and positive relationship would be unusual, particularly for a country that had for years sought to deal with matters of trade on a multilateral basis. The draw to multilateralism was as much an effort to mitigate the concomitant dilemmas posed by continentalism and imperialism with which Canadian policymakers had traditionally struggled. However, by the mid-1950s, the pattern was clear: the ascension of the US economy, coupled with prolonged stagnation in the United Kingdom, meant that the Canadian capacity to pursue a foreign policy independent of either continentalism or imperialism was compromised. US dominance was the reality. On a practical basis, the United Kingdom's shaky economy coupled with the fact that it was already experiencing a trade deficit with Canada meant that isolating its automotive industry for attention would be disingenuous. Meanwhile, in the 1950s Canadians still clung to emotional ties that the United Kingdom represented. Finally, the rejection of the United Kingdom in so far as its automotive industry was concerned would deliver Canada and its consumers into the charge of the US-owned manufacturers that controlled the industry. Until the late 1950s, Canadian policymakers could avoid making choices, at least as far as automotive trade was concerned: domestic production and employment was growing more quickly than imports. However, by the latter part of the decade, those conveniences were no longer available, and the continentally aligned Canadian automotive industry would coalesce to pull Canada even more squarely into the orbit of the United States.

The conclusion reached here is that by 1960 the consequences of policies and practices dating back to the 1930s were being felt across the Canadian automotive industry. Significant structural inefficiencies had been created that could no longer be countenanced. They included uneconomic production runs in Canada and a Canada–US price gap that was compelling Canadians to purchase lower-priced European imports. At the same time, imported vehicle sales were growing faster than overall sales, and the response that the new North American compacts had generated in the Canadian marketplace was disappointing. Export markets for Canadian-made automotive product were declining at the same time as domestic demand for Canadian-made autos was falling. Finally, lucrative auto-sector employment was on the decline in Canada. All of this was happening as imperial ties were waning. Consequently, pressure had grown to the point where the Conservative government of John Diefenbaker felt compelled to take action. It was against this backdrop that Diefenbaker appointed Vincent Bladen in August of 1960 to lead a one-man Royal Commission into the auto industry.[84]

Conclusion

Since Confederation, those charged with the responsibility of developing policy related to Canada's relations with the rest of the world wrestled with competing social and economic pulls. The result was a tendency to lurch from one "ism" to another – from imperialism to nationalism to multilateralism to continentalism, with several back steps and side steps along the way. This balancing (or perhaps vacillation) is manifest in the progression of policy related to Canada's automotive industry. This chapter has explored how that process and those influences unfolded during Canada's earliest years and followed it through to the appointment of Vincent Bladen to lead a Royal Commission into Canada's auto industry in 1960.

Although Bladen's appointment represents a critical juncture in the development of the modern Canadian automotive industry, it should be viewed as the product of a century of evolution – a process involving balance, assessment, and debate about Canada's position in the international milieu. As such, policy invoked decades earlier and the conditions that prompted those measures must also be considered. By viewing Canada's auto industry through this lens, certain aspects not considered in previous work have been brought to the fore. For example, this chapter has included a broader enumeration of the importance that Canada's unique access to other markets afforded its automotive industry throughout its first few decades; it has charted the impact that significant tariff modifications have had on imports of both vehicles and parts; and it has provided context to the tariff adjustment that afforded duty-free treatment to UK-built vehicles in 1932. It has also offered a more comprehensive outline of the conditions leading to the appointment of Vincent Bladen in 1960, and in that vein, has documented the impact on import market share of the devaluation of the UK pound sterling in the late 1940s. In turn, one is reminded that the root cause of each of these outcomes can be traced to the concomitant pull and/or rejection of the influences of imperialism, nationalism, multilateralism, and continentalism.

Eventually, Bladen and the process associated with his Royal Commission made an indelible contribution. Bladen's work compelled the industry to commit and /or submit to a North American, continentalist regime. There would be no turning back. To compete for new sources of investment, the country needed a comprehensive policy framework in place with trading patterns established and legislative measures entrenched. It has been shown that these measures were established over decades of debate and decades of policy and attitudinal evolution. The case provides a fascinating example of ideological and policy dexterity – an application of smart globalization – amidst tumultuous change in the structure and fortunes of the economy.

178 Greig Mordue

NOTES

1 The Auto Pact provided for a managed form of sectoral free trade between Canada and the United States. It was to be of unlimited duration but could be terminated by either the Canadian federal government through an Order in Council or through the US Congress on 12 months' notice. Under the agreement, licensed manufacturers were allowed to import into Canada assembled vehicles and parts for original equipment manufacturers free of duty provided that the following conditions were met: the ratio of net factory sales value of any class of vehicle produced in Canada to the net factory sales value of vehicles of the same class sold in Canada remained equal to the ratio in the base year of 1964 or 75 per cent, whichever was higher, and Canadian in-vehicle value added was at least as great in absolute terms as the Canadian Value Added (CVA) in the base year of 1964. (Note: Inflation was not factored into this second safeguard. As a result, this feature became increasingly meaningless over time.)

2 Canada, Queen's Printer and Controller of Stationary, *Royal Commission on the Automotive Industry* (Ottawa: Queen's Printer, 1961).

3 Sir John A. Macdonald, 10 March 1876, *House of Commons Debates*, Sess. 1876, vol. 1, 573.

4 "The Treaty of Reciprocity Ratified," *Toronto Examiner*, 16 August 1854, 2. (Appeared originally in the *Union*, published in Rochester, New York.)

5 Ibid.

6 "House of Commons," *London Times*, 18 and 19 May 1866, 6.

7 M. Hart, *Fifty Years of Canadian Tradecraft: Canada at the GATT 1947–1997* (Ottawa: Centre for Trade Policy and Law, 1988), 11; D.M. Flynn, "The Rationalization of the United States and Canadian Automotive Industry: 1960–1975" (PhD diss., University of Massachusetts, 1979).

8 "What the United States Has Done for Us," *Hamilton Evening Times*, 26 April 1866, 2.

9 "Upper Canada (from an occasional correspondent)," *Canadian News*, 15 March 1866, 4.

10 Hart, *Fifty Years of Canadian Tradecraft*, 12; B. Forster, *A Conjunction of Interests: Business, Politics, and Tariffs 1825–1879* (Toronto: University of Toronto Press, 1986), 138–9; J. Lanigan, "Foreign Capital – Friend or Foe?" *Quarterly Review of Commerce* (Summer 1937): 147–52.

11 "The New Tariff," *Toronto Globe*, 21 March 1879, 1.

12 Ibid.

13 Ibid.

14 Sir R.J. Cartwright, 9 March 1880, *House of Commons Debates*, 2nd Sess., 4th Parl., 537.

15 Ibid., 541.

16 J. Dykes, *Canada's Automotive Industry* (Toronto: McGraw-Hill Company of Canada, 1970).

17 But even a strong capital underpinning, combined with a solid background in carriage manufacture and cross-border affiliations, was not enough to keep manufacturers like the Brockville Atlas Automobile company from bankruptcy, albeit ten years after formation. Available from: http://www.modelt.ca/atlas.html.

18 This same pattern was to be repeated decades later: recognition that Canada represented an access point for larger markets was crucial in attracting offshore manufacturers. Ironically, instead of granting US firms access to foreign markets, by the 1980s, Canada was attractive to foreigners seeking access to the US market.

19 Motor Vehicle Manufacturers' Association of Canada (MVMA), *Facts and Figures of the Motor Vehicles Industry* (Toronto: MVMA, 1968 [and various years]), 28.

20 "District News," *Renfrew News*, 28 July 1911, 2.

21 MVMA, *Facts and Figures* (1968), 37.

22 Even as late as 1909, Ford was not considered the industry leader. GM chairman, William Durant, for example, negotiated the purchase of Ford for $9.5 million and the GM Board voted approval, but the company's bankers stopped the deal upon deciding Ford was not worth $9.5 million. See S. McLaughlin, *My Eighty Years on the Road*. Available from: http://www.gm.ca/media/about/history/en/history_RSM_en_CA.

 Further, according to Sam McLaughlin, a member of GM Board of Directors from 1910 to 1967: "It is putting it mildly to say that in 1909 the auto industry was in a state of flux … At the time of the Ford negotiations, for example, General Motors was also considering the purchase of the E.R. Thomas Co., makers of the then famous Thomas Flyer, and in automobile circles this deal was considered a much more important and promising one than the Ford negotiations" (McLaughlin, *My Eighty Years on the Road*).

23 C.H. Dassbach, *Global Enterprises and the World Economy: Ford, General Motors, and IBM, the Emergence of the Transnational Enterprise* (New York: Garland, 1989), 65.

24 Dassbach, *Global Enterprises*, 120.

25 H. Colling, "The Automotive Industry in Windsor," in *The Auto Pact: Investment, Labour and the WTO*, ed. M. Irish (The Hague: Kluwer Law International, 2004), 41–52, 43.

26 Ford Motor Company of Canada Limited, *Ford 100 Years in Canada* (Oakville, Ontario: Ford Motor Company of Canada, 2004), 50.

27 Canada, *Royal Commission*, 6.

28 D. Anastakis, "Auto Pact: Business and Diplomacy in the Creation of a Borderless North American Auto Industry, 1945–1971" (PhD diss., York University, 2001), 34.

29 Canada, *Royal Commission*, 7; and Dykes, *Canada's Automotive Industry*, 41.

30 Dykes, *Canada's Automotive Industry*, 41–2.

31 The establishment of a trade organization may appear of little consequence to the development of the industry and, as such, has largely been ignored by critics and commentators (including the history of the Canadian automotive industry written by the association's general manager, James Dykes, in 1970). Notwithstanding, the Canadian Automobile Chamber of Commerce, which subsequently became the Motor Vehicle Manufacturers' Association in 1964, has in fact been an influential body for nearly 80 years – one that has sought to influence government and has been actively consulted on practically every major piece of policy impacting the industry since its formation. MVMA, *Facts and Figures* (1964), 2.

32 "Cut on Auto Tariff Nothing but Sham Declares Premier," *Toronto Globe*, 4 August 1926, 1. The article erroneously misidentified the premier as Arthur Meighen, who was then leader of the Opposition.

33 MVMA, *Facts and Figures* (1959), 20.

34 In the mid-1920s, the main source of automotive imports was the United States. However, further waves of import penetration would occur as the industry matured. In fact, it can be shown that in the history of the Canadian automotive industry, rising import trends consistently prompted concern and debate followed by restrictive policy measures. For example, increasing imports from the United Kingdom in the late 1950s spurred a chain of events that ultimately led to a Royal Commission led by Vincent Bladen in 1960–1 and the Canada–United States Automotive Products Trade Agreement of 1965. Then, in the late 1970s, it was perceptions of market disruptions arising from increasing Japanese imports that set in motion a series of policy deliberations that eventually led to a rush of inward foreign direct investment.

35 Assessed using Statistics Canada, *CANSIM*, Series V737344, Table 326002, "Consumer Price Index (CPI) 2001 Basket Content." A figure of $804 was arrived at by dividing the 2004 scaled rate by the 1932 scaled rate and multiplying by 1931 and 1932 losses per vehicle. Therefore, $(122.3 \div 8.0) \times \$118 = \$1,804$.

By comparison, in 2003, Harbour and Associates (Troy, Michigan: Harbour and Associates, 2004, 152) reported that GM, the global sales leader, showed a loss of US$50 per vehicle, Ford lost US$291 per vehicle, and profit leader Toyota earned US$2,118 per vehicle.

36 W. Ashworth, *A Short History of the International Economy since 1850* (London: Longman, 1975), 250.

37 M. Hart, *A Trading Nation* (Vancouver: University of British Columbia Press, 2002), 101.

38 A.G. Kenwood and A.L. Lougheed, *The Growth of the International Economy 1820–1960* (London: George Allen and Unwin, 1971), 204–5, 216.

39 Dani Rodrik, *The Globalization Paradox: Democracy and the Future of the World Economy* (New York: W.W. Norton & Co., 2011), 68.

40 Dykes, *Canada's Automotive Industry*, 8.

41 Automobile Manufacturers Association, *1970 Automobile Facts and Figures* (Detroit, MI: Automobile Manufacturers Association, 1970), 3.

42 Canada, *Royal Commission*, 8.

43 Canada, Minister of Supply and Service, *The Canadian Automotive Industry: Performance and Proposals for Progress, Royal Commission on the Automotive Industry* (Ottawa: Queen's Printer Canada, 1978), 8.

44 "Major Tariff Schedules Revised as Bennett Lays Corner-stone of all British Economic Edifice," *Toronto Globe*, 13 October 1932, 1.

45 "Horsepower Tax Hits Motor Sales in British Isles," *Toronto Globe*, 13 October 1932, 1.

46 Ibid.

47 Colling, "The Automotive Industry in Windsor."

48 Letter from Edgar Rhodes to George Sedgewick, 13 March 1935, appeared in "Tariff Board to Probe Prices of Motor Cars," *Toronto Globe*, 14 March 1935, 2.

49 "Dealers Expect Little Change in Auto Trade," *Toronto Globe*, 2 May 1936, 1.

50 "Auto Tariff Boost Urged for Dominion," *Toronto Globe*, 7 December 1937, 4.

51 Available from: http://windsorpubliclibrary.com/digi/wow/plants/graham-paige.htm

52 Available from: http://windsorpubliclibrary.com/digi/wow/plants/packard.htm

53 Ibid.

54 Dykes, *Canada's Automotive Industry*, 49.

55 MVMA, *Facts and Figures* (1950), 8, 16; Ford Motor Company of Canada Limited, *Ford 100 Years in Canada*, 64; Dykes, *Canada's Automotive Industry*, 57–8.

56 Ford Motor Company of Canada Limited, *Ford of Canada /1960 Annual Report* (Oakville, Ontario: Ford Motor Company of Canada, 1961), 18.

57 M. Wilkins and F. Hill, *American Business Abroad: Ford on Six Continents* (Detroit, MI: Wayne State University Press, 1964), appendix 6.

58 Canada, *Royal Commission*, 28.

59 MVMA, *Facts and Figures* (1961), 16.

60 "UK Car Parts Tariff Demanded," *Toronto Star*, 30 April 1960, 46.

61 MVMA, *Facts and Figures* (1961), 14; Canada, *Royal Commission*, 105.

62 "European Cars Killing Us, Say Parts Makers," *Toronto Star*, 14 July 1960, 12.

63 The Standard Industrial Classification was adopted in 1960 by the Dominion Bureau of Statistics and was reflected in that year's figures. This meant that statistics previously assigned to the categories of motor vehicle industries and motor vehicle metal parts industries were now also assigned to a new category: the truck body and trailer industry. As such, for the purposes of consistency, statistics cited for

1960 incorporate the truck body and trailer industry and therefore cannot be judged against earlier data. MVMA, *Facts and Figures* (1961), 10.

64 Employment data incorporates all aspects of the automotive industry, including both production and sales.

65 From Statistics Canada, *CANSIM*, Table 281-0014, "Average Weekly Earnings, Industrial Composite, by Selected Urban Areas, Monthly (Dollars)"; MVMA, *Facts and Figures* (1962), 16–7.

66 Ward's Automotive (WA), *Ward's Automotive Yearbook* (Detroit, MI: Ward's Automotive Yearbook, 1965 [and various years]), 177.

67 WA, *Ward's Automotive Yearbook* (1960), 57.

68 "Failure to Sell Small Cars Here Could Mean Disaster," *Toronto Star*, 15 June 1959, 7.

69 MVMA, *Facts and Figures* (1966), 12; WA, *Ward's Automotive Yearbook* (1965), 159.

70 "Compacts Haven't Stalled Yet," *Toronto Star*, 26 March 1960, 10.

71 WA, *Ward's Automotive Yearbook* (1960), 30.

72 Statistics Canada, *CANSIM II*, Series V37694, Table 1760049, "Foreign Exchange Rates, United States and United Kingdom, for January 1960." Available from: http://www5.statcan.gc.ca/cansim/pick-choisir?lang=eng&p2=33&id=1760049.

73 "Kind of Car You Will Purchase May Depend on Prof's Report," *Toronto Star*, 18 August 1960, 12; WA, *Ward's Automotive Yearbook* (1960), 178.

74 Dykes, *Canada's Automotive Industry*; Canada, *The Canadian Automotive Industry*, 1978; J. Holmes, "The Auto Pact from 1965 to the Canada-United States Free Trade Agreement (CUSFTA)," in *The Auto Pact: Investment, Labour and the WTO*, ed. M. Irish (The Hague: Kluwer Law International, 2004), 3–23; Anastakis, "Auto Pact."

75 Statistics Canada, Series J560-567, "Foreign Exchange Rates, 1913 to 1977." Available from: http://www5.statcan.gc.ca/access_acces/archive.action?l= eng&loc=J560_567-eng.csv.

76 "Ford Motor Company: Record Production in Spite of Supply Difficulties," *Times of London*, 31 May 1951.

77 Ibid.

78 "Plain Words, Well Said," *Globe and Mail*, 17 January 1951, 6.

79 Calculated on the basis of the rise in UK imports from 1949 to 1950 of 49,376 divided by the rise in all exports from 1949 to 1950 of 49,831 as drawn from *Facts and Figures of the Automotive Industry, 1959 Edition*, 39.

80 Canada, *Royal Commission*, table IV, 104.

81 Canada, *Royal Commission*, appendix VI, 103.

82 In 1960, of the 129,527 new passenger cars registered from Europe, only 3,756 (or 2.9%) were from Fiat-Simca, which were distributed in Canada by Chrysler. Chrysler Canada's overall sales (as represented by new motor vehicle registrations)

including Fiat-Simca were 44,834 (MVMA, *Facts and Figures* [1961], 30). That meant that European imports represented just 8.4 per cent of Chrysler Canada's sales of passenger cars. By contrast, UK-based Vauxhall-Envoy, which was distributed in Canada by GM, had 35,165 new passenger car registrations that year, representing 27.1 per cent of all European passenger cars registered in Canada and 18.3 per cent of GM's total new passenger car registrations of 191,990. Ford, too, had a more pronounced dependence on European-built Fords to meet North American market demands. New registrations of European-built Fords were 15,356 in 1960, 11.9 per cent of total European-built new passenger car registrations in Canada and 15.2 per cent of the 100,850 new passenger car registrations from Ford that year.

83 "Traitorous to Buy Foreign Car?" *Toronto Star*, 14 April 1961, 10.

84 The Bladen appointment was made after it was discovered that the Tariff Board was booked for an extended period with other business. "Bladen One-man Prober of Auto Industry," *Globe and Mail*, 3 August 1960, 18.

7

The Whisky Kings: The International Expansion of the Seagram Company, 1933–95

GRAHAM D. TAYLOR

One morning in June 1964, a crowd consisting mostly of employees of Seagram Distillers (United Kingdom) and some local dignitaries assembled in the Scottish town of Paisley to celebrate the opening of the Chivas/Glen Keith Distillery, touted by the company's public relations department as "the first new malt distillery built in Scotland since the Victorian Era." The main speaker was, not surprisingly, Samuel Bronfman, the autocratic chief executive (and largest shareholder) of the parent company, Distillers Corporation-Seagram Ltd (DCSL), headquartered in Montreal, but with its largest operation – and its most architecturally outstanding building – in New York City. "It is noteworthy that the three whisky-distilling nations of the world today are Scotland, Canada and the United States," Mr Bronfman observed. "This is undoubtedly due to the influence of pioneers from this country to the other side of the Atlantic who helped make these two other nations great distilling countries."[1]

. It was boilerplate for the occasion, of course, but perhaps revealing of some unusual features of this company and its circumstances at a moment when the Seagram empire was basking in the glory of great achievements and embarking on a new era of expansion. In 1964, in terms of average annual sales volume, DCSL was the largest maker and distributor of distilled beverages in the world – a position it would retain for the next three decades. Its US subsidiary, Joseph Seagram & Sons Inc., held more than one-third of the market there, dwarfing would-be challengers such as Schenley and a Canadian competitor, Hiram Walker; twice in the previous decade, Seagram had been the target of US antitrust investigations, reflecting its dominant role. At this same time, DCSL was in the process of expanding its international operations. Building on its base of operations in Britain and Jamaica, the company extended its sales to 175 countries by the end of the 1970s, with production facilities in 25 countries, acquisitions of French wine and champagne producers (Barton and Guestier and Mumm's), and a partnership with the Japanese brewery Kirin to provide whisky to East Asians. In 1981, DCSL was the second-largest Canadian multinational in terms of its worldwide assets.[2]

But Seagram (and its rival Hiram Walker) were most unusual examples of Canadian multinationals. The largest and most enduring Canadian companies operating in global markets have historically been in two areas: natural resources (Alcan, Inco, MacMillan Bloedel) and finance (banking and insurance). The first is not surprising, given the country's resource base; the success of Canadian financial institutions abroad may reflect the strength of a national branch-based system and their (sometimes exaggerated) reputation for prudence. But in most other fields, particularly in manufacturing and marketing, with the exception of specific firms such as Massey-Ferguson or Research in Motion, Canada has not been a major performer.[3] How can we account for the significance of Canadian firms in the alcoholic beverage industry for such an extended period?

The answer, or at least part of it, may be found in Sam Bronfman's remarks. The alcoholic beverage industry covers a wide range of products, including beer, wine, and a variety of distilled spirits: whisky, gin, vodka, rum, tequila, and so on. Except for beer, the Seagram companies did indeed produce all of these products (as well as mixers), but Seagram's reputation rested for many years on the sale of "blended" whiskies, so much so that Sam Bronfman was frequently criticized by the 1960s for his neglect of "white goods" (gin and vodka) and concentration on whisky.

Although marketing created a kind of cosmopolitan effect in the late twentieth century, historically there have been cultural patterns for the kind of alcoholic beverage (or other inebriant) preferred in various societies. In that context, whisky in various forms has been the liquor of choice in Anglo-American communities – or perhaps more accurately regions settled by Scots-Irish since the 1500s, including the United States and Canada (and to a lesser extent other regions of the British Empire). In Scotland, whisky was distilled from barley; the Canadian distilleries largely focused on the production of rye whisky as did their counterparts in the northeastern United States; and in the American South, corn provided the base for "bourbon" whisky. Bronfman built Seagram's market by offering "blends" of these different varieties, which for reasons unique to the post-Prohibition era proved to be an effective form of branding.[4]

In terms of the main thesis of this volume, what is interesting about the history of Seagram and Hiram Walker is that they flourished in an era (from the

1930s to the 1980s) when barriers to globalization were substantial and complex: their expansion into both the US and British (European) markets were to some extent shaped by the need to adapt to government policies that deliberately sought to stymie foreign competition and protect "domestic" producers. It is perhaps ironic that both companies experienced an eclipse of their fortunes in the 1990s when restrictions on international trade were collapsing. In a sense, these Canadian companies found a way to be "selective" in their strategic adaptation to global markets at a time when the world's trading system was inhospitable to any form of globalization.

Samuel Bronfman was, of course, an improbable purveyor of whisky: the Bronfman brothers who transformed Seagram into a major player in North America in the 1930s to 1940s were not Scots-Irish Protestants, but descendants of Russian Jews who immigrated to Manitoba in 1889. However, the circumstances that propelled them into that role reflected another Anglo-American tradition: the effort to eradicate the consumption of alcohol. The introduction of Prohibition on a local level in Manitoba in the early 1900s paradoxically attracted the Bronfmans into the marketing of whisky across Canada, and the imposition of national Prohibition in the United States in the 1920s provided their opportunity to mount an export venture that paved the way for entry into the much larger American market when the "Noble Experiment" ended in 1933.

The expansion of Seagram into global markets beyond North America could also be characterized as in part a reflection of the economic and cultural predominance of the United States in the quarter century following the Second World War. The initial impetus for expansion was to meet the demands of American military service personnel in Europe and East Asia, primarily for whisky; and although the particular circumstances that led to Seagram's first foray into overseas investment were somewhat idiosyncratic, by the mid-1960s the company was only one of many American (and Canadian) firms seeking to exploit the advantages conferred by prosperity at home by investing in what were seen as the emerging economies of a unified Western Europe and a reviving Japan. After 1980, as Teresa da Silva Lopes has highlighted, the competitive environment in the alcoholic beverages industry (as elsewhere) became more crowded as older companies (Allied Domecq and Pernod Ricard) merged and new entrants (Diageo and Grand Metropolitan) challenged the dominant position that had been occupied by Anglo-American firms. Although Seagram sustained its global sales volume through the 1980s, it no longer held the commanding lead established in the immediate post-war epoch.[5]

Seagram now no longer exists, except as a brand name for some alcoholic beverages marketed by Pernod Ricard and mixers sold by Coca-Cola. The events that led to this ignominious end have less to do with the competitive environment in the industry than with the curious dynamics of family controlled enterprises. In the 1990s, the heir presumptive to leadership at Seagram, Edgar Bronfman Jr (Sam's grandson) decided to abandon the family tradition and transform the company into an "entertainment conglomerate," buying, among other things, the film company Universal Studios and the Music Corporation of America – acquisitions that old-line Bronfman associates such as Leo Kolber termed the "dumbest deal of the century." After several years of stagnant returns, Edgar Jr was persuaded to merge the company with a French entity, Vivendi, whose chief executive, Jean Marie Messier, proved even more incompetent, driving the combined operation into bankruptcy by 2001, less than one year after the merger. By this time, Seagram itself was reduced to a neglected subsidiary, having lost more than half of its market share in the United States, and the remnant was sold to Diageo in the wake of the Vivendi merger. The Bronfmans, although hardly left in penury, had sustained major losses to both their wealth and reputations.[6]

The denouement of the Seagram saga is a reminder that the affairs of a particular company cannot be explained entirely as a result of broader competitive trends, especially in the alcoholic beverage industry where, at least up until the 1980s, proprietary or family-controlled firms such as Seagram predominated. The personal characteristics of key players, intra-family vendettas, and inheritance struggles have influenced business decisions in these circumstances, for better or worse. But in some respects, the bizarre implosion of the Seagram empire may reflect changing cultural attitudes towards alcoholic consumption in general and the decline of whisky in particular.

The Conquest of America

In 1835, a German immigrant named Jacob Hespeler settled in the town of Preston, Ontario, and over the next two decades established a range of business operations, including a grist mill, a sawmill, a gas factory, and a distillery, the Granite Mills and Waterloo Distillery, which produced whisky from the surplus rye of the grist mill and was run by his younger brother William with two partners. In 1864, William hired Joseph E. Seagram as a bookkeeper, who married into the family and acquired Hespeler's share in the business. By 1883, Seagram had bought out the other partners, and in 1911, he renamed the distillery Joseph E. Seagram & Sons, which marketed several locally prominent brands of rye whisky, including Seagram's 83 and Seagram's V.O. Joseph Seagram became involved in Ontario politics and horse breeding as well. Seven years after his death in 1919, the company issued its first public stock.[7]

The Seagram distillery was one of many that proliferated in Ontario during the late nineteenth century. In the Windsor area in southern Ontario, an American immigrant, Hiram Walker, established a general store in 1838 and later a distillery, whose products also found a market across the border in Michigan in the years following the Reciprocity Treaty of 1854. Walker relocated to Detroit a decade later, but his enterprises, which included real estate and a gas and water company in what was designated "Walkerville" continued to thrive. Walker died in 1899, but the various enterprises including the Walker distillery remained in family hands until 1926. A similar path was pursued by an Englishman, Henry Corby, who established a distillery near Belleville, Ontario, in the 1850s to supply his general store customers with whisky, and who, like Joseph Seagram, later entered politics and bequeathed the business to his sons. Two other English immigrants, William Gooderham and James Worts, set up a grain mill in Toronto, followed by a distillery in the 1840s. The Gooderham and Worts distillery, part of an industrial complex that included a woollens mill and stockyard, was the largest in Canada by the late nineteenth century, accounting for almost half of the country's distilled spirits. Like the Seagram, Walker, and Corby enterprises, it remained a family business until the mid-1920s.[8]

For the most part, these companies served a regional market, much like their counterparts in the United States in this era, although Gooderham and Worts exported its products to Quebec and England, and Hiram Walker sold whisky in Michigan. In both cases, however, national and interprovincial import duties and the growing temperance movement provided barriers to larger-scale operations. In that context, the major impetus for the expansion of the industry to national markets was provided, ironically, by the introduction of Prohibition, on a local and provincial level in Canada during the early decades of the twentieth century and across the United States through the passage of the federal Volstead Act and the Eighteenth Amendment in 1919–20. In the early 1920s, however, the prospects for the liquor industry in Canada seemed bleak to the heirs of these family distilleries because virtually every province outside Quebec had adopted some form of restriction on the sale of alcoholic beverages within their jurisdictions. The impetus for change came from a new group of entrepreneurs who were more prepared to take risks on the outskirts of the law.[9]

Among these were the Bronfman brothers – Harry, Abe, Sam, and Allan – whose parents had emigrated from Russia to Manitoba in 1889 to take up wheat farming. When that did not work out, the family moved to Brandon and pursued various businesses. By the early 1900s, the brothers were running hotels in towns around the province and in Saskatchewan. Sam's eldest son, Edgar, later described their "hotels" as "a euphemism for a bar, a pool table, a kitchen and several rooms upstairs."[10] The liquor business was the most profitable part of these enterprises and was threatened by the arrival of Prohibition in the Prairie Provinces in 1915–16. But the Bronfmans discovered that interprovincial mail order sales of liquor were permitted under federal law and moved into this field, with Sam Bronfman preparing catalogues emulating those of the Hudson's Bay Company that were distributed across the country.[11]

This loophole was closed in 1918, but by then a much larger market loomed as the United States moved towards national Prohibition. Neither the federal nor provincial governments in Canada blocked the export of alcoholic beverages to the United States, while collecting excise fees, which the Bronfmans meticulously paid. The export trade of course involved dealing with American bootleggers, which posed some unusual risks: Paul Matoff, a Bronfman in-law was murdered in Saskatchewan in 1922, and soon thereafter, the family reduced its operations there. By the mid-1920s, however, the Bronfmans had set up "export houses" along the Canadian/US border and shifted operations to the French islands of St. Pierre and Miquelon after 1929 when Canada succumbed to US government pressure to ban export sales of liquor.[12]

Supplying the burgeoning American market became a major element in the Bronfmans' liquor operations. In 1923, Harry and Sam Bronfman went to Louisville, Kentucky, acquired a defunct distillery, and moved it to Ville LaSalle near Montreal. Montreal was chosen as the best site because it was the province least likely to adopt Prohibition, the land was cheap (the LaSalle site was purchased at less than C$1,000 per acre), and the Bronfmans already had a warehouse there for its mail order business as well as financial and political connections. The revamped distillery at Ville LaSalle opened three years later and soon was producing 3 million gallons of alcohol per year, three times the scale required for the Canadian market and larger than any other distillery in Canada, including Gooderham-Worts. Montreal was to become the headquarters of the Bronfman interests.

In 1926, Sam Bronfman, who was emerging as the leading figure in the family business, and his younger brother Allan, went to Glasgow to meet with the heads of the Distillers Company Ltd (DCL), the largest consortium of scotch producers in that country. Although the Bronfmans produced a range of alcoholic beverages for their illicit American clients, scotch was regarded as the highest-quality whisky, and DCL, which had taken on new partners and expanded its production, was anxious to develop its export market. After some bargaining, and a visit by DCL representatives to the LaSalle distillery, a deal was struck in 1927 through which the Bronfman family became the main recipient and distributor of DCL scotch in North America through a new company, Distillers Corporation Ltd, capitalized at US$2.5 million.

Shortly thereafter, the partners acquired the properties of Joseph E. Seagram & Sons. Although the Waterloo distillery was operating at a relatively low level, the province of Ontario had moved from Prohibition to a system of government-controlled liquor sales; and more crucially, Seagram had a large inventory of whisky, which could be marketed under the established Seagram's 83 and V.O. brands to US customers. The partnership was reconstituted as Distillers Corporation-Seagram Ltd, with Sam Bronfman as vice president but de facto chief executive.[13]

The Bronfmans, however, were not alone in exploiting the opportunities presented by Prohibition. The Hatch brothers, Harry and Herb, had been bartenders in Belleville and Whitby, Ontario, in the early 1900s. Like the Bronfmans, they moved into the mail order liquor business during the First World War, establishing a warehouse in Montreal, and then into supplying bootleggers in the American Midwest, relying on fast boats across Lakes Erie and Ontario. In 1921, Sir Mortimer Davis, a Montreal businessman prominent in the tobacco and liquor industries, hired Harry Hatch to run the Corby distillery in Belleville (Hatch later purchased control of Corby). Two years later, Hatch, with financial backing from Davis, acquired control of the Gooderham-Worts distillery. In 1927, Hatch took over the Hiram Walker operation in Windsor, which provided him with a large distillery with a well-known product, Canadian Club whisky, just over the border with the United States. Sam Bronfman rightly saw Hatch as the most substantial rival for control of the Canadian liquor business and sought to lure away key managers whenever possible, including Fred Willkie, who designed Hiram Walker's distilleries, and Maxwell Henderson, an accountant who later became auditor general of Canada.[14]

The imminent repeal of Prohibition in the United States in 1933 excited a flurry of activity on both sides of the border. Hatch formed a partnership with National Distillers in the United States (which had survived Prohibition by producing "medicinal" whisky) to build the largest distillery in the world at Peoria, Illinois. Sam Bronfman returned to Glasgow with a proposal to maintain the partnership with Seagram (scheduled to end that year) and to join forces with another US company, Schenley, which, he assured the "scotch lords," would give them a virtual monopoly over the American market. But the DCL directors turned down the offer, and Sam, having been alerted by his brother Harry to the availability of the large Rossville Union distillery in Lawrenceburg, Indiana, proposed instead to buy out the Scottish partners, giving the Bronfmans control of DCL-Seagrams. This was accepted; after returning to the New World, Sam Bronfman's negotiations with Lew Rosenstiel of Schenley's also collapsed. This set the stage for Seagram's entry into the United States.

Although conceived in some haste, the strategy pursued by the Bronfmans for their American invasion was well thought out. First, in contrast to Hatch and Hiram Walker, they chose not to build new plants but rather to acquire existing distilleries, many of which were still moribund and relatively inexpensive. The Indiana distillery was reorganized as Joseph E. Seagram & Sons, which became the corporate identity of the company. Later in 1933, Harry located another distillery in Maryland, the Calvert Company, set up as a second company under DCSL. The Seagram and Calvert companies then became the umbrella for the acquisition of eighteen other distilleries between 1934 and 1943, culminating with the takeover of the Frankfort distillery in Kentucky, providing them with a huge inventory of whisky and an established brand name, Four Roses.[15]

Second, the Bronfmans focused their efforts on the marketing of "blended" whisky: this was somewhat risky in a US market in which regional preferences between rye and corn (bourbon) liquor had predominated before Prohibition. But Sam Bronfman correctly perceived that a new generation of imbibers had matured since 1919, less wedded to tradition, and indeed during the Prohibition era they had been fortunate to find anything better than the "white lightning" produced by local bootleggers. The Bronfmans had been developing a "blended" whisky since the late 1920s, based on their access to DCL scotch, and they had a good inventory to draw upon. Third, Sam Bronfman conceived of a marketing strategy that emphasized "quality" and "moderation," in part to circumvent a possible revival of Prohibition sentiment, but also to convey the message that blended whiskies were somehow less potent than "straights" and thus more "respectable" – advertisements for Seagram products featured distinguished gentlemen sipping whisky in their mahogany-panelled clubrooms. In retrospect, this may seem to be a strange approach to selling liquor, but it suited an era shaped by economic hardship and the slow retreat of the forces of social morality.

Sam Bronfman's influence, both in the industry and within his own company, grew steadily through the 1930s. He chose to locate the Seagram headquarters in New York, which over the next decade became his own centre of operations, even though DCSL remained a Canadian company. The decision to establish US production was straightforward because the American government continued to impose a stiff duty on imports; New York was chosen because of the financial support provided by the Bankers Trust, but also because of its connections to the advertising business. Sam Bronfman hired a former military man, Frank Schwengel (usually designated "General" Schwengel in public relations handouts), to run the US Seagram's sales operations. But Schwengel was intended primarily to inspire morale in the troops who fanned out around the country to promote Seagram products. Sam Bronfman retained control over the content of the message. Even in the 1950s, his son Edgar recalled, Sam was the "czar" when it came to marketing, playing a hands-on role in developing advertising copy. By the end of the 1930s, he had transformed Seagram into virtually his personal domain, even though the Bronfmans controlled somewhat less than 40 per cent of the outstanding shares (of which three-quarters were claimed by Sam Bronfman). Harry and Abe were eased out of the company, and Allan was reduced to a minor role. Sam and his family moved to Tarrytown, New York, and built a new headquarters in New York, designed by the European architect Mies van der Rohe, which opened in 1957.

But for all the Bronfmans, the move into the US market had been a major windfall. In the mid-1920s, their collective assets were worth US$3.5 million; by 1951, this had risen to close to US$20 million. Until that time, Seagram in the United States was in close competition with Schenley: each held about 25 per cent of the market for alcoholic beverages, with Hiram Walker lagging at 10 per cent. But by the end of the 1950s, Seagram had moved well ahead of its rivals, with one-third of the American market and a widening array of products, including rum from Jamaica, California wines, scotch from Scotland, and a growing presence in Latin America through arrangements with local distillers.[16]

Expansion Overseas

Before the Second World War, the consumption of whisky, like Prohibition, was largely a North American affair. Scotch whisky of course had an international reputation, reflecting in part the ubiquitous presence of the British Empire and the Scots who populated its far-flung borders, but even in the home isles, gin and rum had a larger market. Not surprisingly, Seagram did little overseas business in its early years under the Bronfmans.

The post-war years opened up new opportunities, however, as American forces stationed abroad in occupied Germany and Japan, and then more widely deployed as the Cold War spread into East Asia, provided a captive market of sorts for American goods, including alcoholic beverages. Sam Bronfman would later be criticized for focusing almost exclusively on the post exchange stores, but this was not entirely fair. In the early 1950s, he established a Seagram Overseas Corporation hiring Quintin Gwyn and Frank Marshall to coordinate sales efforts in Western Europe and Latin America. These ventures were not without hazard, however, as Seagram managers had to deal with local sales representatives of uncertain quality in an unfamiliar environment. One example was Prince Dimitri Romanov, who was reputed to be a (somewhat distant) claimant to the throne of the czars and boasted numerous contacts with the European aristocracy. Unhappily, Prince Dimitri had to be let go eventually because he was found to be spending more on social events for the likes of the Duke and Duchess of Windsor than was likely to be recouped through sales.[17] Other perils included the loss of an admittedly small market in China with the Communist takeover there and the more damaging imposition of Prohibition by the King of Saudi Arabia (site of the large American-owned Aramco oil operation) in 1952. Nevertheless, Marshall could claim in 1957 that Seagram had increased overseas sales of whisky and gin from 150,000 to 500,000 cases in the previous ten years (although this represented about 5 per cent of total sales for 1957).[18]

More critical for the longer-term international expansion of Seagram were steps towards production outside North America. Here development was shaped less by strategic thinking than by a convergence of unanticipated events and unpalatable (at least to Sam Bronfman) choices. In 1935 he discovered that Harry Hatch had once again stolen a lead, by acquiring the Ballantine distillery in Dumbarton, Scotland, providing a steady supply of aged scotch and, more important, a brand name to be added to the Hiram Walker line. Sam's response was to recruit James Barclay, who had handled the Ballantine negotiations for Hatch, to help Seagram find its own supplies of scotch. Barclay obliged by assisting in the acquisition of Robert Brown (United Kingdom) Ltd in Glasgow. Maxwell Henderson, DCSL's financial vice president, described the Robert Brown operation as "a three room office," with some "stocks of whisky in various bonded warehouses ... which Barclay happened to own."[19] But Barclay spent the next few years gathering odd lots of scotch to add to the Brown inventory (which required at least ten years' aging before it could be marketed in any case); most usefully, in 1950, he brought to Sam's attention the prospect of acquiring Chivas Brothers of Aberdeen, a company that did not produce its own scotch but was the supplier of whisky and grocery needs to the royal family, enabling it to display a "Royal Warrant" on its trademark to boost sales to aristocrats and gentry throughout the British Isles. Combining the purchase of Chivas Brothers with the acquisition of a distillery at Strathisla/Glenlivet, and a warehouse of bonded scotch, Barclay's deal gave Seagram the base for its own brand of "high class" whisky.[20]

Meanwhile, Sam Bronfman had discovered a potential new market that involved investment abroad. During the Second World War, when there were restraints on the use of grain for alcohol, limiting new whisky production, he began using molasses imported from the Caribbean to produce rum, marketed under the "Captain Morgan" label. In the post-war period, he enthusiastically set out to become "rum king of the world," acquiring plantations in Jamaica and several smaller rum distillers. The British market seemed the best for expansion of this new venture, and he arranged for the construction of a large warehouse and processing plant at Liverpool, which eventually was folded into the Robert Brown organization.[21]

All of these activities involved the investment of funds from North America, and by 1953, Robert Brown had advances of more than £3.8 million from DCSL and the US subsidiary Joseph Seagram. At this point, however, Sam Bronfman had to confront the maze of restrictions on capital exports that had been erected in Britain since the end of the Second World War. Confronted by the loss of overseas assets during the war and the country's need to rebuild its export markets, the Labour government had established a range of controls over imports of goods and capital, and repatriation of foreign assets and income, administered by a variety of agencies, including the Board of Trade; Exchange Control, administered by the Bank of England; the Capital Issues Committee, which monitored new investments from abroad; and, of course, Inland Revenue. Bronfman had set out to avoid (or at least reduce) import duties by bottling rum in England imported from Jamaica (which as part of the Sterling Bloc was not subject to duty) and, incidentally, to market Seagram's own whiskies in the United Kingdom by having them bottled in Scotland by Robert Brown. He may have anticipated that the return of the Conservatives under Churchill in 1952 would lead to a dismantling of controls, but given the continuing weakness of the pound, the new government chose to retain them. So Sam Bronfman was faced with the fact that neither the investments in Robert Brown nor the earnings from rum sales (nor for that matter from exports of scotch) were likely to be released soon.[22]

While Sam fumed in New York, Maxwell Henderson and John Chiene, the manager of Robert Brown that Henderson had brought in to replace Barclay, argued that Seagram should convert its short-term loans to the Scottish company into a permanent capital investment that would enable it to secure more financing to expand operations in the rum and whisky business, not only for the United Kingdom but prospectively for the European Common Market, which came to fruition in 1957 (although Britain was excluded for fifteen years as it turned out). After further sterling crises in 1957 and 1959, and pressure from his son and heir apparent, Edgar, Sam reluctantly agreed to the proposal. In 1964, a new distillery for Chivas opened in Paisley, and one year later, Seagram (United Kingdom) Ltd took over all the Seagram operations in the United Kingdom.[23]

This event inaugurated more than a decade of international expansion. Seagram (United Kingdom) moved into Ireland, eventually taking over the long-established Bushmill's Irish whisky concern. In France, acquisitions included the wine exporters Barton and Guestier, a "major interest" in the vermouth maker Noilly Prat, and 50 per cent of the Mumm family companies. An even more ambitious alliance was made with the brewery company Kirin, in Japan, to exploit the newfound Japanese enthusiasm for American whisky. Alliances were formed with established distillers such as the Ibarzal family in Argentina and others in Mexico and Venezuela. Although the results of these initiatives took some time to take effect, they would substantially transform Seagram's operations: in 1971, overseas sales accounted for less than 15 per cent of the revenues for all DCSL companies. By 1987, international sales surpassed volume in the United States, and 35 per cent of Seagram's assets were located in twenty-five countries outside North America.[24]

A variety of elements played a role in these developments. By the mid-1960s, Sam Bronfman's one-man rule of the Seagram companies was beginning to diminish, and in any case, he became more receptive to new initiatives overseas – although clinging to his loyalty to blended whisky as the centrepiece of the company's operations. His son, Edgar, who was appointed president of the Seagram Company in New York in 1957 (but by his own admission did not exercise real control until the late 1960s), was interested in overseas business. He published an article – or at least the article bore his name – in the *Columbia Journal of World Business* that emphasized the significance of international investment for American business.[25] When he finally wrested authority from Sam, Edgar established a Seagram Overseas Sales Company (later christened the "House of Seagram") to coordinate operations abroad, and he lived for a time in London to demonstrate his commitment to foreign initiatives.

In a larger context, the decade of the 1960s (up until 1973) was an era when American businesses generally were enthusiastically moving overseas, albeit not always wisely: between 1960 and 1970, US private direct foreign investment more than doubled from US$32 billion to US$78 billion, with the largest increases in European and Asian markets.[26] Seagram was, of course, a Canadian-owned company, but the US subsidiary played the lead role in international expansion, and both Sam and Edgar Bronfman increasingly saw themselves as Americans, at least in terms of their business orientation (Sam's younger son, Charles, chose to remain in Montreal and retained a stronger identification with Canada as well as a more sceptical view of the antics of his brother's family). Being perceived as "American" may have been an advantage in this era: as Jurgen Osterhammel and Niels Petersson have noted in their history of globalization, during the period from the end of the Second World War through the mid-1970s, American culture and its products attained a greater degree of influence, even among Europeans, than previously or in the more recent past.[27]

This dramatic expansion abroad boosted sales by 128 per cent between 1965 and 1975 but could not mask a longer-term problem: the erosion of its traditional market and declining profits. In 1955, earnings had run at 11 per cent of sales, but this deteriorated to 6.5 per cent a decade later and to 4.5 per cent by 1975. A fundamental issue, in addition to the cost of expansion, was the decline of demand for blended whiskies, Seagram's staple, in the United States: between the late 1940s and the 1970s, blends had fallen from more than 80 per cent to less than 30 per cent of the market for alcoholic beverages. The challenge was less from "straights" (rye and bourbon) than the generational shift to "whites" (gin and vodka) and wine, and more broadly, a return if not to Prohibition, then to a healthier, or at least less inebriated, lifestyle. The Bronfmans had not ignored these trends: as early as the 1940s, Sam was buying California wineries (Paul Masson and Christian Brothers) and bringing out gin and vodka lines; Edgar's international investments had focused on acquiring French wines and cordials. In 1977, Edgar hired Philip Beekman, who had directed marketing for Colgate-Palmolive, to secure a new image for Seagram products. But in the world of liquor, branding is fate, and Seagram was inevitably associated with whisky – and "blended" whisky at that.[28]

Fugue

Respite for Seagram came from an unusual quarter: investments made decades earlier by the Bronfmans in the oil industry. After the Leduc oil strike in 1947, Allan Bronfman had taken a more than casual interest in the industry, persuading Sam to invest in a Canadian company, Royalite, in 1950. Three years later, Sam arranged for the US Seagram company to take over a small Oklahoma driller, Frankfort Oil – Edgar Bronfman maintained later that he had pointed out to his father that under the US Oil Depletion Allowance rebate, losses incurred by the oil company could offset taxes on Seagram's profits. When he became president of Seagram in New York, Edgar expanded Frankfort Oil's operations and, by the mid-1960s, could point out that the tax benefit had accrued US$38 million in tax benefits to Seagram over the previous decade. In 1963, Edgar tackled a bigger prize, the Texas Pacific Oil & Coal Company. Although Seagram was obliged to put up US$65 million and borrow another US$50 million for the acquisition, by 1975 the cost had been covered through Depletion Allowance tax reductions, and Texas Pacific was contributing almost half of Seagram's revenues.[29]

Although he had supported expansion into the oil business, Edgar Bronfman was appalled by the capital demands required in this industry; and after the 1973 energy crisis, he feared that a new round of oil price hikes could result in the US government imposing price caps that could seriously affect smaller companies like Texas Pacific. When the next energy crisis struck in 1981, he put the company up for sale, finding a buyer in Sun Oil, which paid Seagram

US$2.3 billion (more than four times the book value of Texas Pacific) for the prize. Caught up in the excitement of the era, Edgar took Seagram into a bidding contest for an even larger oil company, Conoco. At this point, however, much bigger players – Shell, Mobil Oil, and the Du Pont chemical company – entered the contest. Edgar wisely withdrew but parlayed the leverage provided by the Conoco shares that Seagram had acquired into an astonishing 24 per cent equity position in Du Pont, one of the largest corporations in the world.[30]

The Du Pont connection was hailed as "the deal of the century," by Jean de Grandpre, chief executive of Bell Canada and a DCSL board member. "It gave [Seagram] a stability that few other companies had. They were not exclusively at the mercy of the liquor business anymore."[31] Between 1981 and 1995 when Seagram sold its interest back to Du Pont, income from Du Pont dividends rose from US$120 million to US$300 million annually, equal to three-quarters of the revenues Seagram generated from its own operations. Possession of this large cash flow provided Seagram with the capacity to sustain itself without incurring new debt or diluting the Bronfman family's equity position.

But this season of prosperity created a state of complacency at Seagram that allowed it to ignore the rising tide of competition in its own industry and to postpone dealing with continuing underlying problems. After his success in orchestrating the Du Pont deal, Edgar devoted more time to his philanthropic interests, particularly his activities with the World Jewish Congress, and with a busy social life (involving many marriages) in New York. Meanwhile, major changes were taking shape in the international markets. Up until the mid-1970s, Seagram's capacity for global expansion reflected not only its own corporate strategy, but the relative decentralization of its rivals: brewers, distillers, and winemakers were focused on their particular products, catering to local tastes, and under family ownership to some degree – a characteristic recognized by Seagram in its negotiations with companies such as Mumm and Noilly Prat in the 1950s and 1960s. In the next twenty years, "globalization" would come to the alcoholic beverages industry, far beyond anything Sam Bronfman envisaged.

In the 1970s, a hotel chain in Britain, Grand Metropolitan, moved into the English brewery business, taking over Watney's among others; it then acquired International Distillers, which included Smirnoff Vodka, J & B Whisky, and Bailey's, followed by Heublein Wines, with a fillip of diversification into fast foods, including Burger King. In 1997, Grand Metropolitan merged with the Guinness brewers to form Diageo (which eventually ended up with most of the Seagram whisky and rum brands, as well as Barton & Guestier). At the same time, two formerly family-owned French aperitif makers, Pernod and Ricard, merged. Subsequently, they acquired Irish Distillers and, in 1994, merged with the British company Allied Lyons/Pedro Domecq (itself the product of a merger of the English Allied Breweries and a Portuguese sherry producer). By this time, Pernod-Ricard included the remnants of Hiram Walker (Canadian Club, Ballantine's scotch, and Courvoisier cognac), Mumm's (acquired from Seagram), and Beefeater gin, among other brands.[32]

Meanwhile, Seagram was undergoing an apparent generational change in leadership. In 1986, Edgar announced, to the surprise of many of his colleagues, including his brother Charles, that he was stepping down as president of Seagram in the United States, to be succeeded by Edgar Jr, his younger son. Junior had gone through a somewhat accelerated period of apprenticeship in the liquor business under the tutelage of Philip Beekman and had run the European subsidiary, House of Seagram, for a couple of years; however, he had previously displayed no interest in the family enterprise, pursuing a rather feckless career as a failed songwriter and movie producer. Nevertheless, Edgar Jr for a while at least did his duty: in 1987, Seagram triumphed over Grand Metropolitan in a bidding war for the cognac company Martell, which had a strong market position in East Asia; and a few years later, Edgar Jr acquired a license to market the Swedish vodka Absolut – at a price that Charles Bronfman thought was excessive, but which did represent a major new international initiative in "white goods" for Seagram.

But Edgar Jr's heart remained in show business: in 1993, he made a failed attempt to take over the media conglomerate Time Warner. Two years later, he was more successful, acquiring Universal Studios/Music Corporation of America from the Japanese company Matsushita, which had experienced alarming losses in its few years in Hollywood. Both Edgar Sr and Edgar Jr set out to persuade the DCSL board to sell Seagram's equity position in Du Pont back to the Delaware behemoth – "the stupidity of it was breathtaking," commented Charles's close associate Leo Kolber who had managed the Bronfman's real estate holdings. Although the final act was not played out until 2000–2001 with the Vivendi merger and bankruptcy, from this point on the earnings of the combined companies (rechristened Seagram-MCA/Universal and eventually simply MCA/Universal) stagnated. The Seagram liquor divisions became neglected if not unwanted relatives, and with little new capital available, its share of the market dwindled even before the Vivendi disaster. In order to finance the floundering movie studio, Seagram closed down virtually all the distilleries in Canada (including Ville LaSalle and the original Seagram site in Waterloo) and sold off the profitable champagne lines, Mumm and Perrier-Jouet.

Before embarking on this misbegotten odyssey, Edgar Sr and Edgar Jr had gone through the motions of conducting a strategic planning review that presented what turned out to be completely unrealistic comparisons of the revenue and earnings prospects of the entertainment business with those of the alcoholic beverage industry, and these were used to persuade the DCSL board to proceed with the divestment of its Du Pont shares. But underlying the rationales were their personal views about the family business. Edgar Sr famously declared that the liquor industry was "boring," a statement that aroused derision even before the final debacle.

But even as he had dutifully carried out his tasks under his father's stern commands, Edgar Sr had expressed uneasiness over the nature of the business, the past association with racketeers, and the alcoholism that he believed had even affected the family, ultimately undermining Sam's judgment. He too had contemplated a leap into show business, proposing to buy into MGM in the 1950s, a venture that his father opposed and that eventually came to naught. Investing in the oil business, wheeling and dealing with the Du Ponts, and presiding over the World Jewish Congress were more rewarding than another year of tracking declining whisky sales and devising new advertising campaigns for vodka. For Junior, there was, as Leo Kolber put it, an "inherited sense of shame at being involved in the liquor business." Not only was the peddling of whisky rather unrespectable, it was out of fashion. How much more exciting to be at the forefront of the predicted "convergence" of new technology and the entertainment business![33]

The Seagram debacle is generally seen as a cautionary tale of the degeneration of family enterprises, a vivid illustration of Sam Bronfman's often-quoted fear: "shirtsleeves to shirtsleeves in three generations." In some respects, the Bronfman saga represented a classic version of what has been called the "Buddenbrooks syndrome," purportedly exemplified by Thomas Mann's fictional account of the decline and fall of a German business dynasty brought about by the internal weaknesses of a family-run enterprise.[34] But the popular image of the founding father's wealth dissipated by the fecklessness and disinterest of the succeeding generation may not be entirely appropriate in this case. Sam's sons Charles and Edgar Sr brought in professional managers and introduced organizational systems in place of their father's arbitrary one-man rule. Even Edgar Jr underwent a period of managerial tutelage before assuming the mantle of chief executive and relied (perhaps to his detriment) on experienced managers in the entertainment business during his ill-fated foray into Hollywood.[35]

It may be worthwhile to contemplate this story in the context of the changing environment of the alcoholic beverages industry: the shifting demand from whisky to "lighter" drinks, the growth of international competition, the mergers that permeated the industry from the 1970s, and the decline of the traditional family firms that had dominated the business throughout much of the twentieth century, in contrast to many other industries. The fate of Seagram's Canadian rival, Hiram Walker, provides a less melodramatic but interesting counterpoint.

Harry Hatch died in 1946, but the Hiram Walker Company had never been quite the "one-man show" that prevailed at Seagram under Sam Bronfman. Professional managers kept the enterprise running, adding a few acquisitions, such as Courvoisier cognac, over the years. In the 1960s, now under the lead- ership of Harry's son, Clifford Hatch, Hiram Walker embarked on a strategy of international expansion. Although Hiram Walker never reached the global dimensions of Seagram, by the end of the 1970s one-quarter of the company's sales were overseas, and there were distilleries operating in Mexico and Spain. Like Seagram, however, Hiram Walker had to deal with shifts in demand: Ca- nadian Club was a well-known brand but in the declining market for whiskies, and consumer confidence dropped when it was revealed that Hiram Walker had surreptitiously reduced the alcohol content (for cost-cutting reasons).[36]

With Seagram apparently surviving on its oil investments, Hiram Walker set out in 1979 to develop a foothold in this field as well, acquiring Consumer Gas Ltd, a Canadian gas utility, and Home Oil of Alberta, which, despite set- backs in its Arctic ventures, was still seen as a major player, with operations in the North Sea, Indonesia, and Australia. Unfortunately for Hiram Walker, Home Oil had also recently taken over a US company, Davis Oil, which had overextended itself with poor results. Nevertheless, by 1981 Hiram Walker had diversified, creating an oil and gas subsidiary, Hiram Walker Resources, which subsequently acquired a share of Interprovincial Pipelines, in partnership with Imperial Oil.

After Clifford Hatch's retirement in 1983, Hiram Walker Resources was seen as a tempting prize by Gulf Canada, or more properly, the real estate tycoons of the Reichmann family who had taken over Gulf. What followed was a very complex bidding war for control of the various parts of Hiram Walker that brought in a variety of players, including at one point a rumoured Seagram interest, which might have been a logical alliance but was rejected by the Hiram Walker board and, in any case, was not a high priority for Seagram's emerging chief executive, Edgar Bronfman Jr. At the end of the contest in 1986, which involved lawsuits and raids by American junk bond speculators, Gulf Canada took over Hiram Walker Resources, and the liquor end of the company wound up in the hands of Allied Lyons, the British brewery consortium that eventually became part of the Pernod Ricard beverage empire in 1994. So the Hatch fam- ily lost control of Hiram Walker, which soon disappeared from the scene as a company more than a decade before the more spectacular crash of Seagram.[37]

Sam Bronfman and Harry Hatch would probably have developed successful enterprises in one industry or another; they chose to enter the whisky field, however, at a fortuitous moment. Before the era of Prohibition, the compa- nies they eventually resuscitated, Seagram and Hiram Walker, served essen- tially local and regional markets, catering to particular tastes, in common with makers of distilled spirits in North America. US Prohibition did not itself cause the creation of an American and continental market, but it temporarily shut down most of the competition and endured long enough to erode traditional commitments to particular types of whisky. This presented an opportunity for the Bronfmans and Hatches to develop national distribution networks and inventories that could be exploited when Prohibition ended, establishing their Canadian "blends" as popular brands in the re-emerging market in the 1930s and 1940s. It was, however, not so much the blended whiskies themselves that produced success, but rather the marketing of them as somehow more "moderate" and "respectable" than the traditional bourbons and ryes.

Similarly, in the decades following the end of the Second World War, Seagram in particular found itself with the core US market that gave it the financial capacity to expand outside North America and to establish a foothold in foreign markets that post-war US military commitments provided in both Europe and East Asia. Seagram and, to a lesser extent Hiram Walker, could flourish in an era of US cultural as well as economic power overseas, advertising their brands as the essentially "American" alcoholic beverages, and acquiring foreign distillers and vintners when they could not sell their own products.

But Canada's "whisky kings," by tying their fortunes so closely to the American market and its growth, were also vulnerable when that economic power began to recede at the same time that domestic (US) consumer preferences began to shift – trends that were becoming evident by the end of the 1970s. In other countries, the alcoholic beverage field was transformed by amalgamations and regional alliances that eclipsed the traditional proprietary firms that had populated the industry for centuries. Perhaps, under different management, more committed to defending their role in the liquor industry, both Seagram and Hiram Walker could have survived, by merging or by forming their own sets of international allies. But there was no such sense of commitment in either case, and so the companies of Canada's whisky kings perished, although their spirits linger on in the brands that can still be found on the shelves of liquor stores – Canadian Club, Crown Royal, Ten High, and Chivas Regal, products purveyed now by Diageo, Pernod Ricard, and the Coca-Cola Company.

NOTES

1 Samuel Bronfman quoted in "The Seagram Structure in the United Kingdom," *BEV/Executive*, 1 May 1966, 12.
2 On DCSL's sales vis-à-vis its competitors, see Teresa da Silva Lopes, "Evolution of Corporate Governance in Global Industries: The Case of Multinationals in Alcoholic Beverages," *Oxford University Economic and Social History Series* (2004): 8–9.

On Seagram's international expansion, see "Seagram's Late Awakening," *Forbes*, 1 February 1973, 25–6; "Offshore Ties Spur Growth at Seagram," *Toronto Globe & Mail*, 21 March 1987.

3 See Jorge Niosi, *Canadian Multinationals* (Toronto: Garamond Press, 1985), 165.

4 Andrea Mandel-Campbell, in *Why Mexicans Don't Drink Molson* (Toronto: Douglas & McIntyre, 2007, 1–5, 141–9), excoriated Molson brewery (and a range of other Canadian companies) for failing to establish "national" brands that could be marketed globally (e.g., the Netherlands and Heineken, Mexico and Corona). Although she proceeds to focus on more familiar themes about Canada's business failings – caution, complacency, and overdependence on government support – the issue of effective branding is interesting. Sam Bronfman (one of the few Canadian entrepreneurs to win praise from Mandel-Campbell) did not market Seagram as a specifically "Canadian" product but rather set out to associate the brand with certain more general characteristics: "quality," "responsibility," and "moderation in drinking." These themes were particularly suitable to the US market after the repeal of Prohibition but also provided a longer-term image for Seagram products. See Lisa Jaconson, "Consumer Reeducation and Industry Rehabilitation: Seagram's Advertising and the Muddled Meanings of Moderation after Repeal" (Paper presented at Business History Conference, St Louis, Missouri, April 2011).

5 Teresa da Silva Lopes, "The Growth and Survival of Multinationals in the Global Alcoholic Beverages Industry," *Enterprise and Society* 4, no. 4 (2003): 592–8.

6 On the fall of Seagram, see Graham Taylor, "From Shirtsleeves to Shirtless: The Bronfman Dynasty and the Seagram Empire," *Business and Economic History On-Line* 4 (2006): 28–36; Nicholas Faith, *The Bronfmans: The Rise and Fall of the House of Seagram* (New York: Thomas Dunne Books, 2006), 246–98; Rod McQueen, *The Icarus Factor: The Rise and Fall of Edgar Bronfman Jr.* (Toronto: Doubleday, 2004).

7 Andrew Thomson, "Seagram, Joseph Emm," in Dictionary of Canadian Biography, vol. 14 (Toronto: University of Toronto/Université Laval, 2003), http://www.biographi.ca/en/bio/seagram_joseph_emm_14E.html.

8 Ronald G. Hoskins, "Walker, Hiram," in Dictionary of Canadian Biography, vol. 12 (Toronto: University of Toronto/Université Laval, 2003), http://www.biographi.ca/en/bio/walker_hiram_12E.html; Dianne Newell, "Gooderham, William, (1790–1881)," in Dictionary of Canadian Biography, vol. 11 (Toronto: University of Toronto/Université Laval, 2003), http://www.biographi.ca/en/bio/gooderham_william_1790_1881_11E.html; and David M. Calnan, "Corby, Henry," in Dictionary of Canadian Biography, vol. 11 (Toronto: University of Toronto/Université Laval, 2003), http://www.biographi.ca/en/bio/corby_henry_11E.html.

9 On Prohibition in Canada, see Craig Heron, *Booze: A Distilled History* (Toronto: Between the Lines, 2003); Gerald Hallowell, *Prohibition in Ontario, 1919–23* (Ottawa: Ontario Historical Society, 1972).

10 Edgar M. Bronfman, *Good Spirits: The Making of a Businessman* (New York: Putnam, 1998), 25.

11 A federal law had been passed in 1878 that allowed "local option" for Prohibition. A national plebiscite in 1898 reaffirmed a commitment to Prohibition, but Prime Minister Laurier, in deference to his Quebec constituents (who alone among the provinces opposed the proposal) declined to proceed with a law to implement it.

12 On the Bronfmans and bootleggers, see James Gray, *Booze: The Impact of Whisky on the Prairie West* (Toronto: MacMillan, 1972); Peter C. Newman, *Bronfman Dynasty* (Toronto: McClelland and Stewart, 1978).

13 Michael Marrus, *Mister Sam: The Life and Times of Samuel Bronfman* (New York: Viking Press, 1991), 109–29; Michael Moss and John Hume, *The Making of Scotch Whisky: A History of the Scotch Whisky Distilling Industry* (Edinburgh: James & James, 1981), 27–9.

14 On Hatch and Hiram Walker, see "Hiram Walker Digs In," *Fortune*, March 1939, 68–73, 95–102; C.W. Hunt, *Booze, Boats and Billions: Smuggling Liquid Gold!* (Toronto: McClelland and Stewart, 1988). Hatch was also involved in the development of the wine industry in Ontario in the 1930s.

15 Mira Wilkins, *The History of Foreign Investment in the United States 1914–1945* (Cambridge, MA: Harvard University Press, 2004), 397–9; Herbert Marshall, Frank Southard Jr, and Kenneth W. Taylor, *Canadian-American Industry* (New York: Atheneum, 1936), 183.

16 "The Seagram Saga: The Man with the Golden Shovel," *BEV/Exec* 28 (1966); "Seagram in the Chips," *Fortune*, December 1948, 98–100.

17 The misadventures of Prince Dimitri can be traced through his correspondence with Quintin Gwyn in the Joseph E. Seagram Papers, Accession 2173, Series II, Box 27, International Expansion (1952–64) files [hereafter designated Seagram Papers].

18 Frank Marshall, "The Story of Seagram Overseas Corporation in the Markets of the World" (Address to Seagram Centennial Sales Conference, 17 September 1957), Seagram Papers, Accession 2126, Series IV, Box 116, Sosco file.

19 Maxwell Henderson, *Plain Talk! Memoirs of an Auditor General* (Toronto: McClelland & Stewart, 1984), 58.

20 Maxwell Henderson, "Robert Brown and Subsidiary Companies," July 1950, Seagram Papers, Accession 2126, Series III, Box 42, Robert Brown files, 1949–50.

21 Samuel Bronfman, *From Little Acorns: The Story of Distillers Corporation-Seagrams Limited* (Montreal: DCSL, 1970), 43–4. This "history" was distributed with the company's 1970 annual report to shareholders.

22 On British import-export controls after the Second World War, see Peter Burnham, *Remaking the Postwar World: ROBOT and British Policy in the 1950s* (London: Palgrave, 2003); Susan Strange, *Sterling and British Policy* (London: Oxford University Press, 1971).

23 See Graham D. Taylor, "Seagram Comes to Scotland: The Role of 'Local Players' in the Overseas Expansion of a Canadian Multinational, 1949–1965," *Business and Economic History On-Line* 7 (2009).

24 John McCarthy, "Seagram's around the World," *Wine and Spirit Magazine*, December 1973, 52–3; "Seagram's Late Awakening," 24–9; Philip Beekman, president, Seagram Co. Ltd, to Montreal Society of Financial Analysts, 7 March 1979, Seagram Papers, Accession 2173, Series II, Box 27, Corporate Operations 1979 file.

25 Edgar M. Bronfman, "Name Your Brand – In Any Market of the World," *Columbia Journal of World Business* IV (November/December 1969): 31–5.

26 Mira Wilkins, *The Maturing of Multinational Enterprise: American Business Abroad from 1914 to 1970* (Cambridge, MA: Harvard University Press, 1974), 330–1.

27 Jurgen Osterhammel and Niels P. Petersson, *Globalization: A Short History* (Princeton, NJ: Princeton University Press, 2006), 132–3. See also Victoria de Grazia, *Irresistible Empire: America's Advance through 20th Century Europe* (Cambridge, MA: Belknap Press of Harvard, 2005); D. Clayton Brown, *Globalization and America Since 1945* (Wilmington, DE: Scholarly Resources, 2003).

28 "Seagram's Late Awakening," 24; Faith, *The Bronfmans*, 200–4.

29 Faith, *The Bronfmans*, 143, 179. Frankfort Oil Company, Net Cash Expenditures and Oil Revenues, 1957–1963, Seagram Papers, Accession 2126, Series I, Box 2, Murray Cohen files; Bronfman, *Good Spirits*, 6–8.

30 Bronfman, *Good Spirits*, 16–20; Adrian Kinnane, *Du Pont: From the Banks of the Brandywine to the Miracles of Science* (Wilmington, DE: E.I. Du Pont de Nemours, 2002), 215–17.

31 Quoted in Rod McQueen, *The Icarus Factor*, 110.

32 Teresa da Silva Lopes, "Brands and the Evolution of Multinationals in Alcoholic Beverages," *Business History* 44, no. 3 (2002): 1–30. Curiously, Burger King ended up under the ownership of Texas Pacific Oil Company.

33 There are many accounts of the collapse of Seagram: Brian Milner, "Broken Spirits," *Globe & Mail Report on Business*, September 2002, 26–36, provides a view from what might be considered Charles Bronfman's perspective. Edgar Bronfman Sr offered his explanations in *Good Spirits*, 165–70. Kolber's comments about Edgar Jr are in Faith, *The Bronfmans*, 246. See also Rod McQueen, *The Icarus Factor*; Jo Johnson and Martine Orange, *The Man Who Tried to Buy the World: Jean Marie Messier and Vivendi Universal* (New York: Viking Press, 2003); Devin Leonard, "The Bronfman Saga: From Rags to Riches to …" *Fortune*, 25 November 2002, 108–18.

34 See Fermin Allende, "Poor Thomas Buddenbrook! Family Business in Literature," *Business & Economic History On-Line* 7 (2009). Allende noted that Mann's novel did not exactly match the popular notion of the "Buddenbrooks syndrome," as the family maintained its prosperity through at least four generations before

succumbing. Allende attributed the first use of the concept to Walt W. Rostow, *The Stages of Economic Growth* (Cambridge: Cambridge University Press, 1960).

35 Probably the best analysis of the structural weaknesses of family firms is offered by Roy Church, "The Family Firm in Industrial Capitalism: International Perspectives on Hypothesis and History," *Business History* 34, no. 4 (October 1993): 17–43. For a more extended discussion of the pertinence of this critique to the Bronfmans, see Graham D. Taylor, "From Shirtsleeves to Shirtless: The Bronfman Dynasty and the Seagram Empire," *Business & Economic History On-Line* 4 (2006): 33–6.

36 "Hiram Walker Resources Ltd.," *International Directory of Company Histories* (Chicago: St. James Press, 1988).

37 On the Hiram Walker takeover, see Walter Stewart, *Too Big to Fail: Olympia & York Behind the Headlines* (Toronto: McClelland & Stewart, 1993), 111–13, 124–30; Anthony Bianco, *The Reichmanns* (New York: Crown Publishing, 1996), 466–70. Clifford Hatch Jr, who had succeeded his father as president of Hiram Walker worked for a time for Allied Lyons, then went into investment banking.

8

I Was Canadian: The Globalization of the Canadian Brewing Industry

MATTHEW J. BELLAMY

Why is it that Canadian beer brands and brewers do not have a significant global presence? After all, one would be hard pressed to think of a nation more naturally advantaged when it comes to brewing. The vast northern territory has all of the natural ingredients – barley, hops, and fresh water – necessary to manufacture a world-class beer. Furthermore, there is a legacy of commercial brewing in Canada that stretches back over three and a half centuries. Canada's oldest and most successful brewers – Molson, Labatt, Carling, Sleeman, and Alexander Keith – began their operations earlier than most of the global firms that have since taken them over. It is not that Canadian beers are inferior. Beginning in the late nineteenth century, Canadian ales, lagers, and stouts won international awards for taste, quality, and uniqueness. Many of these award-winning beers were once copiously consumed at home. A strong beer-drinking culture has existed in Canada since the Conquest. But Canadian brewers have had a difficult time penetrating foreign markets, leading one commentator to ask recently: "Why don't Mexicans drink Molson?"[1]

This chapter will explore that question and the interrelated one, why is it that Canada's oldest and largest beer companies no longer exist as autonomous agents? By analysing the country-specific, industry-specific, and firm-specific determinants of growth and survival, this chapter offers a multilayered institutional analysis of the historical determinants that have prevented Canada from creating global enterprises in what was one of the earliest, most successful, and most diverse industries in the history of Canadian manufacturing.

Layers of Institutional Analysis

When theorists speak of "growth," they are referring to the increase in size of a firm as a process of development. This can happen either organically or through mergers and acquisitions. The concept of "survival," on the other hand, refers to the maintenance of a firm's autonomy of action. In this respect, non-survivals, or "exits," include firms that have either been liquidated, dissolved, discontinued, or absorbed, as well as firms that have been acquired by, or merged with, other firms, even if they were able to retain their corporate identity and continuity of existence for a significant period of time.[2] Growth and survival therefore have a dynamic element and as such can only be fully understood as historical phenomena.

In her classic study *The Theory of the Growth of the Firm*, Edith Penrose argued that growth and survival are consequences of a complicated interaction of a company's resources, capabilities, and market opportunities. The pace and direction of growth is determined by a firm's technical and managerial capabilities as well as by developments in the marketplace. According to Penrose, growth is strongly associated with the number of competitive advantages of the firm. In the long run, the profitability, growth, and survival of an enterprise depend on its ability to establish "relatively impregnable bases" (e.g., by raising barriers to entry or using restrictive practices) from which to adapt and extend their operations in an uncertain, changing, and competitive world.[3]

Although Penrose and other theorists concede that there is no "secret recipe" that explains survival and sustained growth of the firm, they do maintain that it is possible to monitor the evolution of firms by making systematic comparisons between the largest multinationals from different countries and assessing the type of relations they have developed among themselves.[4] The distinctive nature of studying the evolution of multinationals is that, beyond the multiproduct and multiplant dimensions, the firm also needs to possess other ownership advantages over competing indigenous firms when dealing with different economies and cultures.[5] What is unique to the alcoholic beverage sector, of which brewing is a part, is that it is a case of a non-science-based industry in which firms have both survived a long time and grown very large.

So why have some firms in the alcoholic beverage industry come to dominate global markets while others, like Molson, Sleeman, and Labatt, have failed to survive as autonomous firms? In order to answer this question, the chapter analyses the industry-specific, country-specific, and firm-specific determinants that have led to growth and survival in the brewing industry.

The first section of this chapter analyses the industry-specific determinants of growth. These determinants are predominantly exogenous (i.e., beyond the control of the firm) and affect all firms within the industry equally. The three industry-specific determinants that had the greatest impact on the global brewing beverage industry since the 1960s are the changing patterns of consumption, the level of industry competition, and the nature of the industry's structure.[6]

The second section of the chapter examines the country-specific determinants of growth and survival. Such determinants are embedded in the institutional and natural environment and include government regulation, taxation, the national system of corporate governance, and the processes, structures, and cultures that have fostered or hindered the growth of the firm. Since the publication of Geert Hofstede's monumental study, there has been a growing body of literature on the role of culture in the growth, survival, and internationalization of the firm.[7] Culture, corporate or otherwise, affects everything from consumer behaviour, to industry structure, to the nature of government-business relations, to appraisals of performance, to management objectives and the humanization of work.[8] As will be seen subsequently, this was the case in the Canadian brewing industry, and it is a helpful lens through which to examine why Canadian brewers have been relatively unsuccessful at penetrating foreign markets.

The third and final section of this chapter analyzes the firm-specific determinants of growth and survival in the Canadian brewing industry since 1960. The focus is on Canada's biggest brewers, those firms that have dominated the domestic brewing industry and thus had the greatest chance of going global. Unlike country- and industry-specific determinants, these determinants of growth are endogenous to the firm; that is, they are factors that a firm can control. Such determinants include strategic choices, corporate structures, brands and marketing knowledge, entrepreneurial talent, first-mover advantage, technology and economies of scale and scope. In her recent study of the evolution of multinationals in the alcoholic beverage industry, the business historian Teresa de Silva Lopes argues that firm-specific determinants "are fundamental to explaining the growth and independent survival of firms."[9] As a result, more space will be dedicated to examining these determinants of the growth and survival of those firms operating in the global brewing industry.

It is important to note that these three levels of determinants do not operate in isolation. Rather they over overlap and complement one another, with each level providing important determinants for the growth and survival of firms.

Industry-specific Determinants

Globalization came late to the Canadian brewing industry, as it did to the brewing industry elsewhere.[10] Since the second Industrial Revolution in the late nineteenth century, many firms – with competitive advantages derived from economies of scale and scope – had established production facilities in foreign markets. Geographical expansion into distant markets provided a way for modern industrial enterprises to continue to exploit their comparative advantages. The automobile industry, for instance, began to globalize in the earliest days of mass production. By 1928, Ford and GM were assembling vehicles in twenty-four countries, including Japan, India, Malaysia, and Brazil. Ten years later, both companies were operating large-scale integrated "transplant" facilities in Europe. After the Second World War, an increasing number of businesses – a few of them Canadian[11] – embraced a strategy of foreign direct investment as a means of global growth. Firms from around the world became successful challengers to what the eminent Harvard business historian Alfred Chandler termed "first movers" – those Parsonian industrial organizations like Ford, GM, RCA, Du Pont, and Dow, which had established branch plants in distant lands early in the twentieth century.[12] Having relentlessly expanded the output of their standard production line (i.e., increased their scale) and introduced new sorts of products (i.e., increased their scope), post-war industrial firms invested in new products and new geographical markets in order to grow.[13] The global enterprise thus evolved naturally out of the successful national corporation.

For those firms in the brewing industry, however, globalization did not occur until the end of the twentieth century. Consumer taste, entrenched regional brands, barriers to trade, and convoluted distribution systems made brewing a form of trench warfare: gains for those with global aspirations came only slowly. Until the end of the Second World War, the only international brewer was Ireland's Guinness, which, in reaction to falling sales at home and increased protectionism following the First World War, introduced advertising in Great Britain and established a brewery in London.[14] After 1945, two other brewers that dominated their small home markets, Holland's Heineken and Denmark's Carlsberg, set out to turn their beers into global brands. In most countries, however, brewing remained a local business.

In Canada, the period between 1945 and 1965 witnessed the rise of the "national brewers" and a consolidation of the Canadian brewing industry. As other industries were going global, the brewing industry in Canada was finally shedding its regional skin and stretching out across the nation. Three brewers emerged to dominate the Canadian beer market. By acquiring existing breweries and building new production facilities from the ground up, Canadian Breweries Limited (which later became known as Carling-O'Keefe), Molson, and Labatt came to dominate the national marketplace. By 1965, more than 95 per cent of the total volume of beer consumed by Canadians was being produced by these three firms. They thus became known as the "big three."

Fittingly, the first Canadian brewery to become truly national was E.P. Taylor's Canadian Breweries Limited. Having built a regional giant in Ontario,[15] Taylor set his aim on the national market place.[16] Given the regulatory regime (see "Country-specific Determinants"), having a national reach meant maintaining a physical presence in each of the provinces. As Taylor made note in

a confidential company memo, it was "not practical" for breweries in central
Canada to ship beer to the west and east and compete with local breweries.
Taylor was profoundly aware of the provincial tariff barriers against imports
from other provinces. Therefore, he determined that the proper course was to
purchase two or three prosperous regional concerns.[17] South of the border and
in the beer-producing nations of Europe, going national was far less capital
intensive, leaving them with more capital to diversify geographically. By 1960,
Canadian Breweries Limited had a significant presence in every province except Prince Edward Island,[18] and Carling, O'Keefe, Brading, and Dow had become distinctively national brands.[19] The problem was that while a few brewers
in Canada were developing national brands, a few brewers elsewhere were taking their national brands global (see "Firm-specific Determinants").

For a time, Canadian Breweries reaped the rewards of being the industry's
"first mover," but soon the innovative corporation had competition on the national scene. During the 1950s and 1960s, Molson and Labatt similarly constructed plants across the nation. By the mid-1960s, each of these firms had
a national presence. In Canada, therefore, the brewing industry was characterized by a high degree of concentration. A relatively stable cartel of three
firms, which was supported by the government and maintained by its policy of
erecting high barriers to entry, dominated the national market. Between 1960
and 1990, the big three brewers manufactured between 96 and 98 per cent of
the beer consumed by Canadians. Although concentration was occurring the
world over, the unique character of the Canadian case was that the system of
government regulation mitigated against price-based competition, hampering
the global competitiveness of Canadian firms in the long run (see "Country-
specific Determinants").

By 1990, the biggest beer market was still the United States, and the biggest American brewer was Anheuser-Busch, which made it the indisputable
market leader in the world. That year, the American brewing giant produced
104.6 million hectolitres of beer, which accounted for just over 9 per cent of
total global beer market volume (see Table 8.1). Anheuser-Busch and the other
leading US brewing companies (i.e., Miller and Coors) based their operations
predominantly in the United States and had an exclusive focus on beer.[20] Indeed, Anheuser-Busch derived 85 per cent of its sales from its home market.
As in the past, its foreign expansion took place primarily through exports and
licensing agreements covering production, distribution, and commercializa-
tion activities.

In those less populated countries, like England, Scotland, Germany, and
Canada, where there was a strong tradition of brewing, but where brewers

Table 8.1. World top brewing groups in 1990 (35.1%)

Rank	Brewery	Production Volume (in millions of hL)	Percentage of World Beer Production
1	Anheuser-Busch	104.6	9.1
2	Miller	62.2	5.4
3	Heineken	46.5	4.0
4	Kirin	34.6	3.0
5	Foster's	30.5	2.7
6	Danone	26.0	2.3
7	SAB	25.8	2.2
8	Brahma	25.5	2.2
9	Guinness	24.3	2.1
10	Coors	23.7	2.1

Source: Teresa Da Silva Lopes, *Global Brands*, p. 262.

remained focused on the domestic market and therefore generally lacked international experience beyond exports, the size of the firms remained relatively small from a global perspective.[21] But the size of the home market did not necessarily determine the growth and survival of the firm. Exceptional enterprises like Heineken of the Netherlands, Guinness of Ireland, SAB of South Africa, Foster's of Australia, and Kirin of Japan were able to become large and globally dominant despite the relatively small size of their domestic markets. These firms succeeded by developing corporate strategies, global brands, and market knowledge that allowed them to penetrate foreign markets. Nevertheless, in comparison to other industries, in 1990, brewing remained relatively unconsolidated and local.[22]

However, that changed during the 1990s, as the industry became very concentrated and truly global. Whereas in 1990 the top ten brewers represented 35.1 per cent of the world's market share, by 2000 the top ten brewers controlled 36.9 per cent of the world's beer market. The concentration accelerated thereafter. In 2005, the world's top ten brewing groups represented 54.9 per cent of the world market share. And by 2010, the top ten brewers controlled just under three-quarters (74%) of the world's beer market. Since the 1990s, therefore, leading brewers in advanced economies have launched aggressive global campaigns, resulting in an unprecedented global consolidation. The global consolidation has become a key factor shaping global development as brewing companies achieve greater scale and their beer brands grow in more international markets.

Several factors propelled the industry towards globalization. On the demand side, traditional markets had gone flat. In the main markets of Northern Europe and North America, consumption remained static or declined gently after the mid-1970s, making it difficult for brewers to raise prices in established markets. In the United States, for instance, per capita consumption of beer increased by less than 0.04 per cent between 1975 and 1995, from 80.63 to 83.65 litres of beer per person, per annum.[23] During the same period, per capita consumption of beer in the Netherlands, the home of Heineken, increased from 78.96 to 85.80 litres. In the United Kingdom, the consumption of beer actually increased until 1980 and then declined just slightly over the next decade.[24] This might help explain why most British brewers continued to focus on the domestic market. In Belgium, on the other hand, per capita beer consumption declined substantially during the period, from 130.5 to 104.0 litres.[25] Similarly, per capita beer consumption declined in Denmark from 129.3 litres in 1975 to 124.4 litres in 1995. As a result, Belgium's biggest brewer, Interbrew, and Denmark's Carlsberg geared up their global quest. Canada faced a similar decline in beer consumption. Having reached a post-war high of 86.8 litres in 1975, per capita consumption of beer fell to 80.7 litres in 1985 and then to just 77.1 litres in 1990. By 1995, the level of per capita consumption had fallen even further to 70.1 litres.[26] Unlike Interbrew and Carlsberg, however, Canada's biggest brewers chose to diversify out of beer, for reasons explained subsequently, rather than to seek out new markets elsewhere. Although other brewers were looking beyond the nation's boundary for growth, Canada's big three brewers remained defensive and inward looking.

This was unfortunate because while traditional markets were stagnant, emerging markets were rapidly expanding. Between 1975 and 1995, per capita consumption of beer in Mexico, for instance, increased by 33 per cent.[27] Brazil also witnessed a rapid rise in beer consumption. But it was China, with its large population, demographics, and rising real incomes that held the greatest promise for brewers. In 1995, the *Asian Business Review* predicted that "China is set to become the world's largest beer market by the year 2000."[28] The magazine was wrong in only one regard: not until 2004 did China move ahead of the United States to become the world's biggest beer market, with annual consumption of 300 million hectolitres that year. As barriers to international trade were lowered during the last two decades of the twentieth century, brewers from established markets rushed to gain a foothold in the emerging markets of the world. For country- and firm-specific reasons discussed subsequently, Canada's largest brewers were unable to acquire a lasting share of the global market.

Country-specific Determinants: "Rich by Nature: Poor by Policy"

When it comes to brewing, Canada has long had a comparative advantage. The nation is ideally suited to produce beer. All the necessary natural ingredients – barley, hops, and fresh water – are located within the national boundary. It is not surprising therefore that beer was one of the first commodities to be manufactured in Canada. The history of Canadian commercial brewing stretches back three and a half centuries.[29] Admittedly, a number of other nations could claim a longer legacy. Commercial brewing in Holland, Belgium, Denmark, and Germany dated from the Middle Ages. Nevertheless, Canada's breweries were among the first established in North America. When John Molson took over the operation of a 36-by-60-foot log-built brewery in Montreal in 1786, he laid the foundation for a firm that would go on to be the longest-lived family business in Canadian history and the oldest continuous brewery in North America. In the decades that followed, Alexander Keith (in 1820), John Carling (in 1843), John Sleeman (in 1847), and John Labatt (in 1848) founded the firms that would later dominate the Canadian market, Thus, Canada had not only the natural resources but also the historical legacy that should have enabled, at least in theory, the nation's brewers to compete in the global market place.

One therefore returns to the original question: Why haven't Canadian brewers come to dominate world markets as much as global players have come to dominate the Canada beer market? Part of the answer lies in the nature of government business relations and the country-specific character of regulation and taxation. Perhaps no industry has been as heavily taxed and regulated as the brewing industry. The uniqueness of the Canadian case is that brewers faced a dual system of regulation and taxation. Under the terms of the nation-forming British North American Act of 1867, the provinces had the constitutional power to regulate the retail sale and distribution of intoxicating drink, while the federal government had the power to regulate the production of beer and other alcoholic beverages. At the dawn of the twentieth century, provincial governments took these powers to the extreme when they attempted to legislate the brewing industry out of business. Prohibition had a destructive effect on the Canadian brewing industry. Nationally, the number of breweries in operation was cut in half, from 112 in 1915 to just 66 in 1935.[30] The relatively strong and dynamic growth of the Canadian brewing industry up until the 1920s was retarded by the country-specific determinant of government regulation. Although growth was also restrained during the period of Prohibition south of the border, it was not held back in the beer-producing nations of

Europe. Thus, they continued to grow, while brewers in North America were
battling just to survive.

Bottom feeders like Edward Plunkett Taylor – later dubbed "Excess Profits
Taylor" by his critics – used the opportunity created by Prohibition to capture assets at rock-bottom prices and to construct large breweries that could
capitalize on modern production techniques and advertising. By 1935, Taylor's
company, Canadian Breweries, was twenty times the size of most turn-of-the-
century breweries and represented a new post-Prohibition Canadian reality.
Taylor's aspiration was to create a brewery with national scope. But Canadian
Breweries again ran into the bugbear of provincial legislation. In the period
following Prohibition, provincial governments instituted tariffs and imposed
import quotas that limited out-of-the-province beer or stopped it altogether. As
a result, beer sold in the province had to be produced in the province. Although
good for provincial treasuries, the move ultimately prevented firms within the
Canadian brewing industry from benefiting from economies of scale. The
"shipping brewers" south of the border could sell their products across the nation, which led to larger breweries concentrated in relatively few cities. It also
gave US brewers, like Pabst, Anheuser-Busch, and Coors, a substantial head
start in creating and marketing a few "national brands" – brands they would
eventually take global. Brand development is critical to the growth and survival
of the multinational enterprise in the alcoholic beverage industry.[31] The world's
most successful alcoholic beverage brands have been long established, some
being created as far back as the eighteenth and nineteenth centuries.[32] Although
brewers elsewhere began to look beyond the national boundary for growth, Canadian brewers were concentrating their efforts on dominating and protecting
their share of the domestic market (see "Firm-specific Determinants").

After the Second World War, the nation's brewers – through their lobbying
agency the Brewers' Association of Canada – successfully pressured the federal
and provincial governments to protect them from foreign competition. The
battle with the Prohibitionists during the late nineteenth and early twentieth
centuries had taught the brewers the value of lobbying.[33] And after the war, they
again put this practice to use. The federal government responded to the brewers' pressure tactics by increasing the tariff on imported beer to a minimum
of 12.5 per cent per gallon.[34] The brewers had come to embrace the Canadian
tradition. As the business historian Michael Bliss has argued, few Canadian
businessmen have liked dangling on the strings held by Adam Smith's invisible
hand of free-market forces: "They looked to government to cut those strings, to
liberate them from the harsh discipline of competition by taking them under its
protective wing."[35] This was especially true of Canada's biggest brewers during
the post-war period.

In addition to having to pay the federal tariff, foreign brewers seeking to sell their product in Canada had to hurdle three non-tariff barriers used by provincial authorities to discourage the domestic consumption of non-Canadian beer (i.e., listing practices, distribution requirements, and discriminatory mark-up policies). Each province had its own unique distribution system, with its own distinct policies and practices. These added to the foreign brewers' cost of doing business in Canada and thus further protected domestic brewers from competition. Liquor control boards routinely imposed conditions on the supply of imported beer. For example, sales quotas and performance standards had to be continuously met. Distribution systems restricted the sale of imported beer to provincially run liquor board outlets, where foreign brewers were forced to pay extra fees and meet additional requirements. For example, in Ontario, imported beer was only allowed to be sold in six-packs instead of full cases. In other provinces, restrictions were placed on the type and size of bottles sold. In addition, mark-ups and handling charges were higher on foreign beer sold in Canada.[36] Thus, many foreign brewers, including US brewers with plants close to the Canadian border, found it next to impossible to compete on a price basis. As a result, for most of the post-war period, domestic brewers regularly manufactured more than 98 per cent of the beer consumed in Canada.[37]

But the same regulatory regime that so successfully protected Canada's brewers from foreign competition led to plants of suboptimal size. According to a Conference Board of Canada report, the minimum plant size necessary to achieve ideal manufacturing efficiencies produced an annual output of at least 2.2 hectolitres.[38] Other reports put that figure higher.[39] But by the mid-1980s, only five of Canada's twenty-eight brewers were operating at the 2.2 million hectolitres in capacity (all of them were in Ontario), and about half of Canada's production came from suboptimal plants. The same study concluded that beer production per plant in Canada was just over one-quarter the level, on average, of US plants.[40] Canadian breweries were thus operating at a disadvantage relative to the optimal US plants. As a result, when the news reached the boardrooms of Canada's brewing establishment that the federal government of Brian Mulroney was negotiating a free-trade accord (FTA) with the United States, the brewers' lobby quickly mobilized in an attempt to hold back the laissez faire tide.

Free trade, the brewers maintained, would be the death knell of domestic brewing.[41] Even Canada's biggest brewers were far too weak to compete in an open marketplace. The structure of the Canadian beer industry was such that it worked against economies of scale. Because of the system of provincial barriers to trade within Canada, the industry's productive system was hopelessly fragmented in numerous uncompetitive plants across the country. Provincial rules forced the operation of breweries of suboptimal size. In a position paper presented to James Kelleher, the minister of international trade, the brewers lobby argued:

> Bilateral free trade with the United States in beer must be considered in the context of the historical and continuing highly-regulated and trade-restricted domestic market environment, resulting from high interprovincial trade barriers and restrictions on inter-provincial shipment of beer. This environment has led to the development in Canada of numerous small-scale breweries which, while they have attained international recognition for their quality products, are not cost effective or cost competitive with their larger scale international competitors.[42]

A number of academic studies later gave some objective weight to the brewers' position, although most weren't willing to advocate continued protection.[43] The brewers therefore asked that the protective practices be grandfathered under the new accord and threatened that if they weren't, then the brewers would come out publicly against the entire FTA. The threat worked, and as a result, brewing was one of only three industries to be exempt from the FTA. The protectionist regulatory regime remained in effect until 1995 when trade barriers finally came down. Canadian brewers could no longer hide behind the traffic wall, in an artificial environment free of price-based competition. Now, for the first time, they were forced to compete in an increasingly open, integrated, global marketplace. To survive, they would have to have significant international activity and firm-specific advantages in relation to foreign firms. As will be seen subsequently, this did not happen.

Firm-specific Determinants

Success in the brewing industry is determined in large part by a firm's ability to development global brands.[44] The loyalty of consumers lies with brands, rather than producers.[45] The world's largest beer companies manufacture the world's most popular brands of beers. For example, Anheuser-Busch InBev, the world's biggest brewer, owns and manufactures Bud Light, Skol, Budweiser, and Brahma – the world's second, third, fourth, and seventh bestselling beers, respectively. The world's third-largest brewer, Heineken, owns the world's sixth most popular brand and the world's bestselling international beer, with a non-domestic volume in 2008 of more than 25 million hectolitres.[46] Not a single Canadian brand is listed among the world's top twenty-five most popular beers. Part of this is explained by the industry- and country-specific determinants analysed previously. The regulatory regime in Canada fragmented the Canadian industry for most of its history. As a result, the development of national brands that might later be taken global was delayed. However, these exogenous determinants are only part of the explanation. Firm-specific factors played an equally critical role.

In an attempt to reduce costs and increase shareholder value, executives at Canada's big three breweries made the short-sighted strategic decision to enter into licensing agreements with foreign firms to manufacture and promote their beer within the national boundary.[47] Licensing agreements had the advantage of circumventing international trade barriers. Foreign beers that were brewed in Canada under license were not subject to either the federal tariff or the discriminatory mark-ups that other imported beers faced at the provincial government outlets. However, the advantages did not end there. Licensing agreements substantially reduced transportation costs and allowed brewers to get their product to market more quickly. For these reasons, brewers began approaching other brewers around the globe, particularly in the largest beer-drinking markets, to get them to brew their beer.[48]

In 1965, Labatt became the first Canadian brewery to sign a licensing agreement with a foreign competitor. The license with Guinness Overseas gave Labatt the exclusive right to brew and market their famous Guinness Stout brand in Canada. The landmark agreement was a sign of things to come. After a decade of unsuccessfully attempting to persuade Canadians to purchase domestic imitations of American light beers (e.g., Labatt's Cool Springs and Special Lite lager), Labatt opted instead to produce the "real stuff." In the spring of 1980, Labatt announced that it had licensed the right to brew Budweiser – the "King of Beers" – and distribute it to thirsty Canadians. Labatt had initially approached Anheuser-Busch with a proposal to brew Michelob north of the border. The undisputed brewing leader in the United States rejected that idea, however, suggesting instead that Labatt brew its Budweiser. Anheuser-Busch was harbouring as-yet-unannounced international ambitions. Although the American beer giant controlled 32 per cent of the US market, by 1980 growth had become stagnant. Executives at Anheuser-Busch decided that in order to grow in the future, the company would have to tap into external markets.[49] With that goal in mind, executives at Anheuser-Busch decided that Budweiser, and not Michelob, had the best chance of becoming a global brand.

At Labatt, there was a sense that the international brewing industry was moving in a new direction, that in the future there would be a homogenization of tastes and a globalization of brands.[50] "We saw the globalization of brands," stated Don McDougall, the company's president in 1979, "and thought being ahead of everyone else might be a good idea."[51] Having joined Labatt shortly after receiving an MBA from the University of Western Ontario in 1961,

McDougall quickly moved up the ranks at Labatt. Between 1973 and 1979 he held the titles of president and senior vice president and was a driving force behind the licensing agreement with Anheuser-Busch. The deal that he signed gave Labatt a ninety-nine-year license to brew Budweiser in Canada.

In the summer of 1980, Labatt rolled out the product in Alberta and Saskatchewan, a region where there had been a long tradition of brewing and drinking American-style lagers.[52] It wasn't until the following year that the Canadian brewer made Bud available to beer drinkers in Ontario, Quebec, and British Columbia. By 1982, Budweiser accounted for about 7 per cent of the total Canadian beer sales.[53] The Americanization of Canadian brewing was underway.

The other big Canadian brewers took immediate notice. For Canadian Breweries Limited, which had been renamed Carling O'Keefe after the sale of the company to the British tobacco giant Rothmans in 1969, licensing the right to brew and market American beer in Canada held out the possibility of reversing its fortunes. Once the industry leader, Carling O'Keefe had suffered during the 1970s from not having a "national brand." Executives hoped that licensing the right to manufacture a well-known American beer would give them a brand that they could promote nationally. The decision was made that Miller High Life would be Carling-O'Keefe's Bud.

Miller was launched in the summer of 1983. In an effort to make its new beer stand out, Carling decided that it would sell Miller in a tall-necked bottle of the same proportions as the US Miller bottle. It marked the beginning of the end of the "stubby" bottle – perhaps the single most distinctive feature of Canada beer in the post-war period. Miller quickly gained a 7 to 8 per cent market share.

In November 1985, Molson Breweries of Canada Ltd joined its major Canadian competitors in offering a domestic version of an American beer. Molson was rarely a "first mover." The corporate culture was such that conscious and conservative conduct was promoted and celebrated. As Molson's president Jacques Allard stated in 1985: "We watched to see how successful the other brands would be. Then with an eye on the future we moved."[54] After two years of talks with Coors of Golden, Colorado, Molson signed an agreement to brew Coors and Coors Light under license in Canada. Viewed through the prism of domestic market share, Molson's slow and deliberate action paid off. By the early twenty-first century, Coors Light was Canada's largest-selling light beer and the second bestselling brand in Canada overall (although the gain in market share came at the expense of Molson's historic brands). Viewed through the prism of global competitiveness, however, the move undermined the development and promotion of the firm's own brands, and ultimately compromised the growth and survival of the firm.

The success of brands like Coors Light led executives at the big three to con-clude that the licensing and then brewing and promoting of American brands was the way to go. However, this was short-sighted in the extreme. To be sure, owning the right to brew the most popular American brand could add to the firm's bottom line. After all, brewing in Canada was a zero-sum game. Little revenue was generated from the big three's beer sales outside of the national boundary. Brewing and licensing these American brands made financial sense given the institutional environment, but the signs were already pointing in the 1980s to the globalization of the beer industry. What product would Canada have to offer the world if its beer was American?

Beyond developing global brands, successful alcoholic beverage firms are diversified in terms of geography and the products that they produce. Diver-sification has always held a special place in the minds of executives faced with stagnant or declining markets for their original product, as was the case in the alcoholic beverage sector after 1975. As Alfred Chandler has noted, during the 1970s, the drive for growth through diversification into related and unrelated products "had almost become a mania."[55] This became the age of the protean multinational corporation, an enterprise dedicated to internationalization and the pursuit of synergies – a seemingly magical mixture of business activities that were stronger and more profitable together than they were apart. Diversifi-cation could be rewarding, but it took substantial resources and continual com-mitment. The timing and type of diversification was also crucial in determining its success or failure. For those firms in the alcoholic beverage industry, diver-sification generally produced positive results when it related to the firm's core competencies – that is, when there were physical and/or knowledge linkages to the firm's assets that could be easily exploited. For example, when Louis Vuitton Moët Hennessy diversified into perfumes in the 1990s, it allowed the firm to exploit not only its marketing knowledge in terms of the general management of brands and distribution, but also its knowledge about specific markets, such as the Far East.[56] On the other hand, diversification often went wrong when a firm expanded into industries that were unrelated to its core business, and thus when physical and knowledge linkages were absent.

During the 1970s and 1980s, Labatt had joined many other companies, both at home and abroad, which were diversifying in an effort to sustain their growth. More so than elsewhere, Canadian corporate managers believed that having "all your eggs in one basket" was a dangerous strategy. This mentality emerged out of a conservative corporate culture that stretched back to at least the late nineteenth century. There had long been unwillingness on the part of most Canadian businessmen to believe in the global appeal of their products, beyond natural resources. This collective corporate culture led brewers to be derivative, first in copying and selling American brands at home, and then by diversifying into unrelated businesses within Canada or the United States, rather than concentrating their efforts on taking their principal business overseas. Consequently, Labatt diversified into media and entertainment, food businesses, dairy products, fruit juices, chemicals, and retailing.[57] These diversifications did not bring the anticipated profits. The large dairy operations and packaged foods, for example, brought in revenues that showed only a thin margin of profit. Milk and the products made from it could not be marked up in price with the same ease as beer. As a consequence, whereas Labatt's brewing division returned a profit of C$218 million in 1993, the dairy division, which had a book value of C$140 million that year, showed no profit at all.[58] Like a number of Canadian companies, Labatt had diversified beyond what was optimal.

It was a similar story at Molson. Under the leadership of Mickey Cohen, a cultured corporate lawyer who had become Molson's president and CEO in 1988, Molson diversified into chemicals and the home improvement sector, spending hundreds of millions to purchase Beaver Lumber, a 45.1 per cent interest in the Quebec-based Réno-Dépôt Inc. chain, and a 25 per cent stake in Home Depot. The diversifications were as disastrous for Molson as they had been for Labatt.[59] If Molson had diversified into spirits, wines, or even soft drinks, there would have been at least the potential to exploit physical and knowledge linkages as well as to foster economies of scale and scope. But the firm chose instead to diversify into unrelated industries, where it had little expertise. For this, Molson paid a heavy price, not only in terms of its short-term financial results, but also in stripping it of the cash it might have used to promote its core business overseas.[60]

More important to the success of firms in the global alcoholic beverage industry than product diversification is geographical diversification. Indeed, some of today's most successful multinationals in the alcoholic beverage industry only briefly diversified out of alcohol. For example, even at the height of the diversification mania in the 1970s, Heineken still derived close to 90 per cent of its total sales from the sale of its alcoholic beverages.[61] It appeared that the business theorists of the post-diversification craze were right: the wisest strategy for big business was to "stick to the knitting."[62] The mentality of the global age was to do what you do best and do it the world over. As a result, firms in the alcoholic beverage sector intensified their efforts to expand into new markets. As the economist Charles Kindleberger succinctly put it, "[I]n going abroad, they grow abroad."[63] Some firms had a "first-mover" advantage, which greatly benefited them in the long run. For example, Heineken and Guinness had long derived a substantial percentage of their sales from outside their home continent.[64] Initially, they did this through exports, then by entering into licensing agreements with foreign firms, and then by way of foreign direct investments. As a result, by 1990, 40 per cent of Guinness's total sales and 25 per cent of Heineken's came from outside of Europe.

This was not the case in Canada, however. Canadian brewers had never established a significant presence outside of the continent. Indeed, as late 1990, fully 99 per cent of Canada's beer exports went to the United States, representing only 10 per cent of total beer production.[65] There had been some earlier, but generally unsuccessful, attempts at geographical diversification through mergers and acquisitions. For example, in 1987, Labatt launched Labatt Lager (Blue Light under a foreign guise) in England by way of a licensing agreement with the regional brewery Greenall Whitley. Not content to let others manage the brand, Labatt soon began pouring resources into the United Kingdom, a market that quickly proved to be far different from the cosy Canadian oligopoly to which it was accustomed. Its initial £6.5 million advertising campaign for Labatt Lager was a series of television commercials starring a red-coated character named Malcolm the Mountie. The campaign, which ran during most of the brewers push in Britain, boasted the tag line: "Malcolm the Mountie always gets his can." The campaign served to anger Canada's national police force more than win over beer drinkers in Britain. In 1991, Labatt Lager ranked a lowly number nine among lager brands in Britain.

When George Taylor took over as CEO of Labatt in 1992, he was determined to control more of the North American market. In 1994, he made his intentions clear when Labatt paid $720 million for a 22 per cent stake in Mexican brewer FEMSA Cerveza SA. This was not a plan to slowly break into a foreign market, as was the case in the United Kingdom. FEMSA controlled 48 per cent of the Mexican market, which was twice the size of Canada's. FEMSA's largest brewery at the time produced 6 million hectolitres of beer annually (or about 220 million cases of beer), triple the amount produced in Labatt's largest Canadian brewery.

Mexico also represented an opportunity for brewers in North America. Lucrative as it was, stagnant population growth and an aging population made the Canadian business a zero-sum game of expensive market-share swaps and no growth. Once Labatt had mastered domestic quality control and marketing, the main challenge for senior management was to invest the resulting stream of earnings. In an absence of serious, competitive price wars, the structured and regulated domestic brewing business was a powerful engine that made substantial amounts of capital available for acquisitions. The strategic logic of the purchase in Mexico made sense given its size, proximity, and demographics. Furthermore, like Canada, it was a government-protected duopoly, with FEMSA and Groupo Modello, the brewer of Corona, controlling the market.

Perhaps if the timing had been right, Labatt would have made money in Mexico. But, unfortunately for Labatt, the timing could not have been worse. Just a few months after the Canadian brewer paid out almost three-quarters of a billion dollars for FEMSA, a currency crisis struck the Latin nation. In December, the peso began a free fall as two political assassinations, a guerrilla insurgency in southern Mexico, and a change of government led foreign investors to pull billions out of the country. And although US officials and powerful media outlets like the *New York Times* told people that the currency crisis "does not reflect fundamental flaws in Mexico's newly liberalized economy,"[66] the peso continued to fall. By 10 March 1995, the Mexican peso was worth only half of what it was when the financial crisis began in mid-December.

The usually conservative Canadian brewer had not hedged its Mexican purchase against a possible devaluation of the peso, and as a result, the firm lost heavily. On the day that the peso hit a new record low, Labatt president George Taylor conceded that "there is no question whatsoever that the devaluation is a significant setback for the company."[67] Just nine months after buying its stake, Labatt was forced to write down the carrying value of its FEMSA holding by $272 million and expected a further $110 million reduction in the investment's carrying value.[68] The market was tremendously bearish about the prospect of turning a profit in Mexico in the near future. "You can't be positive about it," stated Jacques Kavaflan, an analyst with Lévesque Beaubien Geoffrion Inc. in Montreal. "There's not going to be an earnings contribution from Mexico until the end of the century."[69]

The Mexico fiasco brought an abrupt end to Labatt's global aspirations. Still, at home beer sales were still strong. Labatt Blue and Budweiser were selling particularly well in Canada, and, as a result, Labatt's share of the domestic beer market increased from 44.2 per cent in 1993 to 45 per cent in 1994.[70] The company continued to turn a healthy profit, making it an attractive target for those multinational enterprises in the industry looking to further diversify geographically.

As the mega breweries raced to tap into China and other emerging markets, they simultaneously sought to acquire existing breweries in established markets, rationalizing their operations. The goal was to upgrade and enhance the marketing of local and regional brands while concomitantly introducing their "global brands" in some markets. The approach was pioneered by Belgium's Interbrew SA, which had been making beer in Europe since 1366.[71] In 1995, the debt-free, family-controlled company was Europe's fourth-largest brewer, with sales of more than $2 billion. In the early 1990s, Interbrew began gobbling up breweries in emerging markets such as Romania and southern China. At the same time, it began to eye the $30 billion North American beer market. But Interbrew's big brands, beers such as Stella Artois and Jupiler, were virtually unknown to North American beer drinkers. And after exhaustive study, Interbrew's executives decided that it was impossible to penetrate that highly competitive, mature market through exports alone. Thus, in April 1995, Interbrew offered to acquire Labatt for $2.7 billion, or $28.50 per share. Once the deal had been approved by the shareholders, Interbrew quickly set Labatt on a course to get "back to basics." As Interbrew's Belgium-based spokesman Gerard Fauchey noted: "It's very simple. We're brewers, not managers of hockey or baseball teams or television stations."[72]

The acquisition of Labatt by Interbrew left Molson as the biggest Canadian-owned brewer. Having acquired Carling O'Keefe a few years earlier, in 1995 Molson had a 46.5 per cent share of the $10 billion Canadian beer market. Nevertheless, in international terms, Molson was small. "It may look like a giant in Canada," wrote one beer industry analyst, "but when it crosses the border it looks more like Tom Thumb."[73] To make matters worse, Molson's own brands were losing their grip on the Canadian consumer. Admittedly, Molson wasn't the only Canadian brewer to suffer declining sales at home. Sleeman, Canada's third-largest brewer, had seen its share of the market decline over the past decade. This was a result of two factors: the microbrewery revolution, which had been underway since the mid-1980s, and the rise in imported beer, particularly from the Netherlands, the United States, and Mexico.[74]

In a belated effort to gain a presence outside of North America, in March 2002 Molson took the audacious step of paying $1.1 billion to acquire Cervejarias Kaiser SA, Brazil's second-largest brewer. Molson had already missed its chance to become an autonomous global player. Although its conservative corporate culture had served it well domestically, that culture had held it back internationally. A "fast follower" at home, Molson was simply a follower on the global stage. Still, the purchase of Kaiser was a risky move into what was at the time the world's fifth-largest beer market. The deal gave Molson 17.8 per cent of the South American country's beer sales, when combined with Bavaria, which Molson had purchased from Ambev two years earlier.

But the deal was marred from the start. The key to success in Brazil, as in other emerging markets, was to have a strong distribution system. This led a number of the leading multinationals in the global alcoholic beverage industry to form joint ventures with local partners to produce, bottle, and distribute locally. Molson's Canadian counterpart in the alcoholic beverage industry, Seagram, understood the value of forming alliances to distribute its distiller spirits worldwide. In 1972, it formed one of the world's first joint ventures in Asia with the Japanese brewer Kirin. Seagram brought its manufacturing technique, while Kirin contributed its sales network and market knowledge to sell Seagram's brands Robert Brown, Dunbar, Emblem, Burnett's Gin, and Nikolai vodka in Japan.[75] But unlike Seagram, Molson arrogantly chose to go it alone. To make matters worse, the company did not integrate vertically through wholly owned distribution units. Rather, the firm relied on sixteen Coca-Cola bottlers to distribute its beer to the country's more than one million points of sale. Molson lacked market knowledge: a situation not helped by the fact that the man appointed to oversee Molson's Brazilian operations brewery was a financier who had never lived outside of Quebec and who didn't speak Portuguese. In 2004, Kaiser's market share was down to 11 per cent. Just two years after the purchase, Molson sold its ill-fated billion-dollar Brazilian brewery for a mere $108 million. Just a few months after the sale of Kaiser, Molson merged with Colorado's Adolph Coors Company.

Conclusion

So why is it that Canadian beer brands and brewers do not have a global presence, and why is it that Canada's oldest and largest beer companies no longer exist as autonomous agents? The answer to that question lies in the interwoven layers of industry-specific, country-specific, and firm-specific determinants of growth and survival.

In the period before the gale winds of globalization gained full force, it was possible for the big three Canadian beer companies to grow and survive without constantly rebuilding their firm-specific advantages. This was attributable to the fact that industry-specific and country-specific determinants were not adverse for those firms within the brewing industry that lacked significant international activity, like Molson, Labatt, and Carling-O'Keefe. This was a period when brewing was a relatively unconsolidated and fundamentally local industry. Added to which, consumption patterns of beer were primarily specific to the regional culture in which the beer was being sold. The period was also one in which the regulatory regime in Canada protected the big three brewers from foreign competition, allowing them to survive despite not having firm-specific advantages relative to their international counterparts. The regulatory regime in Canada was such that it fragmented the industry along regional lines, leading to cost inefficiencies and suboptimal production levels that hampered the development of large, internationally competitive firms. Safe behind the tariff wall, Canadian brewers had little incentive to internationalize through foreign direct investment. Rather, they spent millions of dollars a year on national advertising campaigns in an effort to gain a larger share of the domestic market. The doppelgänger of federal and provincial legislation protected existing firms and enabled them to survive without developing managerial capabilities, marketing skills, and global brands. When the protective trade barriers were dismantled in the mid-1990s, Canadian breweries were forced to compete on an even playing field.

When one reflects on the firm-specific strategies of the big three brewers in Canada since 1960, one is reminded of Adam Smith's scorn for the feudal lords who traded their leadership for a pair of silver buckles. The principal decisions made by executives at the big three were myopic, in that they were aimed at maximizing short-term profits rather than promoting longer-term growth and survival. Instead of manufacturing, marketing, and developing their own brands, they decided to manufacture the brands of their foreign competitors and to promote them within the national boundary. Although lucrative in the short term, the move served to cannibalize the sales of their existing brands. More damaging to their future survival was the fact that the strategy served to strip Canadian beer of its "Canadian-ness." By choosing first to brew American styled-beers and promote and package them in an American way, and then by licensing the right to brew popular American brands, Canadian brewers Americanized the Canadian brewing industry. At the same time that they were derivative in terms of their marketing, they were derivative in terms of their diversification strategy. As a consequence, when the brewing industry became truly global after 1990, Canadian brewers no longer had unique, distinctively Canadian brands to offer the world.

One might argue that the brewers were just responding to a consumer demand – that Canadians wanted American-style beers, and thus the big three brewers sensibly supplied them. To a certain degree, the assertion has an element of truth. In the 1980s, a thirst for differently styled beers existed, in part because the institutional environment stifled innovation at Canada's big breweries. This lack of ingenuity on the part of the big three led to the microbrewery revolution. But one must remember that between 1960 and 1990, the big three brewers controlled between 96 and 98 per cent of the market. What did they have to gain by such a move? The answer is a slightly larger share of the domestic market. And that is the point. The Canadian brewing industry was emblematic of the Canadian corporate condition: an inability on the part of all but the most dynamic of Canadian corporations to look beyond the national boundary for opportunities for growth.

NOTES

1 Andrea Mandel-Campbell, *Why Don't Mexicans Drink Molson: Rescuing Canadian Business from the Suds of Global Obscurity* (Toronto: Douglas & McIntyre, 2007), 141–7.

2 Neil M. Kay, *Patterns of Corporate Evolution* (Oxford: Oxford University Press, 1997), 78–81.

3 Edith Penrose, *The Theory of the Growth of the Firm* (Oxford: Oxford University Press, 1959), 137.

4 Peter E. Hart and Robert D. Pearce, "Growth Patterns of the World's Largest Firms, 1962–1982," (Discussion Papers in International Investment and Business Studies, No. 83, University of Reading, Reading, Berkshire, UK, 1984).

5 John Dunning, "Trade, Location of Economic Activity and the MNE: A Search for an Eclectic Approach," in *The International Allocation of Economic Activity*, ed. B. Ohlin, P.O. Hesselborn, and P.M. Wijkman (London: MacMillan, 1977), 395–418. These ownership advantages must be sufficient to compensate for the costs of setting up and operating a foreign value-adding operation in addition to those faced by indigenous producers or potential producers. Elsewhere, Dunning identifies three types of ownership-specific advantages: (1) those that stem from the exclusive privileged possession of or access to particular income generating assets; (2) those that are normally enjoyed by a branch plant compared with a de novo firm; and (3) those that are a consequence of geographical diversification or multinationality per se. See J. Dunning, *International Production and the Multinational Enterprise* (London: Allen & Unwin, 1981), 27.

6 Teresa Da Silva Lopes,*Global Brands: The Evolution of Multinationals in Alcoholic Beverages* (Cambridge: Cambridge University Press, 2007), 21.

7 Geert Hofstede, *Culture's Consequences: International Differences in Work-Related Values* (Beverly Hills, CA: Sage, 1980); Mark Granovetter, "Economic Action and Social Structure: The Problem of Embeddedness," *American Journal of Sociology*, 91, no. 3 (1985): 481–501.

8 Geert Hofstede, "The Business of International Business is Culture," in *The Internationalization of the Firm: A Reader*, ed. Peter J. Buckley and Pervez N. Ghauri (London: International Thomson Business Press, 1999), 381–93.

9 Lopes, *Global Brands* 46.

10 Jens Gammelgaard and Christopher Dörrenbächer, eds., *The Global Brewing Industry: Markets, Strategies, and Rivalries* (Northampton, MA: William Pratt House, 2013).

11 Between 1945 and 1970, Canadian corporations such as Inco, Brascan, Noranda, Cominco, Alcan, MacMillan Bloedel, and Massey-Ferguson made substantial investments abroad. See D. Campbell, *Global Mission: The Alcan Story* (Toronto:

Ontario Publishing Company, 1985); MacKay, *Empire of Wood: The MacMillan Bloedel Story* (Toronto: Douglas & McIntyre, 1982), 245–75; E.P. Neufeld, *A Global Corporation: A History of the International Development of Massey Ferguson Limited* (Toronto: University of Toronto Press, 1969), 290–302.

12 A. Chandler, *Scale and Scope: The Dynamics of Industrial Capitalism* (Cambridge, MA: Belknap Press, 1990), 117, 122, 171–5, 213–17, 446–52.

13 Ibid.

14 S.R. Dennison and Oliver MacDonagh, *Guinness 1886–1939: From Incorporation to the Second World War* (Cork, Ireland: Cork University Press, 1998), 229–82.

15 J.C.H. Jones, "Mergers and Competition: The Brewing Case," *The Canadian Journal of Economics and Political Science* 33, no. 4 (1967): 551–68.

16 Taylor did this by acquiring ownership and control of existing Ontario breweries and rationalizing their operations. Largely as a result of his actions, the number of breweries declined sharply in Ontario from thirty-six in 1930 to just five in 1958. See Albert Shea, *Vision in Action: The Story of Canadian Breweries Limited from 1930 to 1955* (Toronto: Canadian Breweries, 1955), 68–128.

17 Shea, *Vision in Action*, 61–4.

18 In 1958, Canadian Breweries Limited had a 14.9 per cent share of the Nova Scotia beer market, a 5.7 per cent share of the N.B. market, 51.8 per cent share of the Quebec market, a 60.9 per cent share of the Ontario market, a 41 per cent share of the Manitoba market, a 34.2 per cent share of the Saskatchewan market, a 7.9 per cent share of the Alberta market, and a 36 per cent share of the British Columbia beer market. See J.C.H. Jones, "Competition in the Canadian Brewing Industry," table II, 556.

19 Ibid., 554–6.

20 M. Stack and G. Myles, "The Repeal of Prohibition and the Resurgence of the National Breweries: Productive Efficiency or Path Creation?" *Management Decision* 43, no. 3 (2005): 420–32; Joan Holleran, "It's a Small World for U.S. Brewers," *Beverage Industry* 87, no. 5 (May 1996): 10.

21 Chris Lewis, "The Future of British Brewing: Strategies for Survival," *Strategic Change* 10 (2001): 151–61.

22 The concentration was substantially less than in related industries. In the soft drinks sector, for instance, the top four players shared 80 per cent of the world market.

23 Ed Gregory, Wendy Hurst, and Thomas Gussman, *Alcoholic Beverage Taxation and Control Policies* (Ottawa: Brewers' Association of Canada, 1997), 498.

24 Ibid., 472.

25 Ibid., 50.

26 Ibid., 70.

27 Ibid., 276.

28 Sarah Gregory, "Brewers Target Asia's Developing Markets," *Asian Business Review* 1, no. 1 (1995): 58–61.
29 M.J. Bellamy, "'Rich by Nature, Poor by Policy'? The Premature Birth and Quick Death of Commercial Brewing in Canada, 1667–1675," *Brewery History* 137 (Fall 2010): 48–70.
30 M.J. Bellamy, "The Canadian Brewing Industry's Response to Prohibition, 1874–1920," *Brewery History* 132 (Fall 2009): 6–7.
31 Lopes, *Global Brands*; Demetris Vrontis, "Strategic Assessment: The Importance of Branding in the European Beer Market," *British Food Journal* 100, no. 2 (1998): 76–84.
32 Paul Duguid, "Developing the Brand: The Case of Alcohol, 1800–1880," *Enterprise and Society* 4, no. 3 (2003): 405–41.
33 Bellamy, "Canadian Brewing Industry's Response to Prohibition," 2–17.
34 The 12.5 per cent tariff was the rate at which beer from British preferential or most-favoured-nation countries (e.g., the United States) were taxed. See Brewers' Association of Canada, *Brewing in Canada* (Ottawa: Brewers Association of Canada, 1965), 97.
35 Michael Bliss, "Rich by Nature, Poor by Policy: The State and Economic Life in Canada," in *Entering the Eighties: Canada in Crisis,* ed. K.R. Carty and P.W. Ward (Toronto: Oxford University Press, 1980), 86.
36 In Ontario, for example, the handling charge for domestic brewers was 30¢ cents a case, while foreign brewers were required to pay $1.25. See James Sherbaniuk, "Regina vs. Canadian Breweries Ltd: An Analysis of a Merger Case" (PhD diss., University Washington, 1964), 97.
37 Brewers Association of Canada, *Brewing in Canada*, 97; Wendy Hurst, Ed Gregory, and Thomas Gussman, *Alcoholic Beverage Taxation and Control Policies* (Ottawa: Brewers Association of Canada, 1997), 75.
38 Conference Board of Canada, *The Canadian Brewing Industry: An Assessment of the Impacts of Liberalized Interprovincial Trade in Canada* (Ottawa: Conference Board of Canada, 1990), 7
39 Kathryn Collins, *The Canadian Brewing Industry* (Toronto: Midland Walwyn Research, 1991), 11.
40 Ibid.
41 Bruce Doern and Brian Tomlin, *The Free Trade Story: Faith and Fear* (Toronto: Stoddart Publishing Co., 1991), 78–9.
42 Brewers Association of Canada, *Perspectives on Canada-United States Free Trade - Submitted to the Honourable James Kelleher, Minister of International Trade* (Ottawa, May 1985), 1.
43 See, for example, I.J. Irvine, W.A. Sims, and A. Anastasopoulos, "Interprovincial versus International Free Trade: The Brewing Industry," *Canadian Journal of Economics/Revue canadienne d'economique* 23, no. 2 (May 1990): 332–47.

44 Lopes, *Global Brands*.
45 P. Kolter, G. Armstrong, J. Saunders, and V. Wong, *Principles of Marketing* (Hemel Hempstead: Prentice Hall, 1996).
46 *The Global Drinks Market: Impact Databank Review and Forecast* (New York: M. Shanken Communications, 2010), 439.
47 Jeffery Karrenbrock, "The Internationalization of the Beer-Brewing Industry" (Report of the Federal Reserve Bank of St Louis, St Louis, Mo., November/ December 1990), 6–8.
48 Ibid., 6.
49 Maureen Ogle, *Ambitious Brew: The Story of American Beer* (San Diego, CA: Harcourt, 2006), 321.
50 Paul Brent, *Lager Heads: Labatt and Molson Face Off for Canada's Beer Money* (Toronto: Harper Collins, 2005), 63–4.
51 Ibid., 63.
52 Wiliam A. Hagelund, *House of Suds: A History of Beer Brewing in Western Canada* (Surrey, B.C.: Hancock House, 2003).
53 Brent, *Lager Heads*, 69.
54 Fran Halter, "Molson Launches Coors Beer," *Gazette*, 7 November 1985, D-1.
55 Chandler, *Scale and Scope*, 622.
56 Lopes, *Global Brands*, 115.
57 *John Labatt Annual Report* (London, Ontario: John Labatt Ltd,,1987), 9–11.
58 Albert Tucker, "Labatt's: A History – From Immigrant Family to Canadian Corporation" (unpublished manuscript), 431.
59 Tucker, "Labatt's," 431.
60 Molson's financial results were mediocre at best in the early 1990s. Sales rose from $2.55 billion in fiscal 1990 to $3.09 billion in fiscal 1993, but earnings vacillated from $117.9 million in fiscal 1990 to a net loss of $38.67 million the following year, before rebounding somewhat to $164.69 million in fiscal 1993.
61 Lopes, *Global Brands*, 242–3.
62 R. Biggadike, "The Risky Business of Diversification," *Harvard Business Review* (May–June 1979): 101–17; B. Hayes and B. Abernathy, "Managing Our Way to Economic Decline," *Harvard Business Review* (July–August 1980): 67–77; C. Markides, "Back to Basics: Reversing Corporate Diversification," *Multinational Business* 4 (1991): 12–25; T. Peters and R. Waterman, *In Search of Excellence: Lessons from America's Best-Run Companies* (New York: Harper Row, 1982).
63 Charles Kindleberger, *American Business Abroad: Six Lectures on Direct Investment* (New Haven, CT: Yale University Press, 1969), 6.
64 Lopes, *Global Brands*, 242–3.
65 Hurst, Gregory, and Gussman, *Alcoholic Beverage Taxation and Control Policies*, 75.

66 "Mexico: Don't Panic over the Peso," *New York Times*, 29 December 1994.

67 Mariana Strauss, "Labatt Caught in Peso Plunge," *Globe and Mail*, 10 March 1995, B1.

68 Ibid.

69 Ibid., B2.

70 Ibid., B2.

71 H. Schumacher, "The Global Beer Industry 2001 Review: Toto, We Are Not in Kansas Anymore," *Modern Beverage Age* 36, no. 5 (2002): 7–9.

72 Quoted in Andrew Will, "The Winning Brew," *Maclean's* 108, no. 25 (1995): 44.

73 ·Peter Reid, *Modern Brewery Age*, 13 September 2004.

74 Carlo Rupnik, "Canada's Beer Trade: A Swing to Imported Brands" (Analytical Paper, Statistics Canada, Ottawa, February 2006), 14.

75 Lopes, *Global Brands*, 99.

List of Contributors

Dimitry Anastakis is an associate professor of history at Trent University. His research interests include twentieth-century Canadian and US economic and political history, post-1945 trade policy, and the role of public policy in shaping the automotive industry. His publications include *Auto Pact: Creating a Borderless North American Auto Industry, 1960–1971* (University of Toronto Press, 2005) and *Autonomous State: The Struggle for a Canadian Auto Industry from OPEC to Free Trade* (University of Toronto Press, 2013).

Matthew J. Bellamy is an associate professor of history at Carleton University. He specializes in Canadian business, political, and economic history. His publications include *Profiting the Crown: Canada's Polymer Corporation, 1942–1990* (McGill-Queen's University Press, 2005), for which he received the 2006 National Business Book Award. In 2005, *Maclean's* magazine named him as one of Carleton's most popular professors.

Andrew Dilley is a senior lecturer in history at the University of Aberdeen. His research interests are in the history of the British Empire, and especially in the history of Britain's relations with the "Dominions" (Australia, Canada, South Africa, and New Zealand). His publications focus on the influence of British financial institutions upon colonial businesses and politics.

Livio Di Matteo is a professor of economics at Lakehead University. He specializes in public policy, health economics, public finance, and economic history. He is a member of the CIHI National Health Expenditure Advisory Panel, is a contributor to the economics blog Worthwhile Canadian Initiative, and is a senior fellow of the Fraser Institute.

J.C. Herbert Emery is a professor of economics at the University of Calgary. He is currently the Program Director for Health Policy in the School of Public Policy at the University of Calgary and the Managing Editor of *Canadian Public Policy/Analyse de politiques*. From 2007 to 2012, he was the Svare Professor in Health Economics, which was a joint appointment between the Department of Economics and the Department of Community Health Sciences in the Faculty of Medicine.

Michael N.A. Hinton is a partner in Hinton and Co., Montreal, a consulting firm with twenty years of leader, team and organization consulting, coaching, and facilitation experience. He also teaches in the Executive MBA program at Concordia University's John Molson School of Business. He has served as a fellow at the Rimini Centre for Economic Analysis.

Mark Kuhlberg is an associate professor of history at Laurentian University/ Université Laurentienne. He teaches Canadian history, with a focus on environmental and business history. His publications include *One Hundred Rings and Counting: Forestry Education and Forestry in Toronto and Canada, 1907–2007* (University of Toronto Press, 2009).

Greig Mordue is General Manager at Toyota Motor Manufacturing Canada. He completed a PhD titled, "Government, Foreign Direct Investment and the Canadian Automotive Industry, 1977–1987," in Business History from the University of Strathclyde in Glasgow, Scotland in 2007. He has served on the Research Management Committee of AUTO21 Inc.

Martin P. Shanahan is Dean of Research at the University of South Australia Business School. He is also Deputy Director of the Centre for Regulation and Market Analysis and an associate professor of economics in the School of Commerce. He is a consultant editor for *The Australian Economic History Review* and President of the Economic History Society of Australia and New Zealand.

Andrew Smith is a lecturer in international business at the University of Liverpool. His research is on the evolution of international business. His research interests focus on the geopolitical, technological, and cultural forces that have changed the strategies of transnational firms. His publications include *British Businessmen and Canadian Confederation: Constitution-Making in the Era of Anglo-Globalization* (McGill-Queen's University Press, 2008).

Graham D. Taylor is a professor of history at Trent University. His research interests include business history, Canadian history, and US history. His publications include *Du Pont and the International Chemical Industry* (Twayne, 1984) and *The Rise of Canadian Business* (Oxford University Press, 2009).

Daryl White teaches history at Grande Prairie Regional College. He completed his PhD in history at Western University, where his dissertation was titled "Multinational Patriots: Business-Government Relations in the Canadian Aluminum and Nickel Industries, 1914–1945."

Index

Page references in *italic* indicate tables or figures.